PRAISE FOR

THE ART OF GRACE

A BARNES & NOBLE
DISCOVER GREAT NEW WRITERS AWARD
WINNER

"This thoughtful meditation will stay with me for a long while. Sarah Kaufman's thoughts on the rare virtue of grace are both inspiring and uplifting. Humanity at its finest is merely what she is offering here, and we could all use a bit more of that in our lives."

—Elizabeth Gilbert,
author of *Eat, Pray, Love* and *The Signature of All Things*

"Kaufman's deft way with words aligns perfectly with her subject: Smooth and controlled, she writes with authority about an impressive array of subjects. . . . [T]houghtful and inspiring."

—Sarah Archer,
Washington Post

"Sarah Kaufman offers an old-fashioned cure for a modern-day ailment. The remedy for our culture of coarseness is grace—forgetting ourselves, being attentive to others, and approaching our encounters with the effortlessness that comes from being at ease in the world. This is an elegant, compelling, and, yes, graceful book."

—Daniel H. Pink,
author of *Drive* and *A Whole New Mind*

"Both joyful and directive, a celebrity-packed collection of observations and a manual for easing anyone's way through the world. It's a book with a message, delivered with calm command."

—Cathy Lynn Grossman,
Huffington Post

"Sarah Kaufman has nailed it: she has detected precisely what it is that has changed us so for the worse. . . . Her book is itself most graceful, and ever knowing."

—Frank Deford,
NPR sports commentator,
and author of *Alex: The Life of a Child*

"This is a truly eloquent book on moving and communicating with eloquence. Sarah Kaufman paints a charming, dignified portrait of a lost art."

—Adam Grant,
professor at the Wharton School
of the University of Pennsylvania,
and author of *Give and Take*

"As a dance photographer, I have considered myself an expert on the art of grace. Not anymore. Sarah Kaufman has set the gold standard by which I will judge all future subjects."

—Jordan Matter,
photographer and author of *Dancers Among Us*

"Thoughtful and interesting." —*Times*

"[*The Art of Grace*] is one of the most wise, capacious, and multidimensional tributes to this virtue we've ever read."

—Frederic and Mary Ann Brussat,
Spirituality & Practice

OF

ON MOVING WELL THROUGH LIFE

SARAH L. KAUFMAN

W. W. NORTON & COMPANY
Independent Publishers Since 1923
New York | *London*

Printed in the United States of America
First published as a Norton paperback 2016

For information about permission to reproduce selections from this book,
write to Permissions, W. W. Norton & Company, Inc.,
500 Fifth Avenue, New York, NY 10110

For information about special discounts for bulk purchases, please
contact W. W. Norton Special Sales at specialsales@wwnorton.com
or 800-233-4830

Manufacturing by Quad Graphics Fairfield
Book design by Marysarah Quinn
Production manager: Anna Oler

Library of Congress Cataloging-in-Publication Data

Kaufman, Sarah L.
The art of grace : on moving well through life / Sarah L. Kaufman.
— First Edition.
pages cm
Includes bibliographical references and index.
ISBN 978-0-393-24395-6 (hardcover)
1. Grace (Aesthetics) I. Title.
BH301.G7K38 2015
302'.1—dc23

2015028036

ISBN 978-0-393-35318-1 pbk.

W. W. Norton & Company, Inc.
500 Fifth Avenue, New York, N.Y. 10110
www.wwnorton.com

W. W. Norton & Company Ltd.
15 Carlisle Street, London W1D 3BS

1 2 3 4 5 6 7 8 9 0

TO JOHN, WITH LOVE,

AND

TO ZEKE, ASA, AND ANNABEL,

MY THREE GRACES

In life, as in art, the beautiful

moves in curves.

—Edward G. Bulwer-Lytton

CONTENTS

PART THREE

Grace in Action

PART FOUR

Grace under Pressure

PART FIVE

Understanding Grace: Theories and Practice

THE ART OF GRACE

INTRODUCTION

THE BODY ELECTRIC

PARIS, 1962. An Italian restaurant. Audrey Hepburn and director Stanley Donen are having dinner with Cary Grant to talk about teaming up on the film *Charade*. Hepburn—the icon of grace, class, and elegance—is so nervous about meeting Grant that she knocks a bottle of wine into his lap.

People around them start buzzing. Think of the mood!

To everyone's relief, Grant takes it lightly. He laughs off the accident and sits through dinner in wet wool as if nothing had happened. To further comfort the mortified Hepburn, the next day he sends her a box of caviar and a warm note.

Charade comes out a year later, and it's a big success. The chemistry between its two stars draws raves.[1] Few realize that the spark had been ignited months earlier, when a cold, wet shock was met with grace.

Grace is being at ease with the world, even when life tosses wine down your pants.

Grace is rather like wine, actually, or—better yet—a cocktail. Not the snorter of desperation, mind you, but the balanced, well-made palliative, a jigger of this and a twist of that, served up for pure delectation. Whether you perceive grace in a moment of startling compassion, in Roger Federer's miraculous forehand, or even in the minute-by-minute harmony of line cooks during the dinner rush, witnessing it pleases the senses, brightens the mood, and inspires a feeling of ease.

I'll go so far as to say that once grace enters the room, our cold, hard, tottering world becomes a better place in which to live.

The ancients would agree. The Greeks gave us the original Three Graces, the Charites, progeny of the world's coolest parents, by some accounts. Mom was Aphrodite, goddess of love and beauty; Dad was Dionysus, god of wine and Wallbangers. The Charites were the personifications of beauty, festivity, and joy, celebrated by Homer, Hesiod, Pindar, and other poets. The Romans renamed them the Gratiae, from which we get the word *grace*. Gifted with charm, high spirits, and the desire to please, these divine young ladies had the simple task of enhancing the enjoyment of life. Of bringing about ease.

Who couldn't use more of that?

And yet, though grace seems like it should be natural, when we look around us—and at ourselves—we tend to see the jarring angles, the glitches, the raw edges. The jerks.

But grace is within the reach of all of us. Neuroscientists and movement specialists agree that it is within the capabilities of everyone, no matter one's condition or abilities. It is made up of a poised and relaxed body, smooth and efficient motion, attentiveness, compassion. There is a contented silence to grace; it avoids what is loud and intrusive, and what offends the eye.

We need a return to grace. We are all fighting hard battles, and we need all the help we can get. Yet we've lost sight of grace, which for so long was an essential, treasured quality, and which ought to be at the heart of how we interact, how we inhabit our bodies and the world around us. Life in the twenty-first century is often rushed, clumsy, and frustrating, and it is this way because of what we do to one another, and to ourselves. We're overloaded at work. We're overwhelmed at home. We're distracted and we let the door slam on the person behind us, we trip over curbs as we're texting, we're running late, we fail to notice. Our bent postures show us the unfeeling habits we've fallen into—sedentary, weighed down, collapsed over the laptop. We've given in to gravity. We've forgotten how to move through life with grace.

Grace was once a subject for philosophers, poets, artists, and essayists, but you have to dig into French scholarship of nearly a century ago to find the last time it was explored in depth. In 1933, Raymond Bayer published a monumental examination, the two-volume *L'esthétique de la grâce: introduction à l'étude des équilibres de structure* (*The Aesthetic of Grace: Introduction to the Study of Structural Equilibrium*), which dissected grace as methodically as a chef fillets a pike. In twelve hundred pages he analyzed the nature of grace, compiled the history of philosophical theories of grace as a category of aesthetics, used graphs and charts to document the arc of spring and rebound in rubber balls and a sprinter's stride. It is an astonishing work, and very French. Bayer writes about the "secret" grace of animals, which no perfected machine will ever duplicate, and of the *royauté* that women share with felines in matters of movement. This is an intriguing observation; would Bayer, if he were alive, make it today? I doubt it. When was the last time you saw someone on the street with a truly mesmerizing way of moving? Grace has faded as a living aspect of our daily lives since the 1930s. It is ripe for rediscovery.

And in this endeavor, there is no greater guide than Cary Grant.

I HAVE BEEN a dance critic for thirty years and have been looking at grace for my entire adult life. My interest in it goes back even further than that, unofficially, when I consider my childhood fascination with movement. Born with a heart defect that required surgery when I was seven, I was strictly kept away from any physical exertion until a year after I'd had the operation. I watched and absorbed vicariously all I could of others' play and sports. Ballet lessons, with which I became obsessed as an older child and teenager, finally gave me a way in to the much-longed-for world of physical expression.

But it was Cary Grant—with not a ballet lesson to his name—who got me thinking more deeply about grace as an art unto itself. Watching the 1940 film *The Philadelphia Story* one day, I was drawn in by his uncommon gifts of clarity and depth: his deftness with complicated emotions, the way he could flit effortlessly from a zinger to an existential truth, and the way he embodied his finely etched, black-inked character with such vibrant ease. Mostly, it was the way he moved that got my attention.

In *The Philadelphia Story* he takes on the familiar role of the ex-husband still in love with his former wife (played by Katharine Hepburn) and hoping to scuttle her marriage to another man. Mindful of appearances as he reconnects with Hepburn's high-society family, Grant tries to hide his mixed-up feelings. Yet his body tells us something different. He speaks to Hepburn with a clipped indifference, but his torso softens. In the scene in which he comes to her house just before her marriage, Grant shows how much he wants to reclaim her with his long stride that eats up the space between them. What his lips can't say, his body reveals: he stands close, inclining toward her, yielding in the middle like a surrendering wolf flashing its underbelly. He does this all so easily, so effortlessly that we don't consciously think about it as a physical performance, like a dance, though in fact it is.

Movies and television show us possibilities beyond ourselves, so it is fitting to turn first to them for ideals of grace. There we find that, frequently, the most interesting and alluring actors are the ones who move well. Think of Greta Garbo's soft, slightly melting carriage and languorous stride, and Sophia Loren's hypnotic lateral sway. Audrey Hepburn's weightless bearing and (usually!) well-coordinated dancer's body. Big Jackie Gleason, so buoyant and light on his feet. Denzel Washington's glide.

Grace doesn't make a fuss about itself, but it subtly warms and transforms the atmosphere. At its essence, grace is the transference of well-being from one who is calm and comfortable to those around him. The graceful person is an image of our ideal selves, the embodiment of the dream we have of existing easily in the world. This is why we are so moved by graceful people, who carry themselves with ease and unselfconsciousness, who seem at peace. Life—regular life, the way you and I live it—is full of effort and awkwardness, those breathless dashes for the bus or the train, the times we wish we hadn't opened our big mouths. And then there is Garbo, almost floating along, no sharp edges, all chiffon and softness and that sense that she is attuned to some deep vibrations of the universe. We may never saunter as magnificently through a glittering lobby as she did in *Grand Hotel*, but her gracefulness has a broader significance. It exemplifies her ease in the world, the enviable condition of being completely in her element.

Graceful actions sound a note of pleasure in us, an intoxicating buzz we sense in our bones, because they offer an image of that most desirable state of affairs: effortless mastery. Mastery of the situation and of our own bodies, behavior, and emotions. We may feel that we're stumbling and huffing our way along, but a glimpse of graceful movement and manner inspires us with the dream of perfect harmony.

Enter Cary Grant. Alfred Hitchcock said he was "the only actor I have ever loved in my whole life."[2] The famously exacting director wasn't alone in his assessment, though it is especially weighty coming from him. It's been said that Hitchcock regarded actors as animated props. Perhaps this is one reason Grant stood out to him. The former acrobat and vaudevillian was never purely decorative; Grant was an unusually physical performer. He could launch himself into back flips (*Holiday*) and clamber along rooftops (*To Catch a Thief*). He hauled Katharine Hepburn to the top of a dinosaur skeleton (*Bringing Up Baby*) and pulled Eva Marie Saint up Mount Rushmore (*North by Northwest*). One-handed. Both times. Old acrobat's trick, he'd say.

Even more interesting is what Grant did with the common stock of human movement. He knew how to hold the eye and deepen a scene's emotional tone with a precisely formed and timed gesture, one that for anyone else would be perfectly ordinary—drumming his fingers on the steering wheel or shrugging a shoulder at just the right moment. Walking across a room with that loose, rocking stride of his, rising from a chair, leaning on a mantelpiece: Grant infused routine actions with a theatrical sense of purpose and an artist's subtlety. This is the Mozartian mystery of Grant's performances. Dramatic tension exists alongside playful, natural ease. And both the tension and the ease came from his full-body, three-dimensional responsiveness to others.

Yet Grant's screen performances aren't the only reason he is a model of grace. He also possessed the inner dimension, what the ancient Greeks referred to as *kalokagathia*: beauty and nobility of the soul. Tales of his gentlemanly qualities abound. Like all of us, he had his struggles and weaknesses; his included four divorces. But while he was unlucky in love, he managed his marital difficulties discreetly. And if his formality and famed perfectionism didn't make him easy to live with, they were useful professional qualities. If a costar's delivery was slightly off, Grant would flub his lines, too, so the whole scene would have to be reshot, allowing the other actor to save face while also getting a do-over.[3]

Well, it's easy enough to be kind when the stakes aren't terribly high. But Grant was kind when it wasn't easy to be kind. Ingrid Bergman credited him as the first—and one of the few—to stand up for her when her love affair with director Roberto Rossellini ignited an international scandal and, in an atmosphere of sanctimoniousness in excelsis, she was denounced from Hollywood to the Senate floor.[4]

At around the same time, when hardly anyone in Hollywood dared to protest the McCarthy-era blacklisting, Grant had the grace to think beyond himself and express his support publicly for Charlie Chaplin, English-born like Grant, whose visa had been revoked in the anticommunist furor. Grant held a press conference announcing his retirement (prematurely, as it happened), closing it with an unqualified defense of Chaplin, and a clear but understated warning: "We should not go off the deep end."[5]

Grant had a habit of making graceful gestures. Including this: in 1940, when America had not yet joined the war against the Nazis, he donated his entire salary from *The Philadelphia Story* to the British war effort.[6]

Grace can lie in a smooth, well-coordinated motion, or in a humble and tolerant attitude. More often than not, the two go hand in hand. The people who move well tend to be folks you want to be around. Their ease comes from being comfortable in their own skin, and that's what we're drawn to—not to technique or practiced perfection, but to what smooth physicality conveys about a person's nature. Grace has nothing to do with looks or sophistication, and everything to do with compassion and courage. There is grace in the courage, for instance, to step forward with a warm welcome for someone who has been shunned. (Think of Melanie's serene steadfastness toward Scarlett in *Gone with the Wind*; she ignored the scandalous rumors, standing up for Scarlett against the gossipmongers.) I find it is the folks who are humble, unpretentious, and direct who are the most graceful. They are the ones who open up a kind of ease with people, who don't put up barriers.

GRACE HAS POWERFUL ROOTS that reach back thousands, even millions, of years. As mammals, our brains evolved to perceive the subtlest movements of others. An appreciation for smoothness took up early residence in our neural pleasure centers. We depended on smooth, connected, and harmonious motion to survive in the treetops, swinging and climbing with a range of motion that was—and still is—extraordinary in the animal kingdom. Acrobatic agility is our birthright.

The yearning for ease of living, for an untroubled wholeness with the world, is also part of our foundational human heritage. It is inextricably bound up with that often awkward effort to live together that we call civilization.

Allow me to introduce a man named Ptah-hotep, who lived about 4,500 years ago in Egypt. There were no pyramids built in his honor; he was just a bureaucrat, an adviser to a pharaoh. But he left behind an inestimable treasure. He wrote the world's oldest book.

You might expect his hieroglyphics to chronicle heroic deeds in battle, or burial rites or tax collection, things we know were important in antiquity. But Ptah-hotep set forth something else entirely. His list of instructions for his son has been described as a first effort at moral philosophy or etiquette, but those labels miss the mark. Ptah-hotep wasn't setting forth rights and wrongs, nor was he limiting his list to polite behavior. He had a lot to say about showing respect for authority, as you'd expect from a royal insider (and he was writing to his son, after all). But he also urges us to honor the people around us by being "bright-faced," generous, and humble, and by helping them feel comfortable and appreciated. Ptah-hotep's purpose is social harmony.

Things were pretty much falling apart in the twenty-fifth century BC, in his view. Kids weren't obeying their parents, greediness and bad manners were rampant, people at table were more intent on stuffing their faces and arguing than on exercising restraint and listening. Leaders were prone to absolutism. So our ancestral author, composing what would become the urtext of human civilization, made an exhaustive effort to set things right with a plea for understanding, composure, and care.

"Kindness is a man's memorial," he wrote. In the eyes of posterity, "the mild has a greater claim than the harsh." Also: "If thou be powerful, make thyself to be honoured for knowledge and for gentleness."[7]

In other words: Get out of your head and pay attention. Think of the other guy. This theme rings through his maxims, as Ptah-hotep counsels husbands to pamper their wives with liniments, fine clothes, and loving attention. He calls on leaders to be patient with subordinates and to allow them to vent without interruption: "Be gracious when thou hearkenest unto the speech of a suppliant." (From his emphasis on keeping quiet while others gripe, it seems Fifth Dynasty tempers were high and morale was in the dust.) He directs those in power to leave behind a legacy of compassion. "Be not proud because thou art learned; but discourse with the ignorant man as with the sage," he wrote.

As time rolls forward, what humanity holds dear does not change much. Ptah-hotep's message continues to echo through the ages, even as its medium shifts from papyrus to parchment, from books to film. The kind of social sensitivity the Egyptian vizier advocated was taken up in ancient Athens, in Renaissance Italy, and in colonial Virginia, where, as a school exercise, a teenage George Washington copied out his *Rules of Civility and Decent Behaviour in Company and Conversation* in large, looping script. These 110 rules, which Washington held on to for the rest of his life, were a simplified version of a 1640 book by Francis Hawkins, *Youths Behaviour, or, Decency in Conversation Amongst Men*. Hawkins had translated his principles from sixteenth-century French Jesuits, who had likely absorbed them from court traditions borrowed from the classical era, which preserved ways of getting along with others as old and nourishing as the Nile.

"Be not froward," commands Washington's Rule 66, using a wonderful old word for willfully obstinate, "but friendly and Courteous." Rule 70: "Reprehend not the imperfections of others." And 105: "Be not angry at the table whatever happens."

Ptah-hotep's views—rooted, undoubtedly, in even earlier times—express an ideal vision of how to be in the world. How to live with ease, avoiding friction. As far back as we have records to show, humanity has longed for this. And herein lies the attraction of grace. It represents a kind of completeness, bringing all one's noblest desires and actions into harmony.

Seeking out this ideal of harmony animates not only the conduct of leaders and royals, but of middle- and upper-class folks in their parlors and public lives. You hear it, for instance, throughout *The Philadelphia Story*. Take the words of the father character, who, like Ptah-hotep, is imparting a lesson to his child.

"You have a good mind, a pretty face, and a disciplined body that does what you tell it," says actor John Halliday's sage patriarch, speaking to Katharine Hepburn, who plays his cold, sharp-tongued daughter. "You have everything that it takes to make a lovely woman except the one essential: an understanding heart."

Cary Grant is Hepburn's perfect foil in the movie, for he has everything it takes to make a lovely man: the mind, the disciplined body, and, most especially, the understanding heart. In the ancient world as in the golden age of Hollywood, as in our own time, these are the three essentials of grace.

We're living in what I call the grace gap. We hurry through our days, with our eyes and ears plugged into our devices, our minds far away, not noticing the physical or emotional impression we make on others. Our impatient, fragmented, competitive society conspires in many ways against gentleness and understanding. Popular culture stokes delight in humiliation and conflict. "I feel your pain" is a cliché and a lie. In recent years, researchers have seen a sharp drop in empathy and a corresponding rise in narcissism among young adults. A 2010 University of Michigan study found that college students are 40 percent less empathetic than their counterparts of thirty years ago, with the numbers dropping the most after the twenty-first century began.[8] Another set of experiments found that upper-class folks suffer "empathy deficits." The richer the participants, the less able they were to read accurately the emotions of others.[9] Think of what that means for their ability to see others' points of view, to transcend a pressing drama and consider the big-picture effect of their actions.

We tend to associate grace with the highbrow realms of life—royal weddings, state dinners, opera houses. We see it in the cultivated correctness of, say, Jackie Kennedy Onassis, whose social status required her to leave a well-designed impression. Of course, we are suitably impressed by that. There is a certain cool, polished quality to that sort of grace, like the surface of a pearl.

But that ornamental grace doesn't illuminate much that's useful to the rest of us.

The great Italian painter Caravaggio insisted on bringing his subjects down to earth. There is an invigorating energy to his paintings; his dynamic, realistic seventeenth-century saints were unshaven, with dirty feet. Some were young and kind of hot. His madonnas were modeled on prostitutes he knew, and very likely loved. They had grace with grit, grace that's fleshly and a little flawed and stems from an open embrace of life. I'm drawn to that hard-won grace, the kind one might also discover looking back at Motown tours in the civil rights era or on the vaudeville circuit, or today among the fearless stagehands hanging lights for a rock concert, or on a tennis court or a suburban street corner, and in a dance class for people with Parkinson's.

These arenas—as well as science—offer hopeful news for the klutzes among us. Grace is wonderfully democratic. The potential is there for everyone. With practice, grace is a skill we can all develop.

Yet there is something hidden about grace; it is often overlooked, or vaguely felt but difficult to identify. "The last and noblest part of beauty is grace," declared the influential eighteenth-century Scottish philosopher Thomas Reid, "which the author thinks undefinable." Defining things is pretty much what philosophers do, so why did Reid stop short in the face of grace?

I've written this book to locate grace and hold it up for examination. Being aware of grace in others allows us to feel some of their ease ourselves and to enjoy a heightened vitality as we sympathetically move in harmony, too, even if it is only in our imaginations. That alone can do wonders. We are natural imitators, and the more we look at grace, the more we can become graceful, too. The next step is practice: cultivate ease of movement, self-control, and warmth, and the Greta Garbo walk may very well follow.

The third step is to learn to face the world willingly (or at least without obvious panic) and with regard for those around you.

Grace—the kind I'm talking about, everyday grace, honest and disarming—doesn't exist without a test. It is most apparent when we have fallen, when we are bare. It is revealed in the simple act of paying attention, when a subtle change, a bit of hidden choreography or an unexpected show of understanding suddenly becomes a moment of truth. We just have to look.

Or rather, let's go full bore and say: behold. *Behold*, when you break it down to its roots, means "to hold thoroughly." You not only see something but you hold it, you feel it against your body; you drink it in, inhale it as you would a baby's buttery-warm head of hair. A graceful act is a sensory rush.

Let us behold, then, the grace and the grace-full around us. Before examining grace as the art of getting along and how graceful conduct has been passed down through the ages; before looking at grace among celebrities, and the grace of stumbles and falls; before exploring grace in sculpture, painting, dance, sports, science, and theology—we begin with one man. The man who taught me more about savoring grace than all the ballerinas in all the *Swan Lakes* I've ever seen.

PART ONE

A Panoramic View of Grace

Cary Grant tapped into a timeless truth: there is nothing we watch so keenly as the human body in action, because the way it moves tells a story. With Katharine Hepburn in The Philadelphia Story, *the tale is one of yearning and resistance.*

CHAPTER 1

FLAIR TO REMEMBER:

WHY CARY GRANT EPITOMIZES GRACE

The human body is the best picture of the human soul.

—Ludwig Wittgenstein

North by Northwest, Alfred Hitchcock's sprawling 1959 thriller that takes us to the top of Mount Rushmore by way of a near-miss with a killer crop duster, begins with the basics: a man is walking down a corridor.

But because the man is Cary Grant, the moment is anything but ordinary.[1] He has us at the first step, with that long, brisk stride and its steady rhythm, a ticktock pace that telegraphs purpose, clarity, and efficiency. We watch him stroll out of an elevator toward the street, dictating correspondence to the secretary at his side. Grant plays an advertising executive named Roger Thornhill, and he wordlessly tells us he's a boss with heart. There's a relaxed, easy give in his body as he moves and as he leans toward his secretary while he speaks to her. He's so very pleased with his own labors, and yet so exquisitely courteous to his assistant. He's smooth as whiskey, and getting further under our skin with every move.

In this scene, Grant's words are not nearly as important as his movement. It's the movement that hooks us. It always does. Grant tapped into a timeless truth: there is nothing we watch so keenly as the human body in action, because the way it moves tells a story.

A person's way of moving through space speaks to us on a primal level. It's animal to animal, picked up like a scent. Our brains, like those of all mammals, are wired to perceive motion. For most of us, smooth motion is more appealing than jerkiness, especially if the smoothness is variegated, with some unpredictable moments. Think about what your eyes might rest on in the natural world: watching the unperturbed flow of a stream can grow monotonous, while the round, changeable flight of a feather in the wind holds the interest.

Graceful movement is the feather in the wind: smooth but fluctuating. This protean fluidity is a quality that unites all the examples of physical grace to come in these pages. While it may be so subtle that you do not consciously notice it, when an actor, a dancer, an athlete, or anyone else moves smoothly and harmoniously—but not too smoothly, allowing for surprises—your eye will follow him anywhere.

The body comes first. Grace is the transference of ease from one body to another. When we witness grace, we feel that ease echo in our own bodies. Graceful people make us feel good.

Grant's dark beauty, cultured diction, and gift for comedy are unmistakable. But what I find most fascinating about him—and I believe it's the reason he is as watchable now as he was all those decades ago—is his physical grace, his ability to create a flowing performance through physical details. It's not just acting, not just body language, but a movement-infused performance that can be felt as well as seen.

That fluidity is always there, in every role, in the way he walks, the way he slips a hand into his pocket. It's in his comedy and his pratfalls, the way he's never ungainly or clumsy even in well-choreographed moments of panic. (Has anyone ever sprinted through a cornfield with such style?) It's even in the way he stands, and his ability to continue infusing alert physicality into a moment of stillness. He might do this simply through the inclination of his head and the lively focus in his eyes, or by melting his shoulders just a bit toward the costar his character is invariably secretly in love with. He expressed a lot through economical means, which directors, of course, loved.

Grant "never wasted a moment on-screen," said Alan J. Pakula (who directed *Sophie's Choice* and *All the President's Men*, among others). "Every movement meant something to him."[2]

Once you start looking for them, you can see examples of Grant's physical grace in all his films. A scene in *His Girl Friday* (1940) is especially fine because of what Grant communicated so potently in the smallest of ways. Sparks between newspaper editor Walter Burns (Grant) and his star reporter and ex-wife Hildy Johnson (Rosalind Russell) pop the whole way through, but in one scene Grant's nuanced physical maneuvering spins its own narrative. Seated over a polite lunch with his former bride—for whom he still pines—and her new fiancé, Bruce (Ralph Bellamy), Walter aims to show Hildy just how foolish her fantasy of impending domestic bliss sounds.

"Ah yes, a home with Mother," he enthuses—then he smothers a chortle and rolls a shoulder—"and in Albany, too!" It's a picture of devastating mockery, but so slight and slippery that Bruce doesn't notice. Hildy does, and we do, too. Grant orchestrates the moment perfectly.

With every move leading up to it, he's drawn our eye to his shoulders, squeezing them together slightly, not relaxing them until now, this instant, when that little action that starts in his neck and trickles across the top of his suit jacket shouts out loud and clear that Hildy is making a stupid mistake. It's not flamboyant, there's nothing self-indulgent in that gesture, and it's over in a wink. But it reveals the calculating trickiness as well as the feelings of his character. That liquid, nearly imperceptible roll of a muscle hangs there like an echo, a ripple in the airwaves, a shiver in the emotional current that encircles Grant and Russell and us.

You understand something subliminal about him. His inner qualities are projected through his outer presentation. Grant's genius was in how he could show us his state of being through a kind of dance, subtle and quick and more powerful than words.

The director of *His Girl Friday,* that master of exuberance Howard Hawks, deserves credit for unleashing Grant's full-body expressiveness. He and Grant shared a delight in rapid-fire improvisation and made five movies together, including Grant's loopy, falling-down romp with Katharine Hepburn *Bringing Up Baby* as well as *Only Angels Have Wings*, *I Was a Male War Bride*, and *Monkey Business*. But Grant had learned the power of graceful physical expression—the power of making it all look easy—long before he ever got to Hollywood.

Gracefulness was his ticket out of a difficult youth. Grant was born Archibald Leach in Bristol, England, in 1904. He was an only child, and his mother disappeared without a word when he was nine.

She'd been put in a mental hospital by Grant's father, who didn't tell his son the truth about why she'd gone missing until decades later.

Grant's childhood became one of unresolved sadness, solitude, and dreams of slipping away on the steamships leaving Bristol's wharves. His escape became real when he took a backstage job at the newly opened Hippodrome, home to variety shows and revues. Grant was barely thirteen, and he rushed headlong into the welcoming embrace of joyful misfits and roustabouts who helped him craft a new existence in the theater.

Acrobats were a music hall mainstay in those days, and by the time he turned fourteen Grant had become one, joining a troupe of "knockabout comedians," as they were known, led by Bob Pender. (A 1913 training manual called *How to Enter Vaudeville: A Complete Illustrated Course of Instruction,* describes the knockabout act, a vaudeville staple, in a way that could sum up many of Grant's films: "more or less of a plot and a laughable, rough and tumble affair from start to finish. The dialog must be clever and original, as the act is a rapid-fire one all the way through."[3]) Pender was a famous clown and his wife had been a ballet mistress at the Folies Bergère in Paris. From them, Grant learned to discipline his body and use it to tell a story. Without a word.

"Touring the English provinces with the troupe, I grew to appreciate the fine art of pantomime," Grant wrote in an autobiographical article many years later:

> No dialogue was used in our act and each day, on a bare stage, we learned not only dancing, tumbling and stilt-walking under the expert tuition of Bob Pender, but also how to con-

> vey a mood or meaning without words. How to establish communication silently with an audience, using the minimum of movement and expression; how best immediately and precisely to effect an emotional response—a laugh or, sometimes, a tear. The greatest pantomimists of our day have been able to induce both at once.[4]

"Surprisingly, Hitchcock is one of the most subtle pantomimists of them all," Grant wrote of the director with whom he made four films, all of them classics (*Suspicion*, *Notorious*, and *To Catch a Thief*, in addition to *North by Northwest*, arguably the greatest work by either man). Though truly, Hitchcock's nonverbal finesse is no surprise; he began his career making taut, emotionally charged silent films. With his keen sensitivity for movement and rhythm, he was as much a choreographer as a director.

But physical skills weren't enough, Grant realized. To lift his performance above the ordinary, he had to make it look easy. Grant set himself to studying and imitating all he could.

"At each theater I carefully watched the celebrated headline artists from the wings, and grew to respect the diligence and application and long experience it took to acquire such expert timing and unaffected confidence, the amount of effort that resulted in such effortlessness," he wrote. "I strove to make everything I did at least appear relaxed. Perhaps by relaxing outwardly I could eventually relax inwardly."

In 1920 Grant arrived with Pender in New York City, where the troupe was booked between acts by tramp cyclists, magicians, and clowns. It was a life of constant discipline, onstage and off. Everyone, from stars on down, punched a time clock. Grant lived in a communal apartment, washed and ironed his own laundry. Backstage, he studied the comic timing of George Burns and Gracie Allen when they were in town. He learned to fill in for others without rehearsal and to improvise on the fly. He toured the country with the troupe, but when Pender returned to England, Grant stayed behind.

He eventually moved to Hollywood, changed his name, found stardom. But he kept what he learned from vaudeville: the grace that comes from hard work. His ease of moving was earned through diligence and careful observation and all the other lessons he picked up from the wings. For Grant this grace took many forms: the ability to turn flips in *Holiday*, again with Katharine Hepburn, as a way to get her attention, and to take pratfalls with deceptive control in *The Awful Truth*, trying to catch his soon-to-be-divorced wife (Irene Dunne) in an affair. It's in his contained, unearthly calm and gliding presence in *The Bishop's Wife*, all the fine-drawn physical details with which he convinces us he is not a homewrecker but a true angel, sent from Heaven to be a perfect platonic friend by taking the neglected Loretta Young ice skating and buying her a hat. It's in the way he lists from side to side as he walks in *Mr. Blandings Builds His Dream House*, where he is all mortal weakness. His midsection sinks as the routine indignities of middle-class life settle on his everyman's shoulders like dust.

Grant's gracefulness is in the crackling, unselfconscious spontaneity that so inspired Howard Hawks, and in his ever-present, head-to-toe physical coordination and command of himself. He smoothed and polished his vaudeville ways into a more subtle performing style, one that was understated and effortless, but never passive. No matter how lighthearted his character, there is always a corporeal energy to Grant. That alertness can be traced right back to his acrobat's love of physical play and feline reflexes, and to his years of experience learning how to hook a live audience through his body.

Grant can transfix us even with his stillness. Think of *An Affair to Remember,* in which a car accident keeps Deborah Kerr from her much-desired rendezvous with Grant. She is too proud to let him know that her injuries have left her partially paralyzed, and so she simply drops out of his life, leaving her absence unexplained. Grant carries on like a gallant wounded animal for the rest of the film, wincing just under the surface, believing that he was jilted by the woman of his dreams even up to the moment when, years later, they finally meet again.

And then, as he's chattering rather crisply and a little snarkily at Kerr, Grant suddenly halts mid-sentence. Clues about Kerr's concealed condition click together in his mind; his self-pity stops dead in its tracks. It's a frozen moment of agony—and just as swiftly, something opens up inside him. You see it in his expression, a mix of clarity, remorse, and overwhelming love, and it sends him in a flash to Kerr's side. Grant's character experiences a moment of grace, right before our eyes. His hurt pride crashes up against his reawakened moral core and he is changed. Hardly anything chokes me up—hardened spectator that I am, I've usually got the driest eyes in the theater—but I can't watch this scene without tears.

I've never seen a cinematic moment that compares to this one for its economy and its quiet revelation. Many actors make use of controlled blankness, keeping you wondering what's going on inside them. That can be intriguing; I'm thinking of Montgomery Clift, or Paul Newman, or any number of others. But they don't offer us the piercing, instant communication we get from watching another person go through a precise emotional experience with grace. We don't see the sharp transference of feeling that distilled but full-bodied acting produces, where emotion registers through the most economical means possible—physical expression—so we feel what they feel within our own bodies.

Think, for example, of Gary Cooper's quick, impatient stride across town to the church in *High Noon,* when he thinks he'll be able to round up a posse among the worshipers. And his slow, pained walk back after he fails to find help. He doesn't say a word, but the heaviness he feels is right there in his movement. You ache watching him.

Hitchcock was a master at deploying Cary Grant's physical grace. *North by Northwest* is the definitive study of Grant in motion. The film has all the compressed, hyperemotional propulsion of a full-length ballet. There is that churning, driving Bernard Herrmann musical score, for starters. The story unspools in a classic ballet structure, moving from the simple to the complex in the buildup of athletic images, revolving around brilliantly restrained duets and—most delicious of all—Grant's bravura solo turns.

This is the film, after all, where that nice ad exec runs for his life from a crop duster, his gait pinched and strained to show us how bewildered and trapped he feels, even under a wide-open sky; he makes a splayed-out, elegantly finessed dive into the dust that Russian ballet star Mikhail Baryshnikov might envy. Later Grant arcs spectacularly backward, up on his toes, even, from Eva Marie Saint's gunshots. All the comedy, tension, and romance, the racing pace and the plot twists, register on that lean, alive body.

. . .

ARTISTS, POETS, AND GREAT THINKERS from the ancients on have associated gracefulness with charm and allure. "Beauty without grace," wrote Ralph Waldo Emerson, "is the hook without the bait."[5] It's true, without that little jig of lusciousness that grace bestows, beauty can be cold. Take, for example, Katharine Hepburn, whom I find fascinating as an actress, but not graceful. There was nothing giving about her angular frame or her character. She had great panache, great bone structure, innards of iron. She gleamed with studied perfection, but not grace. Why? Grace is simple, effortless, tranquil. Hepburn was upright and sharp-edged, a master of technique but not ease. The strongest impression she leaves in her films is of staccato crispness, like a door buzzer or the flap of sails in a skin-chapping wind.

Now consider the other Hepburn. Audrey Hepburn conveys sensitivity and ease in her weightless carriage, her warmth, the way she listens in a scene, with real attention. Her ability to project sympathy, through her expression and that well-coordinated dancer's body—that too is grace. The nineteenth-century English literary critic William Hazlitt could have been describing the *Breakfast at Tiffany's* star when he defined grace in a woman as "an habitual voluptuousness of character, which reposes on its own sensations and derives pleasure from all around it, that is more irresistible than any other attraction."[6] Tall, skinny Audrey had an austere elegance, like Scandanavian furniture. She didn't have a voluptuous body. But she did have a voluptuous *character*; with those lively eyes and her artless enthusiasm, she convinced you that all her senses were firing, that she was living in the moment without judgment. Grace is what warms beauty and makes it irresistible, because it is open, pleasure-seeking, generous: voluptuous. We feel that the graceful person is giving us something, offering us a true human connection, even if that connection is entirely in our imaginations.

I had the chance to speak about this with Rita Moreno over lunch one day.[7] I was impressed immediately with the actress's grace: even at eighty-two she walked with the smooth, unhurried ease of a dancer. She came by this naturally, after a long career ignited by her Oscar-winning role as Anita, the quick, fierce, confident Puerto Rican who survives sexual assault and more in the movie musical *West Side Story*. Moreno is one of the few living links to a time when stars acted, sang, and danced. When physical grace was a job requirement.

We were sitting by a window in a downtown Washington restaurant at the height of the lunch rush, talking about the difficulty of the dancing she had to do in *West Side Story*, and suddenly Moreno put on a show for me. Anita's steps defined her, and she hasn't forgotten them, so after scooting over on the banquette and hiking up her trousers as if she were clutching Anita's purple skirt, she starting singing the beats. It was a Morse code of jazz: "Da-da-da, DA-da-da, DA-da-da!" Her feet tapped out the steps, sharp and crisp. Her shoulders swayed and rolled. "Bam-bam-bam!" One foot swept to the side and Moreno threw her head back—a full-body sketch of Anita's whirling, explosive kick—while the other foot kept time.

Talk about voluptuousness! Her shoulders pumped, her mouth went *ya-tata, ya-tata*, her sandaled feet darted out and back, swift as minnows. I was swept along by it, too. No wine needed: I was intoxicated by her show of grace. I think she was, too. When she stopped, her eyes were huge behind her wire-rimmed glasses; her cheeks were pink.

"We are dinosaurs," Moreno said, sliding back to the table. "Joel Grey, myself, Chita," meaning Chita Rivera, who originated the role of Anita on Broadway. "We are truly dinosaurs. I don't know that many people who do it all anymore. Everyone specializes."

I asked her if we have lost anything as performers have narrowed their breadth, moving away from physical grace. She looked out the window for a moment. "What musical performers bring to straight characterizations is that physical flexibility that comes with knowing your body so well," she said, turning back to me. "A lot of actors are terribly awkward. Terribly. And I think it's so important for them, when they're young, to work on their physical selves. Because it truly gives you a completely different bent on how you move as a straight actor. Christopher Walken has a fabulous way of moving. He's fascinating, isn't he? He physicalizes so much and I think it's due to a true knowledge of his physical self. That's what's missing from a lot of performers. They are really stiff."

I agree with her about Walken. He started out as a dancer and went on to musical theater before concentrating on films. But his kinetic past has never left him: he whirled through a tap-dance routine in the Steve Martin comedy *Pennies from Heaven*, and he makes full use of his disciplined, expressive body whether he's playing bad guys or goofs. He makes it look easy, which can be both creepy and great, especially when he's cast as a villain.

The physical self is overlooked in live theater, too. "I often get surprised at actors who think acting is just saying things," said John Tiffany, the English director of Broadway's *Once,* for which he won a Tony. He was telling me why he has insisted on an eloquent physical language not only in romantic musicals such as *Once* but also for *Black Watch*, the heartbreaking war play about Scottish soldiers in Iraq, which he also directed. "Theater is about being an athlete. And a musician. And not just for musicals, not just for Broadway. That should be a part of every theater."

If the art of moving well is rare in live theater, it has nearly vanished from movies. In particular, we don't see a lot of male grace in films nowadays. Built-up bulk and aggression on the one hand, or the slump-shouldered regular-guy aesthetic on the other, have taken its place. Actors aren't formally trained in dance and movement as they were in the early years of filmmaking. There was the invasion of psychoanalysis, and the rise of the Actors Studio and Method acting, starting about a half century or so ago. Psychological realism, interior motives, and deep mental preparation were the artistic trends. Emotional truth trumped physical truth. Actors started questioning the precise blocking of action—the choreography of the scene—that directors asked of them.

In an interview about his 1953 film *I Confess*, Hitchcock complained that Montgomery Clift, who starred as a priest suspected of murder, "was too obscure in his methods." In one scene, Hitchcock said, "I asked him to look up, so that I could cut to his point of view of the building across the street. He said, 'I don't know if I would look up.' . . . I said, 'If you don't look up, I can't cut.' It was like that all the way through."[8]

I spoke about this with David Thomson, the British film critic and historian, and author of the essential reference *The New Biographical Dictionary of Film*. (In it, he describes Grant as "the best and most important film actor in the history of the cinema."[9])

Before Method acting came into vogue, "American acting was

much more in line with English acting, where physical grace was a very important thing," Thomson told me. "Approximately with Marlon Brando, we suddenly get physical gracelessness."

Enter slumping and mumbling, exit agility. Broadly speaking, the midcentury's new crop of actors reacted against the poised grace of Grant and his like. *From Here to Eternity*, which came out the same year as *I Confess*, is a neat example of the split. On the one hand, you have Burt Lancaster—onetime athlete and trapeze artist, body cut from stone, forever hot under the collar. Lancaster took the physical to a combustible extreme; his Sergeant Warden is all raw power. Compare him with his costar, the young Montgomery Clift, whose Private Prewitt is freighted with the past, self-absorbed, a head case. Searching for personal truth. Remember Lancaster's roll in the surf with Deborah Kerr, one kiss, one wave, destined to crest forever in American loins? To hell with truth; they wanted contact. They were the body; Clift, the loner, was the soul.

"We're still very much in the vogue of the Actors Studio," said Thomson. "The search for inner truthfulness, abandoning elegance and clarity. We're into a style of more awkward personal truths."

Up to around midcentury, particularly in the art films, actors show a subtler, more detailed attention to their form and use it skillfully to express a complicated richness of character. Actors were admired not just for their beauty but for the way they moved, how they carried themselves. Physical elegance signaled inner elegance. Both Humphrey Bogart and James Cagney possessed terrific physical dynamism. Bogart was famed for his compelling walk. Cagney was a trained tap dancer, quick and light, and that was part of his menace in his gangster roles. You knew he could zoom in for the kill in a heartbeat.

Lauren Bacall possessed a ballsy grace. Raised by two strong women—a Jewish immigrant mother and grandmother—she combined power and glamour, and could be blunt and seductive in the same husky breath. ("You know how to whistle, don't you, Steve?") You can't think of her without picturing the way she moved and commanded space with that slender dancer's figure, that stealth. She worked hard at acting, and turned her moves into an art: the way she smoked, cocked an eyebrow, ducked her chin, glided and swiveled through a room. Yet she despised pretense. Bacall fought Hollywood efforts to thin her eyebrows and straighten her teeth; she never augmented her small bust, didn't hide her wrinkles. She disliked her studio name; to her friends she was Betty, the name her mother gave her. Bacall was comfortable with herself. She wasn't hungry for attention, but she didn't shrink from the camera, either, even in her very last years. (That was her most profound expression of grace: Bacall showed us how to age gracefully, with dignity, laugh lines, and zest for living.)

With his aristocratic looks and a way with comedy that hinted at darkness, Marcello Mastroianni was an Italian Cary Grant. He moved with even more ease and swing, but this looser nonchalance was also detached, as if there were music playing in his head, leading his thoughts elsewhere.

"The eye has to travel," declared legendary fashion editor Diana Vreeland. She knew that to hook a viewer's interest there had to be a sense of movement in a photo or among images laid out on a page. Your eyes want to move. The more you are enticed to visually wander, by a rhythmic pull or the unexpected juxtaposition, the more you'll discover. It's true in film as well. Those actors who use their whole bodies as a canvas for character development give us more to discover about them, and that much more delight.

I think about this when I watch Claudette Colbert, the enormously popular French-born actress from the 1930s and '40s, who insisted on being filmed only from the left because she thought that was her better side. Her scenes had to be carefully choreographed to adhere to this rule. When I watch her films (*It Happened One Night* is the most celebrated), I can think only of the strain it must have been to shoot them. To be so controlling about her appearance, so self-conscious, is the antithesis of grace.

You can't blame Colbert's rigidity on the perfectionistic eye for detail for which the French are famous. Actors can be French and also gracefully open to the moment: look at Jean-Paul Belmondo in the landmark 1960 French film *Breathless*.[10] The story of a thug on the run, restlessly marooned in Paris, helped launch a new cinematic style—the French New Wave—with its spontaneous, stream-of-consciousness form and long, unbroken takes. But this film is also an ode to Belmondo's body, by accident perhaps, as director Jean-Luc Godard doesn't fully exploit Belmondo's gift of physical grace. *Breathless* loses air every time Godard moves in for a close-up. But let Belmondo saunter down a flight of stairs while he's lighting one of his fat cigarettes, or swagger through a lobby, or shadowbox in his underwear, and the film hums with raw, freewheeling grace.

Belmondo may not be as polished as Grant nor as sensuously sculpted as a young Marlon Brando. But here's the artfulness of his approach: he uses his body to take us deeper into his character. Is he really just a petty thief who sees himself as a classy tough? The way he carries himself suggests something else entirely.

We fall in love with this lowlife not because of what he says or his story (neither is terribly profound) but because of his moves. He bursts with an endearing boyish energy, light-footed and carefree, fed by the jittery fantasies of a dreamer. The jacked-up optimism in the way Belmondo moves tells us his character has heart, wit, and promise, even if his words convey the opposite. The postwar era was over, the new decade was dawning as one of irony, nervousness, and suspicion, and this is the poignance of Belmondo's portrayal. He has all the ambition and swagger of a dying era, when an ordinary man could believe he really did hold the world on a string, like a cosmic yo-yo pro.

Head tipped back, posture regal, he's a man brimming with self-assurance and vitality. Best of all is Belmondo's walk, set off by the jazz soundtrack. He's costumed to look big and broad-shouldered, wearing an oversize suit jacket, but it's the fluidity of his stride and the harmony in his whole body that signal his confidence. There's a bit of coiled-up James Dean impatience and Montgomery Clift intensity, but Belmondo adds his own dash. He musters up a full-body expressiveness—a relaxed, outgoing, and uninhibited physicality, as if he's the solo star in the dance of life. He throws punches at the mirror and you feel exhilarated because that's what he's feeling: fresh, alive, seductive.

It wasn't until I started studying Grant that I fully appreciated Belmondo and began looking at other actors with new eyes. Which ones have something of Grant's dancerlike understanding of a role, a sense that acting is a physical exercise, not just an emotional one? Which ones convey throughout a career the physical intelligence that Grant had? George Clooney is often held up as Grant's heir for the way he looks in a tuxedo. He has some of that physical flair, though he channels it in a very different direction. He doesn't have Grant's reserve, the sense of mystery that keeps you guessing and looking for clues about what he's really up to. Clooney is direct. He's more of a Clark Gable type—rough, impatient, boldly virile.

Denzel Washington has a profound understanding of grace in acting. His physical elegance gives the hostage negotiator he plays in Spike Lee's *Inside Man* an extra dimension of truth; he has everything smoothly under control, or at least he thinks so. You might actually believe him, even if you were a psychopath. His physical details, little studies in style, make you pay attention. With his floating, dipping walk, is he slooping through water, or treading on smoke?

Bill Murray delivers a Grant-like sense of comfort in his own skin in the masterfully underplayed *Lost in Translation*, which is essentially a movie about energy. High energy alternates with low: the jangly buzz of Tokyo's nightlife contrasts with the somnolent unease that brings together Murray and Scarlett Johansson. But it's not just sleeplessness that joins this pair of misfits who meet at a hotel. Their motors run at the same leisurely rpm.

Through his slowness, his unhurried, unfussy elegance and languid physicality, Murray creates a character we can trust, who comes across as confident, humble, and wise. As Johansson's unappreciated young wife is slowly trying to figure out her place in the world, Murray's comfortable has-been celebrity is a model of self-assurance. In divulging the secret to his own mellowness, he captures the essence of moving gracefully through life: "The more you know what you want, the less you let things bother you."

The popular British television series *Downton Abbey*, with its fictional family of aristocrats and their servants, shows us how essential physical grace is to the drama's post-Edwardian period and the social hierarchy. This was a time when restrictive corsets encouraged (and even forced) proper posture. As the series moves into the 1920s with its looser, linear fashions, the actresses still maintain the upright bearing that allows their flapper dresses and sleek beaded gowns to drape properly. Etiquette also dictates that spines do not touch the backs of chairs, and slouching is a no-no, so young and old sit at the table with a lifted, slightly forward-leaning pose that makes a person look alert and lively. The cast's awareness of physical detail extends well beyond the dining room: it is in the serene, leisurely way the Crawley family members stroll around their Yorkshire estate, and in the swallowed-down energy of the servants, who strive to be inconspicuous as they scoot by with aspics and puddings.

Dignity is found downstairs as well as up. Scottish actress Phyllis Logan portrays the unflappable housekeeper Mrs. Hughes with evocative simplicity. It is an inspiring portrait of calm good-heartedness, told with a brilliantly light touch. She is all about presence: a silent, floating stride through the hallways, an ability to command her staff's attention merely by entering the room. As Mrs. Hughes absorbs the domestic crises of each episode with poise and compassion, you feel the importance she places on excellence.

But to me, the screen star who most embodies Cary Grant's lusciousness today is Cate Blanchett, who moves with a dancer's energy. There is a reined-in elegance about her, a sense of explosiveness carefully under wraps, which gives her an active presence even when she's not moving. With that comes firm self-possession and a watchful intensity, even in so small a role as that of the elf queen Galadriel in *The Lord of the Rings: The Fellowship of the Ring*. She seems to float as she descends the stairs in her midnight scene, breastbone high, a slight arch in her back. She communicates a mystical depth in that taut, gliding physical presence.

In an interview for an entertainment website about how she approached her role in *Notes on a Scandal*, in which she plays a teacher who sleeps with her fifteen-year-old student, Blanchett revealed her thinking about the physical dimension of playing such an unpalatable character. In the novel that inspired the film, she says, her character is "described as having a dancer's body," which Blanchett distilled into a posture that communicated being drawn to intense sensation, even suffering: "that sort of presentation that some women have, chest bone forward, that's a little bit, 'I'm dashed against the rocks.'"[11]

Blanchett performs onstage as well as in movies, as did Grant, Walken, Moreno, and so many of these other graceful actors. She knows how to make that physical connection with her audience, how to reach out to us as if we are her intimates, how to project full-bodied human warmth. To watch her feels like a luxury and makes you realize what so many other films are missing: The body with soul. The human depth that Cary Grant could show us, with a character crafted not only with voice and emotion but through head-to-toe grace.

Seek out Cary Grant. The consummate charmer had a sharp sense of joy, which he shares here with Attorney General William French Smith and his wife.

CHAPTER 2

GRACE AMONG OTHERS:

JAY GATSBY, ELEANOR ROOSEVELT, AND OTHER GOOD HOSTS

The sentiment that reveals grace is too profound to take origin from a purely corporal cause.

—Henry Home

In May 1981, Grant and his fifth wife, Barbara, were invited by President Reagan to a dinner at the White House in honor of Britain's Prince Charles. Other actors were on the guest list, including David Niven. Niven's son Jamie was invited, too, but when his father, who was gravely ill at the time, sent his regrets, Jamie wasn't at all sure about going without him—he wasn't an actor, after all, and he feared he'd feel out of place.

"Don't worry about a thing," David Niven told his son. "Seek out Cary Grant and tell him you're nervous and ask him what to do."

"I did exactly that," Jamie Niven later recounted. "Without batting an eye, Cary turned to a waiter and said, 'We'll have two large vodka martinis.' And we hammered them down."[1]

I find nothing so exhausting as small talk. I run from the obligatory social event. But I'd think otherwise if Cary Grant were around not to judge me but to understand me, and to supply companionship and a little liquid inspiration. In this story he's not only the embodiment of grace but a follower of Dionysus, the Greek god of wine, dear to the Three Graces, and a patron of the arts, whose coterie of satyrs were gentle, companionable creatures. They were fond of dancing and physical pleasures. They were often depicted with a drink in hand.

David Niven clearly had confidence in the willingness and ability of Grant—his friend, fellow Englishman, and costar in the 1947 film *The Bishop's Wife*—to make social magic happen for his son. You just know Niven had seen Grant do exactly that on other occasions. Grant made a quick read of the situation and offered an understanding heart, and the perfect fix—friendship and a shared cocktail to loosen the nerves and relax the mind—while betraying no effort, so as not to add to the younger Niven's troubles. The actor, surely the biggest celebrity in the room, welcomed and rescued the lad with what you can easily assume was pleasure. (That drink was shaken, not stirred, no doubt. It's no secret that Ian Fleming based his hero James Bond on Grant, from the way he looked in a tux to his martini preference.)

In *The Great Gatsby*, F. Scott Fitzgerald's sharp-eyed narrator Nick Carraway finds himself in something of a similar spot the first time he meets Jay Gatsby. Carraway, a misfit among the monied Long Island social set, was a guest at one of Gatsby's parties, though he hadn't yet met the storied millionaire. In his impatience to put a face to the name, he finds himself making the innocent, if awkward, mistake of lightly griping about the evening to the host himself. When Carraway realizes his blunder, you can imagine his hot shame, his guts turning to mud, and you expect Gatsby to express a little frostiness. Yet he does the opposite. In Gatsby's response, Fitzgerald pinpoints the quality of grace that made this most enduring of American protagonists truly great:

> He smiled understandingly—much more than understandingly. It was one of those rare smiles with a quality of eternal reassurance in it, that you may come across four or five times in life. It faced—or seemed to face—the whole external world for an instant, and then concentrated on you with an irresistible prejudice in your favor. It understood you just so far as you wanted to be understood, believed in you as you would like to believe in yourself and assured you that it had precisely the impression of you that, at your best, you hoped to convey.[2]

Grant, like Gatsby, could have handled the situation differently. He could have feigned sympathy, tolerated Niven's son for a polite interval, and then edged away to find more prestigious company than a nervous noncelebrity.

It's a feeling you never forget, the sweet deliverance from embarrassment, discomfort, and ineptness. It's someone throwing you a rope, reaching out to you when you think you've completely blown it.

Or shielding you from knowing that you've blown it.

In her semi-autobiographical novel *The Bell Jar,* Sylvia Plath describes a time when she was spared mortification by the simple gift of silence. This was an act of extravagant generosity, as anyone who was once a teenager can understand.

"The first time I saw a finger bowl was at the home of my benefactress," Plath writes, recounting the time when she attended a fancy luncheon with the woman who had endowed her college scholarship. On the table was a small bowl of water

> with a few cherry blossoms floating in it, and I thought it must be some clear sort of Japanese after-dinner soup and ate every bit of it, including the crisp little blossoms. Mrs. Guinea never said anything, and it was only much later, when I told a debutante I knew at college about the dinner, that I learned what I had done.[3]

Grace is the unexpected glimmering thing that happens, so subtly that no one else might notice, so tiny that it may barely register until later. But the impact is real and deep. Plath doesn't describe the feelings the finger-bowl incident aroused, but the deadpan humor of her account invites us to fill in the unspoken emotional details, and by doing so we are also stirred. If we don't laugh out loud. Plath's tale could be a skit starring Lucille Ball.

The story is funny in the way so many embarrassing moments

are, once you get through them. It's easy to empathize with the fragile girl in the worst kind of hell, out of her element, face to face with a stranger on foreign turf, unprepared and inexperienced, muddling through a social encounter in a fog of self-consciousness.

That Mrs. Guinea could watch her visitor spoon flowers into her mouth without communicating her astonishment is part of the gymnastics of grace. We know exactly why Plath marvels over this encounter later. Her hostess had the respect, the kindness, and the mental flexibility to silently process the blooper and carry on. She overlooked Plath's ignorance, saw the big picture beyond the immediate moment, and in her silence assured her guest, as Fitzgerald put it, that she had the same impression of Plath that Plath had hoped to convey. We should all be so lucky as to find our own Mrs. Guineas, benevolent creatures who overlook our foibles, with the tact to know that every faux pas need not be shoved up a person's nose.

By the way, there's a similar story concerning Eleanor Roosevelt. At a tea party the first lady was hosting, one of the guests picked up his finger bowl and drank from it; to spare his feelings, she did the same. And all the other guests followed suit. (Would Jackie Kennedy have done that?)

A gracious host is a rare thing, and a gift. She understands the difference between entertaining and hospitality. The first is about flowers and china; the second is about pleasing your guests. Who cares how much the cook fusses over the soufflé if it takes her away from her invited friends? They are the ones who ought to be fussed over. When I was a child, I had a friend from Norway, the daughter of a diplomat, whose mother I'll never forget. A tall, willowy woman, she had a kind of floating presence and a soft, lilting voice, and she made you feel cared for as soon as you entered her house.

Unfussy, down-to-earth Eleanor Roosevelt welcomes UNESCO representatives from Siam (Thailand) and China to her home in Hyde Park, New York, in 1948, when she was a United Nations delegate. A devoted humanitarian known as "First Lady of the World," she possessed the grace of compassion, and an ability to connect deeply with people.

She'd serve up an after-school snack of grilled cheese and ice cream as if it were high tea for the queen, her silvery eyes crinkling as she inquired gently after your every comfort. She had a way of setting a sandwich in front of you as if it were the best possible means of easing the realities of the world, but it was her unwavering kindness that assured you that, if oozing cheese wasn't solace enough and you had burdens to share, she would listen and respond with perfect wisdom.

I hope I was a gracious guest. I think I must have been, unwittingly, because I so appreciated the attention. That's the job of a guest, to appreciate the efforts made on her behalf and to keep out of the host's way. End of story. Easiest, best job in the world, if you ask me, but some manage to make a hash of it. Being a bad guest has become de rigueur in some dark places on the celebrity circuit. When the Duke and Duchess of Cambridge visited Australia in 2014, the Sydney Opera House hosted an event for them. Among the two hundred invited guests were a radio shock jock and his cohost. They made a stink over the airwaves afterward because the royal couple didn't come round to their table, and the radio personalities didn't have the grace to see it as an understandable matter, a nonevent. "I was devastated, and mind you, a little bit pissed," ranted Kyle Sandilands on the radio the next day.[4]

WHO DESERVES TO BE A GUEST, to be one of those invited in? Put a little differently, what happens if you open up to others, beyond what you thought possible?

Tolerance of all, and harm to no one. That is the pinnacle, wrote Chinese philosopher Zhuangzi, more than 2,000 years ago. Like Cary Grant welcoming a nervous newcomer to his table, graceful people know all about tolerance and peaceable acceptance.

When I turned six, my mother told me I could have ponies at my birthday party—a little girl's dream—if I invited everyone in my first-grade class.

Fine by me!

Everyone, she continued. Including Dennis.[5]

Dennis, the boy whose pale skin and hair made him look transparent, barely there. The kid I was very sure had the worst sort of cooties. This I knew, though I didn't know much else about him. Dennis was given to nosebleeds and a kind of spastic jitteriness, and like the other kids in the class, I did my best to avoid him.

I think I shed some tears over the ultimatum, but I really wanted those ponies, so Dennis was in.

This was just a year after the 1968 riots tore through Washington, DC, in the wake of the assassination of Martin Luther King. Our otherwise quiet neighborhood of small homes snugged together on the outskirts of the city didn't escape the turmoil. The National Guard had camped out in the park across the street, and one day my brother brought home a spent tear-gas canister, trailing fumes that sent us both hurtling to the sink to flush our burning eyes. I remember rolling around in the rear foot wells of our VW, diving from the backseat for cover, acting out the tensions that had electrified my block, my neighborhood, my world.

But my parents were more deeply marked. My father had moved us to DC from Texas when the Mexican-American state senator he'd worked for in Austin was elected to Congress. Inclusiveness was part of their lives. It was sweeping the nation, or at least it felt that way. One of its flag bearers was folk song maestro Pete Seeger, who believed in nothing so much as the inevitability of spontaneous public harmony, if you only asked for it. He always wrote a chorus into his songs, and his concerts invariably became brave, joyous singalongs.

Of course, inclusiveness was embodied most courageously, wholeheartedly, and gracefully by King himself. The civil rights leader identified the essential paradox of human community that seems so obvious now it's a wonder it took so long to express: it is separation, rather than inclusion, that brings us into conflict. My folks understood this, and to see their heroes felled and their city in flames only solidified their beliefs even as the chaos shook them.

And so on the appointed Saturday of my party, a horse trailer pulled up the alley; three squat, lethargic, darling animals were saddled up by our gate, and an excited line of children formed for turns around the backyard. I remember hopping up and down a lot. I remember going first. I remember what everything looked like from high atop my pony as I traveled grandly past the dirt patch where I made mud pies, past my little playhouse, past the other children, past Dennis, his pale face flashing even paler in the afternoon sun. He was clapping his hands, hopping up and down, as jazzed up as everyone else.

And I remember gazing over to our gnarled, solitary apricot tree, newly in bloom and magnificent, where my mother stood chatting pleasantly with Dennis's mother. His mom was older, grandmotherly, and the white pinned-up coil of her hair almost disappeared against the blossoms. As I watched them, his mother and my mother together—the surprise of it still electrifies this memory—it registered that my mother was taking care of her guest with the same calm, sensitive attention with which she treated, well, everyone. She was looking after Dennis's mom, making sure she had someone to talk to, delivering the unspoken message to her that her son, so often alone at school, was welcome at our house. He was welcome in the same way that, a couple years later, the new boy from China, who barely spoke English, was welcome when I brought him home with me after school. Welcome in the same way as the newly arrived son of Russian immigrants, with whom I reluctantly but obediently played a disastrous game of chess, my mother whispering moves in my ear so I didn't completely embarrass myself in the face of his crushing expertise.

Later on, when I was in high school, I befriended an endearingly rumpled, bearded classmate who had flunked tenth grade a couple times and was nearly twenty. He wasn't in a position to have a Thanksgiving of his own; I believe he lived in his car. He came home with me, too. I cooked the dinner that year—my mother, caring for my dying grandmother, was out of town; my brother was away at college—and my father and I watched in silence as our new friend consumed more than we'd ever seen another human eat. Was I proud!

It took a while to grasp, but as I put together the view from my pony on that beautiful day in my backyard, I came to understand something as startling as it was liberating, heart-opening: everyone should have a good time at my party, and I wasn't the most important person at it.

Dennis had seemed so alien to me. He might as well have been a helium balloon, fragile, not quite of this world, barely connected to the rest of us. But I learned three things about him that afternoon that anchored him, pulling him back down to earth. I learned that he liked ponies, just as I did; that he had a mother, just as I did; and most of all, that his feelings, and her feelings, mattered as much as anybody else's. My mother taught me that, by her own graceful example.

It was a good party. And a great birthday, where I felt myself grow up a little.

CHAPTER 3

GRACE AND HUMOR:

MAGGIE THATCHER, JOHNNY CARSON, AND MY 105-YEAR-OLD HIGHBALL-SIPPING GREAT-GRANDMOTHER

Well, humor is the great thing, the saving thing, after all. The minute it crops up, all our hardnesses yield, all our irritations and resentments flit away, and a sunny spirit takes their place.

—MARK TWAIN, *What Paul Bourget Thinks of Us*

CARY GRANT WAS A SUPERB ACTOR, a beautiful mover, a gracious man. But before all that he was a great comedian. And what gave his comedy such grace and lightness was this: he didn't take himself too seriously.

To the world he was a gallant boulevardier, but Grant didn't get his ego mixed up with his image. He knew who he was—and wasn't. "Everyone wants to be Cary Grant," he once quipped. "Even I want to be Cary Grant."

He excelled in self-deprecating roles—the thickheaded aca-

A lighthearted master of the absurd, Cary Grant relished poking fun at himself, while preserving the dignity of his leading lady. Especially when she's Rosalind Russell in His Girl Friday.

demic, the gullible homeowner, the smug businessman out of his depth. There is no better eccentric ding-dong than Grant in *Bringing Up Baby* and *Monkey Business*; he wasn't afraid of being the klutz who fell over chairs. In *The Awful Truth*, he let himself be shown up by a dog.

Grant's brand of self-deprecating humor is an instrument of grace because it conveys confidence and humanness. It sends out two messages at once: one, he is humble enough to laugh at himself, and two, he is firmly in control. (This is where Grant's physical aplomb was critical; he could trip but keep his equilibrium, too.) As a result, everyone else could relax.

Compare this style of humor with that of, say, Jim Carrey or the late Robin Williams. Two very funny men, yet I wouldn't call them graceful. Watching them can be exhausting; their comedy is explosive, adrenaline-charged. You're a little unnerved by them even as you're laughing.

Jackie Gleason, by contrast, possessed a smoother style of comedy. Here was a big man, a fat man, who was as buoyant as a beach ball, with the magnificence and floating quality of a Ziegfeld girl. He had a sense of his body in space and used it to great effect, dancing around his kitchen in *The Honeymooners*, as the working-class curmudgeon who always had our sympathies because Gleason never played him as a fool. There was always elegance to his antics; even if his vocal cords strained, his body language was confident and easy. He was comfortable with himself—so comfortable that he could mock himself, too.

Self-mockery is a delicate thing, so very tricky, but so graceful when done right. It's one thing for a practiced entertainer like Glea-

The big easy. Buoyant and light on his feet, Jackie Gleason was a beautiful mover.

son to have the perfect physical touch. It's another kind of achievement for one of the most glittering residents of the political sphere, where the powerful are accustomed to absolute choreographed, cue-card-reading control. This is what made Michelle Obama's outing on NBC's *Late Night with Jimmy Fallon* so remarkable.

In February 2013, the first lady and the comedian-turned-talk-show-host teamed up in a tour-de-farce skit they called "The Evolution of Mom Dancing."[1] Fallon, wearing a preppy pink cardigan, cropped chinos, and a Tina Fey wig, launched into a devastatingly tight-assed portrayal of self-conscious uncool. Then Mrs. Obama swiveled on to join the dance, in her own cardy and capris—spiffier, naturally. But would she truly represent? You could hear a million moms around the country fret. With a few more beats, a few more hip bumps, the Mom-in-Chief's dance cred resolved into smooth, self-mocking genius.

Smooth was the key here, as the pair showed us (with helpful subtitles) some clutch "Out of Sync Electric Slide" moves, the side-swiping arms of the "Sprinkler," the "Where's Your Father? (Get Him Back Here!)." Too bad the president didn't sneak on for that part. Mrs. Obama, famed for her ability to put others at ease in her presence, was supremely self-possessed. Her relaxed ease freed Fallon to be his comic best. But when she did the Dougie, swaying with refined funkiness through the hip-hop moves, all her partner could do was stand openmouthed in awe.

The first lady has been overhyped for her clothing choices, because her deepest impact goes well beyond fashion. She glamorizes middle-aged momness. She concerns herself with the folkways of the mom: worrying about what the kids are eating, keeping up with their interests, trying not to look like a dork. And she invests all of this with some of the magic that follows her from her FLOTUS role. It makes people feel a bit better about their ho-humness to see the president's wife caught up in it, too, poking fun at herself, bringing a sense of humor to it.

On the subject of politics, few world leaders have wielded humor and grace more effectively than Margaret Thatcher, the former three-term prime minister of Britain. Self-deprecating charm and ease—not to mention slight shadings of sexual allure—were potent political tools for Thatcher. "There was always an element of the erotic in the national obsession with her," wrote the novelist Ian McEwan after her death in 2013.[2] (Did she really once spank Christopher Hitchens in front of his fellow reporters? And didn't the term *sadomonetarism*, coined during her reign, suggest something a bit beyond fiscal policy?) From the conflicting assessments of her legacy, it's clear her nation hasn't gotten over her yet.

Some dubbed her "Attila the Hen" for her conservative positions: she favored the wealthy, had no love for coal miners or state-run monopolies. She fed the greed-is-good spirit of the 1980s, and she didn't care an iota if people liked her. But what is beyond dispute is that Thatcher spoke and acted with passion and dedication, tempered by extraordinary poise. For all her toughness, she had a pleasing, serene quality, and that sense of ease—that grace—made her improbably endurable.

As much as I was put off by her policies at the time, I now find the way she carried herself fascinating. Indeed, she was no hen; she was fearless and unflappable (more hawk than hen, really). Intent on building up Britain as a great power, she adopted a style of firm control and vigor. She was supremely self-confident and had a commanding presence. However, she sweetened this with feminine grace: she paid attention to her self-presentation, taking care to dress impeccably in simple, well-tailored dresses and suits.

"Suits always photograph well and even out imperfections—not that she had many," Margaret King, Thatcher's dress adviser, told London's *Telegraph* newspaper. "She had wonderful legs, for instance. She stood beautifully, and presented herself well."[3]

Thatcher adopted a softened hairstyle of swoops and curls. She took the shrillness out of her voice with breathing lessons. She relaxed even her name, adopting the chummy "Maggie." She dimpled. Thatcher used warmth and wit to ease through—or to mask the harshness of—ploys and strategies that might not otherwise have been accepted.

It was a masterful performance. Was it sincere? You believed it was; that was the gracefulness of it. There was no strain. (Compare her with conservative politicians Sarah Palin and Michele Bachmann, who have never mastered naturalness and ease.)

Thatcher was keenly aware of her performance qualities. "When hecklers stand up at my meeting I get a mental jump for joy," she once said. "It gives me something to get my teeth into—and the audiences love it."[4]

When she addressed the House of Commons, she had a witty quip for every interruption from her opposition and a way of silencing objections in serene, rounded tones and a firm but patient plea of "if I could just finish." In a manner that was at once grand and humble, she gave the impression that she was speaking directly to you. She did this with her smooth, connected quality of movement, the way she would turn her head and her body to address every one of her listeners, or so she made it seem.

Most graceful of all was how she handled humor as a way of

putting others at ease, lightening the atmosphere, and conveying the sense—so crucial for the world's most prominent female politician—that she was absolutely in the driver's seat.

In a House of Commons session the day that Thatcher announced her resignation, in 1990, one member of Parliament asked the prime minister if she intended to keep fighting against a single currency and an independent central bank after her departure. As Thatcher rose to answer, a Labour MP teasingly implied that she was planning to run the very bank she had long opposed. "No," he said, "she's going to be the governor."

Thatcher joined in the laughs that followed, laughs (and some jeers) coming at her own expense; she gave every sign she thought the MP's jab was hilarious. When the hubbub died down, she waited a beat, turned, and swept the chamber with her eyes, then quipped huskily, "What a good idea!"[5]

Laughter erupted, louder than before. Not only did she have the last word but, on the very day she admitted defeat, she had the last laugh, too.

Thatcher kept her sense of humor long after her downfall. In one of her last speeches, given in 2001, she addressed a Tory rally in Plymouth, England. "I was told beforehand that my arrival was unscheduled," she told the crowd. "But on my way here I passed the local cinema, and it turns out that you were expecting me after all. For the billboard read, 'The Mummy Returns.'"[6]

Johnny Carson raised self-deprecation to an art. "Is there a revolver in the house?" he ad-libbed once on *The Tonight Show* as his monologue was flatlining. Notoriously shy, he let his guests do most of the talking. And he was open to learning from them. How striking this seems now, when everyone is so certain, so reluctant to admit gaps in knowledge. But Carson, one of the most famous men in America, was modest enough to react with interest to some new thing a guest on his show might tell him, and say, "I did not know that."

His calm, authentic ease is why he reigned as a TV talk show host for so many years. Like Cary Grant, he possessed an exquisitely managed mix of charm and control. This was an intriguing and seductive formula, expressed most profoundly in his stance during his *Tonight Show* monologues, with that lifted, buoyant chest and a sense that his whole body was alert and tuned in to the moment.

But he wasn't going to reveal too much to us, even as he delivered dependable laughs night after night, even as he zeroed in on each guest as if that person were the most fascinating creature on the planet. There was a distinct formality in the way this deeply private man held himself, head high and pulled back. He had this shining confidence and iron reliability. You could trust him with your stocks, you could watch him land a jet. But rather than setting himself above the public, Carson used his natural reserve to take the focus off himself and put it on his guests. His empathy toward them came through in a way that was perhaps missing in his offscreen life.

My great-grandmother and Carson came together in a meeting that must have sucked all the grace out of the air for a few moments, because here were two masters of it, face to face.[7]

Mildred Holt, a stooped, frail-looking woman in a powder-blue dress, was neither a celebrity nor a newsmaker when she appeared on *The Tonight Show* in August 1987. She was just a little old lady from a tiny town in Kansas—and by old, I mean historic. She was 105 at the time. But she had all her marbles, as well as a sharp, straight-shooting wit, and that was enough for Carson.

While sipping a highball from a coffee mug on the set, Mimi—as my family called her—teased the TV king about his many marriages and had Carson so charmed that he kept her on after the commercial break. "Oh, you're fun," he told her, giving her wrinkled little hand a squeeze. When Carson remarked that she was "the oldest person I have ever met and ever had on the show," Mimi chirped with a big, crinkly grin, "I'm too mean to die!"

Mimi's comebacks had Carson laughing so hard at times that he fell back against his chair. Mostly, though, the King of Late Night leaned his chin in his hand and soaked up Mimi's crackling optimism with a smile.

Someone in Ellsworth, Kansas, had gotten in touch with Carson's staff about the extraordinary Mimi. Folks there had long thought she deserved to sit on Carson's set. Who could argue? She was an irrepressible force. The daughter of a Civil War veteran, she was the youngest of ten children. She married a prosperous banker and had three children; the eldest was my mother's father. When Mimi's husband lost his business in the Depression, she took boarders into their roomy foursquare house. She also turned her dining room into a tearoom and served the noon meal (back when it was referred to as dinner) to the local schoolteachers. Mimi loved to cook. Fried chicken was a favorite dish; it began at the chopping block in her backyard. She was said to be unerring with an ax, though her chopping days were over by the time I knew her. She busied herself every day in her small kitchen, which was never updated, never had a dishwasher—she scalded her china in boiling water. If visitors dropped by while she was making a meal, she'd bring a cutting board into the living room and continue chopping vegetables on her lap.

Mimi had the most active social life of anyone I have ever known, making daily calls on friends around town and hosting teas and card games. She lived in her house with her widowed daughter until the very end of her life, and in her later years, as her card-playing friends moved into the old-folks home—none of them, it turned out, were as hale as she was—she'd visit them there. Among her favorite sayings was that she would never eat a meal alone, and by all accounts she never did.

This wasn't surprising, considering she was one of the most agreeable people you could wish to meet. During one visit when I was nine or ten and she was, oh, ninety-something, I asked to see her wedding dress. And then I asked to try it on. And then I asked if I could wear it downstairs. Yes, yes, and yes—and we ended up on her front lawn in a fit of giggles, me with my arms through the sleeves of the shirtwaist, shrunken little Mimi holding the matching skirt against her hips. My mother snapped some pictures, and passing drivers stared from their cars. Maybe we did look a little kooky in our heirloom ivory muslin from 1905, very Gibson Girl, but Mimi didn't believe in letting useful things molder in drawers. She would never choose misplaced reverence over fun.

She was an enthusiastic joiner and knew how to keep a good time going. With Carson she talked about getting her first car in 1914, and how she regretted having to give up driving at the age of 103. She also spoke out against West Coast snobbery: "I met a man at the hotel," she told Carson, "and he said, 'Where're you from?' and I said Kansas and he said, 'Oh, my goodness.' That made me mad."

Mimi was always ready to defend the heartland's honor, but first she paused a beat, looking out to the audience with a sweet, pitying smile for the poor fellow with a low agricultural IQ. "He forgets that Kansas produces more wheat than any state in the Union," she said. "That's where your bread comes from."

She was remarkable on TV, as relaxed as if she were sitting in her own living room. Like her host, Mimi was simply comfortable in her own skin. You could tell how much she was enjoying herself by her physical presence, the way she moved. She wasn't stiff or crumpled in her chair. She gestured with her crooked fingers and swiveled around as she spoke (did I mention she was 105?), bringing Carson's sidekick Ed McMahon, seated beside her, into the conversation.

For a guest to pay equal attention to McMahon was so unusual that Carson good-naturedly jibed the older man: "She obviously recognizes you as one of her own kind." He was right. Whoever happened to be in the room with her was Mimi's own kind.

Mimi's graciousness stemmed from her utter lack of fear. As a child preoccupied with imagined threats lurking in shadows, I once asked her if she were ever afraid of robbers popping out from her closets. Her chipper nonchalance stuck with me: "Well, if they get me, they get me!"

She was so at ease in front of the cameras that after the episode, *Hollywood Squares* called her to ask if she'd be on their game show, too, but she declined. Mimi had seen Los Angeles and preferred Ellsworth.

I'm certain her congeniality played a part in her longevity. Certainly she was no health nut. Mimi took her coffee with thick farm cream, dug into desserts with gusto, and enjoyed a hot toddy before bed. She had lost her mother at ten; she had lived through the Depression and the Dust Bowl and decades of widowhood. But

Mimi didn't truck with stress. She didn't dwell. She let the bad crap go and stayed in the present, where she always found something amusing "to help pass the time," as she put it.

A month shy of her 109th birthday, she caught pneumonia and died, three years after her *Tonight Show* spot. Her obituary ran in newspapers across the country. Her highball-sipping usually made it into the headline. But having a social whiskey was all part of her idea of a good time, along with being engaged in the moment, listening and reacting, seeking to draw people in and spread the good cheer around.

They were a good pair, she and Johnny Carson. All the papers noted that, as Carson's oldest guest ever, Mimi was every bit his equal in cracking jokes.

CHAPTER 4

GRACE AND THE ART OF GETTING ALONG:

HOW THE BABY BOOMERS DERAILED CENTURIES OF MANNERS INSTRUCTION

Manners are the happy ways of doing things . . . 'tis the very beginning of civility,—to make us, I mean, endurable to each other.

—Ralph Waldo Emerson, *The Conduct of Life*

As civilization began, it became apparent that the human race was imperfectly suited for it. Living together took some work. All these years later, there are innumerable examples to show that we're still not terribly good at being civilized, from the student commuter who dashes in front of an elderly woman to claim a seat on the subway to how societies treat their poor and unemployed. The unchanging reality is that people tend to think of themselves first, yet the task of coexistence is made easier if they don't. And so efforts arose many years ago to teach folks how to get along.

The concept of grace—refined ease of movement and manner, as a way of pleasing, assisting, and honoring others—wove through this endeavor. Indeed, the term *getting along* itself, in the sense of being on harmonious terms, implies graceful behavior. It carries a hint of a dance, a peaceable duet, or the falling-in-step impulse that horses have with one another, which helps make them manageable. Grace and manners, the general principles of social behavior, have historically been entwined; each adds luster to the other. To trace the development of grace through time, where grace isn't specifically mentioned, I've looked for an emphasis on the art of getting along. By that I mean manners that are aimed at harmonious interactions and creating a climate of warmth and appreciation, as opposed to formalities about fish forks and introductions, which are in the more detail-oriented domain of etiquette.

Some of the world's most influential books have been instruction manuals on the art of getting along, or what we've come to know as the social graces. These include the oldest writings of the ancient era, the runaway best sellers of the Renaissance, and the must-reads of American colonists, revolutionaries, and early twentieth-century strivers with an eye for elegance and civilized living.

Yet instruction in grace mysteriously dropped out of our lives a few decades ago.

Well, "mysteriously" isn't quite right. There is a pendulum swing in the history of manners, when one era comes up with rules and they grow more and more strict until another generation says, oh, just forget about it—this is ridiculous. And grace gets thrown out for being an act, insincere, phony.

"We have the residue now, with well-meaning parents who say to their children, 'Just be yourself,'" said Judith Martin, when I asked her why the social graces were in decline. Martin is the author of the internationally syndicated Miss Manners newspaper column and many books on etiquette. "What does that mean? Who would they be if they weren't themselves? Parents don't teach their children how to act out being glad for a present, or how to seem pleased to see someone they may not want to see.

"Etiquette has long struggled with the opposing ideas of grace and naturalness, of appearing natural and being natural, which are two entirely different things," she continued. This inherent paradox, of feeling one thing and saying another, leaves etiquette open to the charge of insincerity. "There is a disconnect in what you feel and what you ought to project, which is the opposite of sincerity. For example, the hostess who says, 'Oh, don't worry about it,' when you've just broken her favorite lamp. Of course she cares about it, but the primary goal is putting the other person at ease.

"People say etiquette is artificial. But what they really object to is the obviously artificial," Martin said. "Yes, it is artificial and it's often better than the raw expression of natural desires. Look at dance: Is human movement better when it's totally untutored or is it better when you put thought and work into it?"

Social grace, just like physical grace, requires work. That was the point of the conduct books from centuries past: to make it plain that correct behavior required effort and discipline. Being with people is an art like any other art, or a practice, if you will, just like cooking or riding a bicycle. The more we realize what smooths things over, what pleases people, and the more we want to be graceful and practice being graceful, the better and more convincing we will become. Grace will cease to be something we "act out." But as with any learned activity, there are different degrees of polish here.

There is the hostess who reacts to her broken lamp by saying, "Oh, don't worry about it" through clenched teeth, making you feel terrible. And then there is one who reacts with grace, putting on a better act, perhaps. Maybe she's a Meryl Streep, imperceptibly masking her true feelings with an Oscar-worthy portrayal of nonchalance. Or maybe she really hated that lamp and is glad it's headed for the trash. Or maybe she is really and truly a happy-go-lucky angel on earth whose every impulse is upright and pure. It makes no difference to the embarrassed guest who just wants to be forgiven. He's grateful for grace any way it comes.

Grace lies in the manner in which the rules are followed, Martin says. "Do you follow etiquette rules to the letter, or do you make it seem as if they arise naturally from good feelings and it's easy for you to say, 'Oh, never mind, don't worry about it'? It's not easy for a dancer to leap into the air either, and we don't see the bloody toes and the sweat from a distance. And in the same way, if she's being graceful, we don't see the hostess thinking, 'Oh my gosh, this is going to cost me a fortune to fix.'"

Let's face it, if we all exposed our true feelings all the time, the world would be unbearable. Grace, as Martin put it, "is that covering through which we make the world pleasant."

And yet we're in one of those extremes of the pendulum swing where honesty is overvalued and the brilliant act, the self-discipline, the training that produces grace has faded away. An accumulation of blows has led to its downfall, but they stem from a reaction against the overcomplication of everyday life that picked up strength in the 1950s and '60s. The modern means of self-improvement turned from building up one's character (a rather slow, internal, and never-ending process) to the far easier focus on things we can buy. Buying our way into the good life. With the surge in department stores and shopping malls, with ever-present advertising, with our voyeurism via television into the lives and possessions of others, shopping became the modern means of self-betterment.

This was a 180-degree turn from the previous idea. America's Founding Fathers, for example, were obsessed with inner self-improvement. Striving for "moral perfection," a twenty-year-old Benjamin Franklin worked methodically to acquire a list of virtues, from silence and sincerity to tranquility and humility. He assessed himself each evening and tracked his progress on charts. John Adams, in a typical diary entry, resolved to become more conscientious and socially pleasant: "I find my self very much inclin'd to an unreasonable absence of mind, and to a morose, unsociable disposition. Let it therefore be my constant endeavor to reform these great faults."[1] But two hundred years on, such vestiges of a Puritan past had been swept aside by a greater interest in cars, appliances, and shiny hair.

The spread of the suburbs after World War II, with their backyard weenie roasts, patios, and cheese dips, was also a way of escaping an overcomplicated, formal life. It encouraged a sportier, more casual lifestyle for a middle class newly freed from decades of deprivation. Add to that the great wave of Baby Boomers, born into prosperity and surrounded by products, a Me Generation showered with attention, not inclined to modesty, and little interested in the artifice of social graces and their required self-control. In them, the age-old tendency of the young to rebel against their elders attained an unprecedented critical mass. And with that came even more informality, more "be yourself" free rein. The courtesies of their parents' era were a drag.

Child-rearing practices were also changing. In the new, less formal times, manners instruction for children simply went out of style, and the subtleties of grace were deemed passé, or worse: elitist. Anything implying snobbery was swept aside by a growing middle class, the youth counterculture, and a surging progressive tide. Change was sorely needed, as the civil rights, antiwar, and women's movements demonstrated. But it wasn't only social institutions that were rocked. So was the cradle.

A nation crawling with babies was hungry for advice, the simpler the better. The easygoing child-centered approach advocated by Benjamin Spock in his enormously influential, best-selling *Common Sense Book of Baby and Child Care*, which first came out in 1946, gave parents permission to forgo the feeding schedules and strict discipline of former times and simply enjoy their kids. Hugs were in, spankings were out. But if you're tracking the demise of grace, you can find a few nicks and cuts in his pages.

Since people like children with "sensibly good" manners, Spock writes, "parents owe it to their children to make them likable." But he also put forth the view that "good manners come naturally" if a child feels good about himself.[2]

Yet self-esteem is not the answer to everything. In fact, some researchers blame the self-esteem movement of the 1980s for the rise in narcissism among college students today as compared with those of thirty years ago.[3] Narcissists have a grandiose view of themselves but care little about others; the argument is that parents who fill their children's ears with how special they are (as opposed to, say, how hard they work or how kind they are) create adults with little patience for those who don't recognize their superiority. We've all encountered plenty of people, young and old, with high opinions of themselves and precious little grace. It is one thing to empower a child with self-worth and confidence and to guide her in becoming a good person. But children who are not taught to behave with consideration for others and to respect other people's feelings will not develop empathy and compassion.

While *likable* is a perfectly fine quality, it's a low bar to set for parents. It refers only to how others view the child, and in a bland way at that. Being likable means you're receiving something—someone's approval. Compare it with *agreeable,* which is about giving. It's other-directed, referring to getting along, being warm, supportive, and helpful, while diminishing the focus on yourself. "Be pretty if you can, be witty if you must, but be agreeable if it kills you!" declared the 1930s Home Institute booklet *Charm*. Interestingly, Spock's view of the primacy of likability flips the longstanding Anglo-American notion, prevalent among the Puritans and up through the nineteenth and early decades of the twentieth centuries, that one builds character through service to others, whether God or your fellow man. In this older view, the less you fixate on yourself the better, apart from controlling unruly impulses. Putting priority on others is the right—and graceful—thing to do.

A Culture of Coarseness

What has most threatened grace is what I can only describe as a culture of coarseness. Some folks are insensitive to their effect on other people. They don't think about how others feel when they shoot down their ideas in a meeting, when they court laughs at the expense of others, when they criticize others in front of colleagues. Or when they make it known how little others matter once someone more interesting comes along. I was having lunch with a colleague once when she saw a man she knew passing by on the sidewalk. Waving vigorously through the window to get his attention, she urged him to join us. But the moment he got to our table, before she'd had a chance to introduce us (I'm choosing to believe that was her plan), her cell phone rang. She'd placed it on the table in case this should happen, so of course she took the call, having long forgotten the conversation she'd interrupted by inviting in a guy off the street, and leaving me and a stranger in awkward silence while she also forgot about us.

Our devices are draining us of grace. "We need to e-mail!" a friend I haven't seen in a while calls over her shoulder, because there's no time to talk. E-mail and texting are convenient, but they also crumple us up physically and make us unaware socially, closed off from those around us. Riding the subway can be like nursery school, what with the manspreaders who don't want to share the bench they're sprawling on with wide-open knees and a slump, and the woman who takes up two seats with all her bags and doesn't much care if you have to stand. Or maybe she doesn't notice you because she's very busy texting, like the toy store owner sitting behind the counter who couldn't be moved to help me find a birthday present for my nephew. Silly me, I thought that she was entering important data on her tablet; it was my savvier preteen daughter who detected instantly the gestures of a stealth texter.

With the hours spent hunched over keyboards, no wonder we're awkward when we get up. Hips tighten, necks droop, our backs round. I watch people walking and standing. Most of us sag in the front, with shoulders pitched forward and chests caving, probably from too much sitting and driving and not enough walking, or walking incorrectly. Our footfalls are heavy; we gaze at the ground or at what's in our hands. We've lost the ability to carry ourselves with upright buoyancy and ease. Grace is not only the furthest thing from our minds, it's beyond the reach of our bodies.

Instead, we're drawn to disgrace. No teaser is bigger Internet click bait than the one that promises bad behavior: "Mogul Throws Fit Over Spilt Champagne"; Lindsay Lohan gets kicked out of a hotel; Justin Bieber moons his fans on Instagram.

Reality TV thrives on disgrace. Fans watch it for the awkward moments, for people to be told they're fired, they suck, they're the weakest link. The appeal of *American Idol* used to be Simon Cowell bullying a contestant who had volunteered himself for public shaming. Would we ever be so stupid? Of course not. *Survivor* competitors drag one another through the dirt, physically and verbally; the mothers on *Dance Moms* put the toddler antics of subway riders to shame. Viewers can puff themselves up in comparison, engage in some vicarious ribbing without responsibility.

The glee of disgrace, of course, exists beyond TV. In May 2014, Evan Spiegel, CEO and founder of Snapchat, the ephemeral photo-sharing app, issued an apology after the release of e-mails he'd written to his frat brothers while attending Stanford. Those missives had cheerfully chronicled getting sorority girls ("sororisluts") drunk and musing about whether he'd peed on his date.[4] Typical frat boy fun, some said.

Are we too easily outraged? Or are we numb to what is truly outrageous (torture, for starters), because we're overoutraged? Internet outrage has become a fact of life, a ritual of righteous indignation practiced after the inappropriate tweet. Outrage is such a satisfying cycle: First there is a celebrity faux pas; then the offended take to Twitter, the defenders counterattack, the bloggers repost, a Facebook fight erupts, and after all the time invested in following this trail—trust me, even your respected local newspaper is following this trail—why, there's a new dumb thing to get mad about.

We're in an environment of grabbing and taking: taking advantage, taking control, taking for oneself. Grace, by contrast, is associated with giving. The three Charites of Greek mythology, you'll recall, are the givers of charm, beauty, and ease.

In so many fields of activity—sports, entertainment, business—success isn't just winning, it's crushing. Total domination is the desired image to project. Power is valued over grace; taking is celebrated. Giving is considered a lesser quality, even a weakness. These are the days of category-killing control and sensory bombardments by any means necessary. It's as if society at large has been captivated by the steroid aesthetic of today's sports.

Asked by business analysts if he was going to retire at sixty-five, Boeing CEO Jim McNerney said no, despite it being company custom, and by way of explanation—offered to people he wanted to impress, no less—he chose to depict himself as a monster. "The heart will still be beating, the employees will still be cowering," he said. "I'll be working hard. There's no end in sight."[5]

This prompted another memorable public apology. Yet McNerney's original phrasing was telling, right up to his last words. *There's no end in sight.* Perpetual power: Why give it up if you're on a roll? Why give up anything if you're in a position to take? If those down the rungs have anything to relinquish—if they can be made to cower, to give back benefits and raises and job security—then that must be done, because it can be done.

Bigger may be better, but gigantic is best, whether it's profits, or the wedding of Kanye West and Kim Kardashian, or the tech effects of a Hollywood blockbuster. (Just look at how the intimate, human-scale charm of *The Wizard of Oz* gave way to the massive 3-D spectacle of *Oz the Great and Powerful*, with its CGI landscape, booming soundtrack, explosions, and strained seriousness.)

In all of this, being compassionate and humble, generous and considerate, elegantly restrained rather than a show-off, at ease instead of in-your-face—in short, being graceful—seems rather behind the times.

"Go out of your way to do something nice for somebody—it will make your heart warm," urged a 1935 guide, *Personality Preferred! How to Grow Up Gracefully*.[6] This book, like others of its era, took a holistic view of grace as a way of being that one acquired through habits of the body, mind, and spirit.

"Grace isn't just a set of behaviors you dust off and display on special occasions," author Elizabeth Woodward explained to her young readers. "It's how you carry yourself every day."

Woodward, an editor at *Ladies' Home Journal*, wrote her book after getting hundreds of thousands of letters from young women seeking advice. Before the upheavals in the mid-twentieth century, growing-up advice to young people, such as Woodward's book, generally followed a course set in antiquity. Making one's way in the world was seen as an art, something to be practiced and perfected. It was in some ways like a lifelong dance, with rules and steps and choreography, as well as the need for rehearsal. This art of living incorporated not only what people said and how they behaved at dinner or in the parlor, but how they moved in many ways, large and small. Control of the body through posture and proper body language has long been a part of "conduct books." In *How to Grow Up Gracefully* and publications like it, for example, it is essential to the graceful life.

Carrying Yourself

Carrying yourself wasn't only a question of posture, though that was stressed, too. Carriage was also a matter of taking your time, so you could move with dignity and ease—and so you would stay out of people's way. "Hurry is what makes girls fall up steps, bang into folks, step on people's toes, spill things on dresses, say the wrong thing. Slow down," wrote Woodward. "Give your brain a chance to work out your plan of operation before you dash into things."

"Watch the woman of charm enter a room. She is graceful, unhurried, in complete control of the situation," noted the Home Institute booklet *Charm.*[7] This was one in a series of mail-order how-to guides published in the 1930s and '40s, when homemaking was considered an art and a science, and women were expected to be able to teach themselves music appreciation, gardening, rug-making, and "How to Budget Your Income." Presumably, how to be delightful was on an equal level.

"We should so move," the booklet continued in a chapter titled "The Body Beautiful," "that if every muscle struck a note the result would be harmony."

Emily Post agreed. In her landmark 1922 book, *Etiquette in Society, in Business, in Politics and at Home,* she paraded a fictitious society matron before her readers' imaginations, drawing their attention to her perfect gait.

> How does Mrs. Oldname walk? One might answer by describing how Pavlowa dances. Her body is perfectly balanced, she holds herself straight, and yet in nothing suggests a ramrod. She takes steps of medium length, and, like all people who move and dance well, walks from the hip, not the knee. On no account does she swing her arms, nor does she rest a hand on her hip! Nor when walking, does she wave her hands about in gesticulation.[8]

It's very likely that Mrs. Oldname also undertook some mental preparation before navigating the ballroom. The guides to grace taught that grace begins well before the first step is taken. It begins in stillness, within a mind that is composed and primed for a good time. Are you heading to a party? "Concentrate on your state of mind," writes Woodward. To her, that is the essence of gracefulness: a calm, alert mental attitude. Proper preparation is the way to acquire it. A girl can avoid nervousness by trying on her new frock a few days in advance, Woodward counsels, and by practicing moving around in it. Then she should forget about it and focus on her mood and her mind, so she's able to help others feel comfortable with her. "Fill your ears with good music—it will put you in the mood," Woodward writes. "Too much jazz will make you skittery.

Read some French just before going out, to wake up your brain." In this perspective, loveliness was not just a matter of how you looked, nor did it depend on memorizing rules of etiquette, though this book contained some of those as well. Woodward made clear that it was the quality of your appearance and actions that mattered most, the dignity, ease, and warmth you conveyed. Imagine if such a view was promoted to young women today, instead of the prevailing notion that a new you can be bought off the rack at the shopping mall.

Charm counseled: "When you're self-conscious, think of the other fellow. You cannot think of two things at once, so you cannot be SELF conscious. This is the first lesson in charm."

Inconspicuousness

A consistent theme in this book and others of its time is the virtue of being inconspicuous. Going unnoticed was the goal, unless you were with intimates in an appropriately festive environment. One should blend harmoniously into the surroundings. Don't draw attention in public, the guides cautioned. That will only lead to awkwardness and embarrassment. Consider others first. Think of your fellow patrons when you go to the movies or the theater; don't scramble over their knees and trample their feet on the way to your seat. Strive for a quiet, unobtrusive presence. Eat calmly, speak low. Restraint, restraint, even to the point of leaving your perfume at home when traveling. "A great many people don't feel at their best in a plane, and it's only fair to consider them," writes Woodward, in what must have been rather avant-garde advice for 1935, when air travel was loud, bumpy, and relatively new.

Self-control

For all of this, for dignified, considerate, and graceful comportment, self-control is the foundation. Like hemlines and heel heights, fashions in manners instruction come and go, but as far as grace is concerned, whether one is casual or strict about manners is beside the point. Grace is about the ease that comes from self-control: mastering one's own reactions/needs/concerns and focusing on others to foster smooth interactions and a pleasant atmosphere. But for most of us, self-control does not come naturally. It's a skill that requires practice, gentle but consistent reminders from trusted elders, and abundant everyday examples.

Self-control was important enough to be the subject of a set of scrolls so valued that they were copied over and over and were protected enough to endure, where other writings turned to dust. Their author, the Egyptian vizier Ptah-hotep, thought more than four thousand years ago that in the matter of social grace, self-control was imperative.

"Be thine heart overflowing; but refrain thy mouth," he wrote. Among his admonitions are to practice kindness, pay attention to others, and to listen, quietly and with compassion, when someone else is speaking. He had a particular concern for defusing anger: "Beware of interruption and of answering words with heat. Put it far from thee; control thyself."[9]

With that directive (depicted, aptly, as "control of heart" in the hieroglyphic text, with the heart being considered the seat of reason[10]), Ptah-hotep foretold the overriding theme of the conduct literature to follow, from Moses to Miss Manners. Self-control is the key to order and harmony. To take the Egyptian's image, if you control the heart, the engine of the body, the result is smoother function on many levels: emotional, physical, and social. The little acts of grace that contribute to getting along require some measure of harnessing and refining one's energies, such as allowing others to speak rather than dominating a conversation or easing an awkward moment with an apology when you have, intentionally or not, ruffled feathers. If grace has long been considered an aspect of beauty—beauty of movement, beauty of expression, beautiful behavior—it is discipline, the time-honored writers tell us, that allows it to blossom.

In other words, grace is grounded in work. Inside and out. Practice, concentration, and the self-control to set yourself to it. In this way, you gain the wisdom—the habit, born of practice—of keeping quiet and rethinking those first words or actions that pop into your head.

The common view of grace in the 1930s, as a habitual practice that involves and enhances the whole person, seemed to reincarnate values that had flourished in Renaissance Italy, where writers as well as artists were intent on defining the ideal.[11] Just as Michelangelo and Raphael were perfecting the human form, so too were poets trying to polish human conduct as a way to attain aesthetic and spiritual perfection. Writing in sixteenth-century Florence, the poet and archbishop Giovanni Della Casa equated grace with fine craftsmanship. The way he described it, gracefulness was an art: a way of engaging with others according to timeless design principles of balance, order, and harmony. The refinements that make all the difference between art and schlock go into his definition of grace for social situations.

"It is not enough for a man, to do things that be good: but he must also have a care, he do them with a good grace," wrote Della Casa in *Il Galateo overo de' costumi*, generally translated as *Galateo, or the Rules of Polite Behavior.*[12] His slim and hugely popular book, published in 1558 (two years after his death), helped spark a craze throughout Europe for the Italian social graces. As Della Casa explains, "A good grace is nothing else, but such a manner of light (as I may call it) as shineth in the aptness of things set in good order and well disposed, one with another: and perfectly knit and united together."

Without such "proportion and measure," he continues, even something that is good is not "fair," or beautiful. "And the fairness itself is not pleasant."

Della Casa also gave detailed and concrete instructions about how to achieve this good order. Control of the body was crucial; the idea was to smooth all movements into a graceful whole. Virtually no area of physical activity was ignored.

While seated, one must not claw, scratch, or spit. While standing, there should be no slumping or leaning, and while walking, no rushing or running, for it makes a man "weary, sweaty and puffy."

The art of conversation wasn't just about cleverness and wit; it involved physical discipline. "Moreover, it is a needful observation to bethink yourself, how you do move your body, and especially in talk," Della Casa wrote. Chatty folks can get so carried away in speaking that they become reckless, and as a result, "one wags his head, another looks big and scowls with his brows. That man pulls his mouth away. Another spits in and upon their faces."

Della Casa took his title *Galateo* from a friend's name. But he may also be referring to the myth of Pygmalion, the Greek sculptor who carved an ideal woman for himself, fell in love with her, and through his love managed to bring her to life. The sculpture was called Galatea. Perhaps Della Casa was suggesting that behaving with grace is a way to sculpt ourselves, to elevate what we do, and to turn everyday actions into living art. (He wouldn't be the only writer to link learning manners and creating art; George Bernard Shaw also invoked the Pygmalion myth in his social-transformation play by that name. More on that shortly.)

Nonchalance

Throughout *Galateo,* Della Casa pointed out the paradox of grace. In the physical realm, "such a manner of light," as he charmingly called it, comes about through disguised effort. Anyone who has perfected his craft—or tried to—knows exactly what he's talking about. Gene Kelly spent years training his shoulders to remain soft and calm through his quicksilver tap dancing; Roger Federer has hit mountains of tennis balls to keep his forehand so devastatingly liquid. What sets them apart from other dancers and tennis players—what makes them graceful—is their skill at masking the effort.

This is a kind of genius, really. It has been recognized as essential to grace, both physical and social, for centuries. Writing a few years before Della Casa, in 1528, the Italian poet and ambassador Baldesar Castiglione coined the term *sprezzatura* for that specific nonchalance that makes difficult tasks look easy and through which grace is achieved. In Castiglione's *Il Cortegiano,* or *The Book of the Courtier,* a group of noblemen and intimates of the Duke of Urbino, whose court was one of the most brilliant of the Italian Renaissance, gather to discuss the qualities that make up the ideal royal confidant, and thus the perfect Renaissance man. In essence, this was a self-help book for sophisticated Europeans, offering a humanist view of how to live in the world. Castiglione was so renowned for his vision of a harmonious society governed by beauty, reason, and compassion that Raphael painted his portrait. The affinity that this painter of calm had for his model is evident in the vulnerability and understanding he illuminated in the ambassador's eyes. Composed with a striking similarity to the *Mona Lisa,* from the gracefully turned pose to the muted colors and the tranquil softness of the lighting, the portrait hangs in the Louvre. The writer on grace was a hero of his day, and beyond. *The Book of the Courtier* was an international best seller, and remained a standard for centuries.

Think of it as the sixteenth-century version of Stephen Covey's *7 Habits of Highly Effective People*. In Castiglione's view, a courtier needed to be a master of arms, horsemanship, dancing, and so on. But the number one habit required of him was to be "full of grace in all that he does or says."[13]

Noble birth helped, but it wasn't essential. The most knowledgeable of Castiglione's characters, Count Ludovico, goes on to say that while it is "almost proverbial" that grace of the body is not learned, indeed it can be. One "must begin early and learn the principles from the best of teachers" and he "must always make every effort to resemble and, if that be possible, to transform himself into his master."

This is where *sprezzatura*, the concept that made Castiglione famous, comes in. There can be no grace without it. *Sprezzatura* meant avoiding affectation while also making "whatever is done or said appear to be without effort."

Facility causes "the greatest wonder," says the count, while to labor in difficulty "shows an extreme want of grace." There is something wonderfully Italian about this kind of relaxed grace. Consider the luscious ease, vitality, and naturalness of Marcello Mastroianni and Sophia Loren.

Sprezzatura brings to mind another Italian concept of grace: *bella figura*, literally "beautiful figure," meaning to make a good impression by being well-groomed, well-dressed, and well-behaved. In other words, making the best of yourself before you go out and face the world. This is different from the superficial ego trip of aspiring to be likable.

Sprezzatura takes a light touch. If you really want people to admire how hard you've worked, that's not *sprezzatura*. Or it's *sprezzatura* taken too far. It can be an affectation to strive mightily against affectation. Beware the "Oh, I just threw it together" brag about a meticulously planned outfit or a meal that has been slavishly perfected. Such fauxchalance is intended to put the speaker in an untouchable light, far removed from the stressed-out, last-minute, forgot-to-make-the-salad-dressing rest of us. Our guide to gourmet grace is down-to-earth Julia Child. Think of fearless, charming, genuine Julia, sloshing her potato pancake on the counter, scooping it up, and tossing it back in the pan, all while chattering happily to her television viewers. She made it all look easy, especially the flubs. *Sprezzatura!*

At its best, *sprezzatura* softens the cold rigidity that can accompany perfectionism. Some people have an excessive desire to appear very accomplished. For example, the dinner party host who fusses over his coulibiac of salmon en croute yet neglects his guests. Or the guest who monopolizes the conversation with a stockpile of clever remarks because she must always be the center of attention. There is nothing graceful about such efforts, for they don't project the kind of calm that sets others at ease. Nor do they respond to what those around them want most of all: inclusiveness, human connection, a little joy. Grace is balancing skill with pleasure in doing it.

Theatrical Interlude: The Ungraceful Case of the Manners Police

Pleasure, ease, an inconspicuous hint rather than a heavy hand: these are the small things that contribute to the "manner of light" to which Della Casa refers. Taking pleasure in pleasing others, rather than fussing over minutiae. In making a big deal out of things, there is a willingness only to stand out, not to get along.

It's easy—too easy—to bemoan a world gone crazy over superficial things and swift gratification, however. To be sure, previous generations placed a high value on character, which was defined by one's self-control, service to others, and faith in God. But we have to be careful not to get too nostalgic for those days, when views about righteous living could be suffocatingly rigid. The writer Katherine Anne Porter, a penetrating observer of the judgmental harshness of early twentieth-century American society, called such a rigid view "axiomatic morality."[14] Strict codes of behavior that govern whom one can love and marry, what's appropriate for men but not for women, and who's good enough for Heaven's A-list and who isn't—well, they are beside the point, if you recall that grace, child of Aphrodite and Dionysus, is the fruit of love and pleasure.

George Bernard Shaw, with his precise jeweler's eye, brilliantly exposed what happens when folks focus on behavior to the point of showing off: emotional constipation, lack of compassion and human feeling.

In Shaw's play *Major Barbara*, Lady Britomart Undershaft personifies the bullying side of upper-class gentility, scolding and correcting her browbeaten son as if she had memorized George Washington's *Rules of Civility and Decent Behaviour* but had absorbed nothing of their spirit. She urges self-mastery but sees its use—wrongly—as a barricade against empathy. Only the middle class falls into "a state of dumb helpless horror" at the wickedness of the world, she sniffs. "In our class, we have to decide what is to be done with wicked people; and nothing should disturb our self possession."

Did Shaw have an ironic twist on Della Casa's *Galateo* in mind when he wrote *Pygmalion*? Like the ancient sculptor of the play's title—and like someone who had studied Della Casa's manual, all but the points about grace—Professor Higgins transforms Eliza, the Cockney flower girl, by drilling her in every detail of genteel speech and behavior. She blossoms into not only a proper English lady but a self-respecting equal. She becomes a truly free Galatea, awakened by the social awareness she has gained, mostly from others besides Higgins. Shaw shows us that she is the one with the truly noble character, not the educated super-snob Higgins. For all his sophistication, he remains cold, graceless, sneering. His aim, after all, was to win a bet, not to actually help anyone.

"Dear Boy: Sacrifice to the Graces!"

As this country got started, manners instruction took a hard line that Henry Higgins would appreciate. In the strict social strata of colonial society, the young were to be groomed in deference and obedience to authority. This was the tone of George Washington's prized catalog of behavior.

Things changed when a thick treatise on ease, rather than effort, made its way to an America newly interested in shaking up the social order. *Letters to His Son on the Fine Art of Becoming a Man of the World and a Gentleman* by the Earl of Chesterfield was published in England in 1774, a year after the author's death, and became an instant best seller on both sides of the Atlantic. Though the colonists were keen to throw off English rule, they still appreciated English refinements. Here, in zesty, colorful depth, was how to go through life with freewheeling grace, enjoying wine, women, and good company, for anyone anywhere. Philip Stanhope, the Earl of Chesterfield, had a long diplomatic career; he was an ambassador to Holland, and a friend of Voltaire and Montesquieu. But he'd be forgotten about today if not for his greatest achievement: a monument to the art of living in the form of more than three hundred fatherly letters. They were written from the heart and never intended for publication, which is probably why they sound so alive and unselfconscious all these centuries later.

In the tradition of concerned parents everywhere, Chesterfield was trying to get his kid ready for real life. What he dearly desired, he wrote, was to hear people say of the boy, "What manners, what graces, what an art of pleasing!"[15] But the earl had a lot of work to do to groom his son into a gentleman, because young Philip Stanhope, ambitiously named after his father, was illegitimate.

There's more than a little irony in the fact that one of America's best-loved bibles of behavior should concern the cultivation of a bastard. Yet it's the kind of thing to make Caravaggio proud, as the painter of prostitutes and muddy saints and the transcendent beauty of them all. In fact, it was the very democratic nature of Chesterfield's quest that appealed to a society feeling its way along an uncharted path. You didn't have to be an aristocrat or a Boston Brahmin to adopt elegant ways. You didn't have to be a pious person either. Chesterfield took more of an Italian approach, focusing on the fine details of behavior rather than shading his advice with moralism, as was the prevailing Anglo-American fashion.[16] If he didn't write much about moral duties and service to others, he found pleasing people to be essential. But mostly, he put stock in grace.

For him, grace was subtle, elusive, and indispensable. It was something you intuited after spending time with graceful people, i.e., the French. France made a veritable religion of grace, in his view. Paris was "the seat of the graces," where conversation was an art and the best company was attentive to the precision and elegance of language and enunciation. A charming mien was also part of grace: "*Enjouement*"—cheerfulness—"prevails in all their companies."

Grace surfaced in the way you dressed, carried yourself, moved, and spoke, and it was in your mood. "Dear Boy," he writes in March 1748, "SACRIFICE TO THE GRACES." (Capitalization his.) He continues:

> The different effects of the same things, said or done, when accompanied or abandoned by them, is almost inconceivable. They prepare the way to the heart; and the heart has such an influence over the understanding, that it is worth while to engage it in our interest. . . .

> A thousand little things, not separately to be defined, conspire to form these graces, this je ne sais quoi, that always please. A pretty person, genteel motions, a proper degree of dress, an harmonious voice, something open and cheerful in the countenance. . . . All these things, and many others, are necessary ingredients in the composition of the pleasing je ne sais quoi, which everybody feels, though nobody can describe.

A few months later, he describes a painting by Carlo Maratti whose subject was "The School of Drawing," in which the Three Graces are depicted under a banner reading "Without us, all labor is in vain." Everybody knows that's true in painting, Chesterfield notes. But few consider that it is also the case in "everything that is to be said or done."

Ask yourself why some people please you and others of "equal merit" do not, he writes. You will always find

> that it is because the former have the Graces and the latter not. I have known many a woman with an exact shape, and a symmetrical assemblage of beautiful features, please nobody; while others, with very moderate shapes and features, have charmed everybody. Why? because Venus will not charm so much, without her attendant Graces, as they will without her.

He is right. You can apply this to the puzzle of why the strikingly beautiful actress Anne Hathaway has been criticized for all kinds of reasons, while down-to-earth Jennifer Lawrence can do no wrong. Lawrence has "the Graces": she is natural and unflappable—she even handled the leaking of her nude photos with aplomb—and she seems like she'd be better company.

Much of Chesterfield's advice is timeless. He railed against making others uncomfortable. "Pulling out one letter after another and reading them in company . . . is impolite and rude. It seems to say, we are weary of the conversation." (The same goes for scrolling through e-mails.) He believed life was a banquet and one should enjoy it with appetite. To take full advantage, his son needed the knowledge of a scholar and the manners of a courtier, a union of "books and the world." And by "world," Chesterfield meant the whole ball of wax. "Everything is worth seeing once," he reasoned, and urged the boy to take in operas, plays, and even "the Savoyard's raree-shows," for the earl wasn't above a peep show.

Being well bred meant conversing with ease and respect with people of all classes, "without the least concern of mind or awkwardness of body." Getting the kinks out of the body required discipline—in this Chesterfield linked himself with the self-mastery ethic of his age, and ages past—but that should be leavened into a well-proportioned life. He advised waking early, working in the morning, exercising in the afternoon, and keeping company in the evening.

Beware the "stiff immobility of a bashful booby"! Banish that with "a good air," he wrote: "You cannot conceive, nor can I express, how advantageous a good air, genteel motions, and engaging address are, not only among women, but among men, and even in the course of business; they fascinate the affections, they steal a preference, they play about the heart till they engage it."

As with Castiglione's *sprezzatura*, there was a measure of artifice implied in having an air. Not affectation; this was the opposite of ease. The goal was to appear artless and natural, but you only got that way through practice. This was the point Chesterfield hammered again and again in his letters: a convincing performance took work. Indeed, Chesterfield urged a bit—often more than a bit—of fakery. His philosophy was fake it till you make it.

Readers ate up his advice; if Chesterfield's son could learn the graces, so could anyone. It was a remarkably populist approach, perhaps without meaning to be. "*Les manières, les agrèmens, les grâces,* cannot be learned by theory, they are only to be got by use among those who have them," he wrote. And so he urged his son to weave his way into elite company by imitating its manners, looking around him, and copying how others behaved. With this technique, Chesterfield was letting the average Joe in on how to gain the social graces and advance by them, even if they weren't a birthright.

Some of his advice was loopy. Women, for instance, were "children of a larger growth" and not to be trusted with serious matters. Machiavelli himself might have written the tip about studying the weaknesses of others to know "what to bait your hook with to catch them," though this could also be viewed as politically savvy. But it was the earl's endorsement of using grace and demeanor to gain access to a playboy lifestyle that drew criticism from stiff-necked quarters; the introduction to one edition warned that Chesterfield was "dead to the higher interests of humanity." Of course, this is one reason his letters sold so well. Many editors either excised the racier parts about pleasures with women or apologized and included them anyway, and Chesterfield's renown grew in America through the 1800s until his work exceeded all other conduct books in popularity.[17] Editions were still being published well into the 1900s, many retitled *The American Chesterfield*.

As a final, sad irony in the earl's saga, his instructions served more use to strangers throughout the ages than to their adored recipient: Junior Stanhope died unexpectedly at the age of thirty-six, within days of what turned out to be his father's final letter.

The 2006 film *Idiocracy* takes contemporary trends to their logical extreme of coarseness and gracelessness. In an army experiment on hibernation gone awry, a man is frozen and forgotten; he wakes up five hundred years later in a dumbed-down future where a stumbling population is barely articulate, fast food comes in Extra Big-Ass sizes, and the chief domestic pastime is a show called *Ow, My Balls!* Along with literacy and intelligence, grace is extinct.

PART TWO

Looking at Grace

CHAPTER 5

SUPERSTAR GRACE:

LESSONS FROM MOTOWN

A lady with class can sit on a garbage pail and look good.

—Maxine Powell

PEOPLE ARE FALLING ALL OVER THEMSELVES and their Birkin bags for cramped seats to a nine-minute parade of empty-eyed stick figures in stilettos. Holsteins on a feedlot have more elbow room than a reporter at New York's Fashion Week.

Just when you have groped your way past the crowds, the furs, and the immovable fashionistas to your spot in the bleachers, in come the celebrities and their entourages. They stroll up the runway like avatars of the Almighty. Once enthroned in the front row, they will pretend not to notice the gawkers pooling around them. Celebrities do not appear in this photo-centric arena without a storm of interest.

That's what I thought, at any rate, until one morning when the lights dimmed just before the start of one fashion show. Emerging at the last minute from the shadows, a woman trotted across the runway to take her seat. She was moving as fast as her platform pumps would take her, semi-crouched, her eyes downcast in the mode of someone who doesn't want to draw attention to herself. But because this woman was superstar songstress Beyoncé Knowles, everyone noticed.

She was wearing the silliest-looking dress I'd seen all week (and that's saying something). It barely reached past her bottom and poufed out around her belly before narrowing at her thighs. In fact, she looked like she was stuck inside a marshmallow. But her glow! Beyoncé was barely visible in the near-darkness, but she seemed to carry her own golden follow spot with her. This is one of the Miracles of Beyoncé, for which she is the envy of all womanhood. Could it be she was being favored by the lighting technicians? Ah, even more envy. Never mind—what really got my attention was the look of pleased expectancy in her eyes as she gazed toward the top of the runway.

She sat at attention in her seat, quietly engaged with the atmosphere of anticipation, as if she couldn't wait to see what was going to come down the catwalk.

I have long admired Beyoncé for her ability to balance an unabashedly provocative, sexy stage style with a mostly classy off-stage image. Her glow, that golden follow spot: it seems to come from inside, a kind of inner magic—but really, it's grace. It is grace that has come about because she was raised to treat people well, and by most accounts she does treat people well. Her obsessive work ethic is justifiably famous, she is the utmost professional—never, ever appearing disheveled or out of control—and she stays away from trouble, avoiding tabloid scandals. That would be enough to make her a worthy role model, but in addition she gives an active boost to female empowerment with her all-female band and her songs about strength and self-acceptance.

She may not be the only pop star with self-discipline and a positive message. But none can touch her physical grace. No living entertainer possesses Beyoncé's mix of sensuality and muscle, pleasure and power. Surely she is anchored to some superior force of gravity available only to her. How else to explain the way she can spin off-kilter and whirl hair-flingingly atop those heels with total control? She scoops new mysteries of the human form out of her long, convulsive spine. She also has excellent taste in artistic inspirations. Her Super Bowl halftime show in 2013 was a nod to the cabaret chic and self-possessed sexuality of Marlene Dietrich. (Thank you, pop stars—you too, Madonna—for the occasional reminders of Dietrich's genius.)

I could point to many examples of Beyoncé's grace. There is, for instance, the warmth that spills over in interviews and public appearances, and the coolness with which she handled the flap over whether she lip-synched "The Star-Spangled Banner" at President Obama's second inauguration. That was a lesson in How Not to Enter the Fray: she kept quiet during the swell of accusations until she could silence her critics in a way that was as artful as it was persuasive. That opportunity came a week later, at her pre–Super Bowl press conference, when she surprised and delighted the assembled media by singing the national anthem, live and a cappella. "Any questions?" Beyoncé purred, after sustaining the final loud note and ending any speculation that she couldn't belt.

Yet in that offstage moment I witnessed under a tent at Lincoln Center, Beyoncé displayed a kind of grace that is all too rare to see.

There was no grand Superwoman entrance, no crowd of handlers, no look-at-me show or I'm-really-too-hip-for-this attitude. Instead, she showed humility and respect for her surroundings. And in that strange dress, to boot. Moments later, three models came strutting down the runway in identical frocks. Beyoncé was a billboard for the designer's bubble-belly look, but instead of swanning around in it, she had kept that low-key, too.

Why does that picture of Beyoncé stay with me? Because the diva was an antidiva. Because she wasn't a scene-stealing peacock. She didn't shout out her celebrity and shove it at the rest of us. In a sea of impatience and egos gone haywire, she was a reminder of why we were there. She brought in a spirit of wonder.

What with the traffic and the jostling crowds, I'd begun to hate the world, or at least the part of it that had overtaken midtown Manhattan. But in that dark cavern of claustrophobia, the pop queen's down-to-earth display of grace felt transcendent.

WE'RE USED TO SEEING pop-culture stardom result in big egos and big problems. Chris Brown beats up on Rihanna. Kanye West barges in on Taylor Swift's MTV Video Music Awards moment. Britney Spears, dressed to make a hooker blush, weeps and whines on national television. A hard-partying Lindsay Lohan ends up once again in rehab.

Obviously, money and celebrity don't guarantee an ease with the world. You don't find grace where self-importance runs amok. But so many pop stars are just kids when they become famous. How are they supposed to know how to handle their success?

"Grace is the growth of habit," wrote eighteenth-century French moralist Joseph Joubert. "This charming quality requires practice if it is to become lasting."[1]

Imagine an institution that teaches young celebs to carry themselves with grace, to be considerate of the public to whom they owe their stardom, to govern their bodies and their reputations with care. And to awaken in others a similar respect.

That existed in the early years of Motown.

Indirectly, Beyoncé is a beneficiary of it. Feather-light and intangible as it may be, her equanimity is traceable even beyond her own childhood. You can follow it back through her early years in Houston and connect the dots a thousand miles away to Motown, years before Beyoncé was born, when a tiny woman with uncommon grandeur changed the face of pop success.

Beyoncé's father, Mathew Knowles, looked to Motown in managing his daughter's career for nearly two decades, starting with the girl group that came to be known as Destiny's Child. Knowles took as his model Motown founder Berry Gordy Jr., who made sure the artists signed to his record label were groomed for all facets of celebrity life.

Gordy "taught his artists etiquette. He had real artist development. And his artists were glamorous. That's really what the music world is all about," Knowles told *Ebony* magazine.[2] And so, like Diana Ross and Gladys Knight before her, Beyoncé was coached not only in singing and dancing but also in the finer points of stardom that Gordy oversaw in his own stable of musicians: walking in heels, giving interviews, staying poised no matter what.

In essence, Beyoncé absorbed the legacy of Maxine Powell. Powell was petite and tough-minded, a former model and actress whose convictions about grace gave her a profound influence on

American culture of the twentieth century. For five years in the 1960s, she ran the Motown Artist Development Finishing School, instructing the label's teenagers in how to sit, stand, walk, dress, talk to fans and reporters, and sidestep the public blunders that can tank a career.

"Finishing school" may seem a quaint notion, but in fact Powell was creating a new reality with age-old conventions of dignity, a well-groomed appearance, and personal integrity. At the height of the British Invasion, when the Beatles and other English groups topped the charts, Powell created an indelible look and manner for a new generation of American artists, underscoring the importance of graceful bearing to a charmed public even as she armed her pupils to smash the color barrier with style.

"You are going to be good enough to perform for kings," she announced to her all-star inaugural class, which included the Supremes; the Miracles and their lead singer, Smokey Robinson; Martha Reeves, of Martha and the Vandellas; and the preteen prodigy Stevie Wonder.

"Don't forget, these were kids," Powell told *People* magazine years later. "They came from the street and the projects. They were rude and crude-acting. They didn't know how to look you in the eye or shake hands."[3]

She got a shy Marvin Gaye out of the habit of singing with his eyes closed, which some women found sexy. But Powell firmly believed you should look at people when you're singing to them. She told him, "You're so handsome, I want to be sure you use every ounce of your body in walking."[4] Soon he was channeling his natural reserve into one of the most seductive displays of elegant understatement you could ever wish to see. Gaye's air of contained ease, his light, gliding carriage with that little bit of a tease—a soft bounce in the knee, suggesting a prowl but never revealing all of himself to us—are as much a part of his persona as his high, sweet voice.

Martha Reeves told me that as much as Powell wanted the singers to look and act their best, she also wanted them to transcend what can be an obsessively self-focused environment and think about others.

"She taught us to keep our head erect and be aware of everything that was going on around us, as a way of respecting others and their personal space," said Reeves when I called to ask her about the early Motown years.

Powell had starred in her own one-woman show years before, and she knew how to hold a stage. She corrected the singers' posture by having them balance books on their heads. She taught them to walk in a straight line across the stage. They learned to exit a limousine with their knees together. There was to be no raunch, no crotch exhibitionism coming out of Hitsville under her reign.

What would she make of the sexually explicit style of so many of today's pop stars? In fact, Powell had plenty to say about Miley Cyrus after the twenty-year-old singer's ungraceful twerking display in a flesh-toned bikini at the 2013 Video Music Awards show in Brooklyn. Foam fingers, stuffed bears, and crude gestures were involved, but most of the focus was on the former Disney Channel starlet's pelvis, grinding and flapping like a haddock in its death throes. Viewers responded with widespread disgust. Asked about Cyrus on a local television news program in Detroit, the ninety-eight-year-old Powell delivered a cogent critique.

"You have to dance with your feet," she said, "not your buttocks."[5] She drew out the last syllable for emphasis, imbuing it with queenly dignity.

But that's not all Powell had to say. Her lifelong focus had been on building up her clients on the inside, instilling them with inner as well as outer grace. And she lived her lessons. So while the world was condemning Cyrus for her degrading spectacle, Powell had the grace to offer a way for the young woman to rise above it.

"My advice to her is don't beat yourself up," Powell said, her voice shaky with age but warm. "Try and grow and be better. And promise yourself that you'll never, ever put yourself in that kind of predicament again."

Powell never let her Motown artists get into that kind of predicament. Her cardinal rules: Don't "protrude the buttocks." Never turn your back on the audience. Respect your fans.

And, since fame is fickle, keep your ego in check.

"When they got compliments," Powell told *People*, "I taught them to say, 'Thank you very much, but we're still developing. I hope the next time you see us we'll do even better.'"

Some of the stars chafed at her instruction, but that didn't change a thing. "It didn't matter who you became during the course of your career—how many hits you had, how well your name was known around the world," said Smokey Robinson at a ceremony in Powell's honor shortly before her death in 2013. "Two days a week when you were back in Detroit you had to go to artists' development. It was mandatory."[6]

Powell was running a banquet facility and a finishing and modeling school in Detroit—placing the first black models in automobile ads—when she met Gordy; she came to work for him in 1964.

In addition to modeling, she had studied dance and acting. She was also trained in the grand old discipline of elocution, which emphasized good posture, physical expression, and gestures as well as the voice and pronunciation. Back in the eighteenth century, elocution was aimed at actors, politicians, and preachers, but the art gained traction in middle-class parlors a century later when reading aloud grew popular as an elegant pastime. Women, especially, turned to it for self-empowerment in a society that didn't always offer them the opportunities of higher education.[7]

"Elocution will not make women orators any more than it will make them actors," wrote Anna Morgan, a prominent elocution teacher, in 1893. "It can not confer brains, nor in a great measure impart that good taste which is the fragrance of the individual soul; but it can take that disordered instrument, the body, and tune it."[8]

The graceful tuning of your instrument and the fluency of speech you learned through elocution gave you status, even if, say, you hadn't had much schooling.

And even if you came from Detroit's housing projects, as the Supremes and Smokey Robinson did.

Of course, Powell's influence also helped sell the music. Gordy wanted to produce records that would interest all people, regardless of race or class. His aim was timeless appeal. Consider Diana Ross, Florence Ballard, and Mary Wilson of the Supremes: chic young women in evening gowns (chosen by Powell) with a gentle, swaying way of moving and a subtle sensuality.

The outer trappings of grace can only go so far, however. Powell refined Ross's performance, got her to rethink her ultralong lashes and to quit her wide-eyed mugging for the camera. But she couldn't ease the ungraceful tension in the singer's shoulders, which tended to creep up protectively around her chin. That telltale bit of body language betrays the stresses of those glory days. The Supremes may have been the leading girl group of the 1960s, but their swift rise didn't make for an easy life.

We have to look beyond the gowns and the posture drills for Powell's deepest influence. Where she elicited true grace was in an entirely different arena: the mind.

"What she taught us was class and self-worth," wrote Martha Reeves in a tribute to her mentor.[9]

Grace under pressure? Hemingway, who coined the phrase, didn't know the half of it, not like Motown artists did at the height of the civil rights movement. Powell trained them to maintain their dignity in response to everyday abuses. Wrote Reeves,

> We were not protesters, we didn't go marching or fighting; we had to break down barriers mentally and spiritually. She taught us how to be gracious if we went into a place and they refused to serve us. We would walk out politely and go and find another place. We were taught how to tolerate, to sustain, and to persevere. And she was right. I survived. A lot of people at that time didn't know how to overcome and persevere.

To overcome and persevere: this is a grace that matters. Especially to the Motown artists in those early years, who had to find a way to move through the indignities of the times without damaging their label, their careers, or their spirits.

For some, Powell's lessons merely expanded upon an existing composure. Smokey Robinson, for instance, was smooth from the start. His smooth, high voice and smooth, relaxed presence made the girls scream; he was Motown's equivalent of Elvis Presley, making disguised getaways after his shows with a coat thrown over his head so he wouldn't be mobbed by fans. But his natural grace could also have a deeper effect.

Montgomery, Alabama, 1963. Several of Motown's top groups were performing for a segregated audience in a horse-training arena, as part of the Motortown Revue bus tour of one-night stands. The road show traveled to major East Coast cities, but it also went through the Deep South, which wasn't always welcoming. In that Montgomery arena, two flags hung over the stage: American and Confederate. In front of the flags stood Martha and the Vandellas, the Marvelettes, Mary Wells, the Temptations, the Miracles, and twelve-year-old "Little" Stevie Wonder, along with a twelve-piece band. They had come together for the grand finale, the Miracles' hit song "Mickey's Monkey."

Joining the artists onstage were two men with baseball bats. They stood at the front, one on each side, to make sure the audience didn't dance.

"If anyone got up to dance they would get hit with those clubs," Martha Reeves told me in our phone conversation.

This was customary in the South at that time, when police often kept white and black audience members separated by a rope that divided the performance halls.

Smokey Robinson and the Miracles were the star of the show. "Mickey's Monkey" was one of early Motown's biggest successes, a bouncy song guaranteed to get everyone dancing. Its driving,

After Smokey Robinson gracefully smoothed over racial tensions at a 1963 concert in Alabama, "everyone was hugging and kissing and laughing and celebrating the music."

hand-clapping beat had helped spread the monkey as a national dance craze. So when the time came for Robinson to launch into the infectiously upbeat closing tune, the tension in the arena was high. Everyone onstage knew the itch to dance was going to be irresistible, and their fans were at risk for a beatdown. They had seen it happen before.

Robinson stepped up to the microphone and decided to try something a little different. He spoke first to the men with the bats.

"He told them, 'We're just going to dance and have a good time,'" Reeves recalled. "He told them, 'This music is *dance* music, and you guys can move away.' The whole situation was soothed over by Smokey Robinson's words.

"He's got this calming, high-pitched voice," Reeves continued. "He didn't say it in an angry tone, he said it in a loving, man-to-man tone. And then it was like, 'Okay, man, if that's what you think,' and they moved away just as easily as he said it. He had enough authority that they got up and got away."

When Robinson started singing the familiar chorus, *Lum-di-lum-di-lai-ai,* the bat-wielding fellows "started dancing, too," Reeves said. "And what happened was, the people had broke the barrier down. Everyone was hugging and kissing and laughing and celebrating the music.

"It was the first time we could perform in the South that someone didn't get hit on the head. Smokey stopped that. He stopped it."

He did it with the grace of his voice, his poise, and his friendly appeal to reason. With an understanding heart, imagination, and, especially, courage, he transformed what could have been ugly into an uplifting experience. Robinson had the presence of mind and body to bring about a moment of grace.

Grace reversed the current. A spark of electricity traveled outward from his words and bearing, igniting something unexpected—surprise, wonder, maybe even respect—in the pair of guys ready to crack heads, and in the crowd assembled there. Did they hear the quiet backfire, see the swap of power? Much better: they felt it.

For one night of grace in the Jim Crow South, a divided people came together and danced.

CHAPTER 6

EVERYDAY GRACE:

COOKS, WAITERS, AND ROADIES

At last, the subject matter of art includes the simple intimacies of everyday life in its repertoire.

—LOUIS EDMOND DURANTY, *The New Painting*

THERE IS A LUNCH SPOT near my office that makes a decent stir-fry, but a couple of years ago you took your chances at the counter.

One of the guys who took the orders was an absolute pill. I don't think he's there much now, and this is why: you ruined his day just by walking in, and he let you know it with the kind of frostiness that makes the little hairs on the back of your neck prickle. When your order was up, he'd shove it across the counter to you and zip away before you could bother him for anything else. God forbid you ask for a fork, as I did once. He shot me a look that said he dearly wished he had something sharper than plastic cutlery to slam my way.

The guy didn't just have a bad attitude, he was scrunched up, his shoulders visibly clenched under his T-shirt. He was so tightly wound you could feel his bitterness from a distance. He shouldn't have been working with the public; any job dealing with people demands at least a little bit of grace. Perhaps he had long ago grown tired of waiting on people, and his resentment was boiling over. For some, being in service to the public is a chore, and the sooner they get out, the better.

For others, it's a calling.

There is an art to good service. It's a matter of choice—the choice to be excellent—and a dedication to others that is at the essence of grace.

I was in New York's Guggenheim Museum not long ago to see an exhibit of California artist James Turrell, who experiments with light and space. His works are basically dim, empty rooms with maybe a little window cut into a wall. I walked around wondering what I was missing. People were waiting in line to enter one gallery, and I joined them. Only a few at a time were allowed to see the display inside, a projection of a dark shadow against a slightly darker wall. The far more interesting experience was outside, where the job of managing the line of visitors fell to a short, compactly built security guard with velvety ebony skin and a physical expressiveness to light up the sky.

He became the emcee of the waiting-in-line experience. Was he always this cheerful, or was he just having a good day? He used his arms as wings to wave us into position, spreading them in a wide embrace. "Two minutes," he announced with a beaming smile and a rich, lilting accent. I was dying to know where he came from, as I watched him work the space, fluttering his fingers at newcomers to welcome them to the line, striding into the hallway to see who else might be coming and kicking a leg out with a backward tip of his torso. He moved to some inner rhythm, a silent music.

Seeing me scribbling in my notepad as my turn came to enter the gallery, he said to me nicely, purring his Rs, "Just finish what you are wrrriting; finish your wrrriting before going in." And when I tucked away my pen, he swept me and my fellow linemates inside with that great, broad wingspan.

When I emerged from the gallery, I asked him where he was from. "Doesn't my accent give me away?" he asked, smiling, eyes alight. "Well . . ." I said, silently scrolling through the possibilities. A Venn diagram of African dance traditions and geopolitics began forming in my mind. He saw I was about to guess and, in an act of charity, tossed me a hint.

"Kofi Annan . . . ?" he said, drawing the name out as if we were playing *Password* on TV.

"Um," I stammered, wanting to join the game, hoping my memory was up for it. The encouraging look on his face must have eased open some dusty drawer in my mind. "Ghana?"

"You are rrright!" he said, rewarding me with an even bigger smile and another beautiful trilled R.

This man was joy in motion, and he knew how to use his body to make connections with others. I encountered him again in the rotunda, which was filled with Turrell's shifting colored light, the best part of the exhibit. Or did it just seem that way because I'd been cheered up by the guard? The museum was closing, and in his preparations to head home, the guard whipped off his jacket with a single smooth action, sending a lasso of fabric whirling around himself. He extended his hand to me in farewell, with a royal bow, and

I whooshed through the revolving doors onto Fifth Avenue with an exhilarating rush.

He'd made me feel cared for and invited me into his dance, which is what the graceful action does. We've all felt this: from the man who swings the door open and steps aside for you as you're coming out of a coffee shop juggling a hot cup and a tote bag, or from the young woman on the subway platform who kindly plucks out her earbuds and looks up your destination on her phone to help you find your stop.

This one-on-one connectedness can offer a few moments of unexpected joy. The delight only grows when you witness it on a larger scale. There is a collective grace in busy workplaces where there is no room for error, where people are supremely good at what they do and they tune in to one another's movements. You find this in a symphony orchestra, with the rolling, washing movement of the strings, and among well-oiled surgical teams, NASCAR pit crews, and waiters navigating a busy dining room at the height of service. Their movement coordination is a kind of dance, with its own hidden choreography that you can uncover if you look closely enough. You've heard of strength in numbers, and this is why that's true: moving in rhythm is both soothing and energizing and bonds us more closely together.

It pleases our animal nature. Collective choreography is found all through the wild. As I write this, it is August in Washington, and thousands of bachelor cicadas are massing to give their annual mating concert in the trees. All in a bunch, they sing and fly and sing some more, in what has to be the loudest collective booty call in the insect world.

There is synchrony of movement in swarms of bees, schools

of fish, and herds of horses running gracefully as one. Their synchrony is part of what we find so graceful about them. Horses move together seemingly effortlessly even over rugged terrain and long distances, coordinating their stride and spacing with one another through a sense of body positioning that any ballet master trying to get his dancers in a line would envy.

Flamingos are primitive birds whose fossil record dates back fifty million years; perhaps because of all this evolutionary rehearsal time, they are famous for their crowd consciousness. Whether they inhabit lagoons or lakes, their mating dance has the smooth precision of the Rockettes. Sweeping this way and that at the water's edge, wing to wing, the birds strut, bob, and head-flick in unison. Researchers suggest that with this dancing ritual, flamingos are seeking to pair up in a way that anyone sensitive to grace can understand: they may be searching for a mate whose moves match their own.[1]

At the essence of all these displays, whether among birds or humans, is relinquishing yourself to the flow. The participants merge into a single living, breathing organism, where the group is emphasized over the individual. You forget that you are a separate entity. In the most harmonious corporeal teamwork, there is a transcendent quality, of connecting with something larger than your own ego.

Look at close-order drills in the military. In his book *Keeping Together in Time: Dance and Drill in Human History*, historian William McNeill writes of the "muscular bonding" in this age-old practice, which has outlived its battlefield usefulness but is still employed as a way to tie recruits together on a deep level. In his own World War II–era army training, he recalls feeling a sense of well being, and "of swelling out, becoming bigger than life."[2]

Throughout human existence, synchronized movement has served to pull people together and strengthen connections. And if most of us lack it in our lives, watching others is a window into its pleasures, and its grace.

Observing cadets maneuver through their drills on a parade ground is one possibility. But with open kitchens a growing trend in restaurants, you can catch a glimpse of collective grace over dinner. Great kitchens match drill-field precision with gestural art. The best cooks possess a soldier's obedience and a dancer's grace.

I saw this on a Saturday night at a restaurant called CityZen in Southwest Washington, DC, where alongside his risotto and rib eye, chef Eric Ziebold served up a quiet show of elegant efficiency.[3]

Before coming to Washington in 2004, Ziebold had logged eight years at Thomas Keller's French Laundry in Yountville, California, one of those revered foodie meccas that is spoken of in sighs. Ziebold held the top job of chef de cuisine there and also helped Keller open the ultra-high-end restaurant Per Se in New York.

Keller is painstakingly precise not only about his food but about the way it is served. "He frequently talked about the service as a dance," said one of his former headwaiters, Phoebe Damrosch. Keller brought in French baroque dance specialist Catherine Turocy to train the waiters in the minuet. Why? Because it is all about graceful approach, Turocy told me, and gestures of offering and accepting are important. Originating under Louis XIV, the minuet exemplifies the courtly manners that were all the rage in France at the time. Its responsive, attentive spirit was what the waiters took away, Damrosch said.

"It was a message from the people who opened the restaurant that this is something incredibly important, we're a team, we have to work together or it's not going to work," she recalled. "We talked about the center of gravity, where to hold the plates so our elbows were at a right angle, so if someone bumped into you, you could hold on to it. It was all about how to make sure your body was really comfortable and stable."

This is the atmosphere that Ziebold absorbed and in which he developed his own approach to running a restaurant. He is known for his quiet authority and for working insane hours seven days a week. He is also known for his moves.

"I fell in love with Eric when I saw him move in the kitchen," confesses his wife, Celia Laurent Ziebold. She met Ziebold when they worked together at the French Laundry.

"I saw this man moving around very precisely in a very tight space, and everyone around him was well orchestrated, with very natural movements," says Laurent Ziebold. "I thought it was beautiful."

Those reality TV chef shows may have you thinking that professional cooking is all about crazy creativity with vinegars and organ meats. Or that it's a matter of egos, screaming, and jungle treks in search of Amazonian rodents. But what really matters in a pro kitchen is instant reaction, mindless repetition, and smooth, efficient maneuvers. Restaurants run on the French kitchen-brigade system, modeled more than a century ago after a military hierarchy. There's the chef, a couple of lieutenants (the sous-chefs), and a platoon of line cooks—the kitchen infantry—manning stations assigned by menu category: appetizers, fish, meat, and so on.

It has to be this way. The restaurant kitchen is a highly physical place, and if the saucier lunging toward the stove collides with the meat cook slinging plated quail toward the waiters, there will be a pileup of disaster. Chefs, like generals, know they have two choices: discipline or chaos.

Wearing a starched white chef's coat with his initials monogrammed by the collar, Ziebold could just as well have medals pinned across his chest. His trim physique and crisp appearance announce him as a man steeped in discipline. He has an easy smile and a friendly, boyish face, but something in his chiseled cheekbones and the set of his jaw brings to mind the solemn intensity of a pitcher throwing a no-hitter in the bottom of the ninth.

His staff will produce perhaps a thousand plates a night, but Ziebold has planned the menus so the preparation is evenly distributed among his cooks, there's plenty of variety, and diners receive each course at a controlled, steady pace.

"I keep them focused on the repetition," he says, nodding toward the line cooks as if he's speaking of the corps de ballet. "Me and the sous-chefs, we'll do the one-offs." The proof of this comes as the first guests are shown to their tables. Show time.

In the kitchen, eight cooks are squeezed together like a submarine crew. Still, they swivel with graceful ease from slicing to stirring, swinging stockpots onto burners, bending down to haul meat out of the lowboy fridge, and springing back up to toss it into a pan.

These toqued commandos glide calmly through the same motions again and again. They're a hairbreadth away from ruin, mere seconds from scorched shoat, lost lamb, overdone duck. All that separates them from expensive errors and trips to the hospital is timing, rehearsal, and reflexive grace.

Two sous-chefs oversee the meat and fish orders. The meat cook is the one with fingers full of bandages. The workhorses are the appetizer guys and a gangly fellow named Alex Brown, a one-man band of pots, whisks, spoons, and saucepans, who makes the hot starters—the soft-boiled egg with gourmet scrapple and gravy, the risotto, the soup.

Tickets roll out of a machine on the counter. Ziebold tears them off and calls out the orders. He has a calm, smooth way of moving, no rushing, no lurching. He wields a long spatula like a conductor's baton.

"Three egg, three tartare!"

Steam is rising from the saucepans. Brown grabs a pan, stirs it, tastes it, sets it back on the flame, and swipes the counter. In a chain of swift, blurred motions, he's swirling risotto, sautéing mushroom sauce, and heating up the cabbage soup. Like a shark, he never stops moving, and never loses his quizzical squint.

"Two tartare, one risotto!" Brown pirouettes with the stack of pots that he's grabbed from the window into the dish room, spinning back to the stove. He slides a pan of bacon-wrapped quail on the counter just before Ziebold turns to grab it.

Steps away, in the candlelit dining room, elegant body language is everywhere—in the way lanky sommelier Andrew Myers glides tableside the instant the waiter has left, to pour the Barolo without further interrupting the guests. Ask for the powder room and a waiter will lead you there with a kind of sideways crab walk, so as not to turn her back on you. With a flourish of her arms, she'll land you right at the door.

The kitchen sings with activity. Over at the fish and meat station, Kerwin Tugas, one of the sous-chefs, threads his way through the channel between the backsides of two line cooks. He floats with a kind of weightlessness, balanced and controlled. Doesn't touch anything as he goes by, agile as a cat, darting back to his station.

He spins on one foot to reach around the other men for a pan. Slips between the two cooks before the gap closes.

They're all adrenaline junkies, these aproned aces. They thrive on the buzz. Brown jolts his sauté pan with a hiccuping motion, flip flip flip. Reaching for a pile of shiitake to crown his veal tartare, another cook glides like an ice skater, launching himself from one counter to the other.

"It's like Chef says, 'There's no perfection, it's the pursuit of perfection,'" Tugas says. "So it's just repetition, repetition, repetition."

Toward midnight, as the dining room empties, the cooks turn to wiping off their counters and gulping water from plastic deli containers. Ziebold, looking as fresh as the minute service started, heads over to the bar to chat with Myers as he polishes wineglasses. The chef starts to talk about how he got swept into cooking.

Scrapple and red-eye gravy come out of Ziebold's kitchen because they're fixed in his emotional root system. He grew up in Ames, Iowa, where his father worked at a newspaper and his mother was a teacher. After the three o'clock bell, she went home to cook dinner, which was served promptly at six.

"God help you if you showed up late," he says.

Her cooking was the original slow food: she did her own canning and her own corned beef, brining it in the root cellar near the shelves of Mason jars.

Now Ziebold is especially proud of his corned beef tongue, a reference point to his past. "Some people are looking for blow-my-mind cooking," he says. "Some people are looking for the emotional tie. That's what inspires me."

Memory is a large part of his arsenal, and so is longing. Eating became a highly charged event, thanks to another formative part of Iowa culture: wrestling. Ziebold wrestled in junior high and high school, making the state team and earning a college scholarship. Cutting weight was as much a part of the sport as grueling workouts.

Food cravings haunted him. With his teammates he'd "walk around the grocery store saying, 'After the weigh-in I'm gonna have that and that and that,'" he recalls. He'd come home from practice so weak from exertion on an empty stomach that he'd be shaking.

After high school, he was burned out. Instead of taking the wrestling scholarship, he headed to culinary school, where he could indulge his food fantasies. At five foot nine—and with a father over six feet tall—Ziebold believes the years of food deprivation stunted his growth. The sport left its mark on him in other ways, too. You see it in his intensity, focus, and militaristic discipline.

And you see it in his moves. The athlete's grace remains in his capacity for endurance and consistency, his easy pivot from counter to counter, his confident legato in the midst of the hustle.

The beauty of the dishes, the carefully orchestrated flavors—it all starts with what lives in the minds and muscles of the chef. The hungers, the memories, the appetite for labor. Add the grace of the kitchen, and what ends up on your fork is the outcome of a string of sweet moves. From the cook's body to yours.

Being a graceful waiter is not all about stamina and memorizing specials. The grace is in quietly anticipating desire.

"You have to stay on the floor and just be around," said Damrosch, who was part of the waitstaff at Per Se. "Visiting the table, being close, pouring water, pouring some wine. You don't have to say anything." But if the customer needs something, you're there, before he's said a word: "You have a sense of the other person in the space and you're communicating all the time in a physical way."

Her memoir, *Service Included,* chronicles the year she spent under Keller's exacting eye, rising to become a female captain in the male-dominated world of four-star restaurants. She describes a good waiter as akin to a social worker, someone who can intuit needs, pick up on anxieties and relieve them, and make the guests feel cared for but not cramped. The reason behind every action is "to put the guest at ease," and mindful use of the body is part of that: perfecting a smooth, gliding stride that is neither too slow nor too fast, reaching beside a guest rather than across her, and never approaching from behind.

There is also an art to tailoring your demeanor to different diners. "You're being different people simultaneously," she told me. "A single diner might need more companionship. A table of rowdy gentlemen might need more gentle ribbing. . . . What puts one person at ease won't be the same for another."

Damrosch no longer works in restaurants; she married after leaving Per Se and is raising a family. She may have slightly lost her touch at pouring champagne with finesse, in a slim golden stream without sloshing, she said, but more important skills have stayed with her from her time in service. Waiting tables, she believes, is good training for life. It teaches you about unspoken communication, body language, carrying yourself and responding in a way that makes others feel comfortable. And about the power of simply being present.

"I think there's something innate about being a good waiter, someone who can pay attention and be a good listener. You have a feel for making someone happy. I remember one waiter stopped me in service once and told me I always needed to let the guest go first. No matter what is happening, however busy I was, I had to stop. The guest's movement is more important than my movement.

"I'm a big advocate of waiting tables," she said, "and to elevate it and to be really good at it requires a lot of attention and study. It's not something we think about too much in this culture, and that's sad."

ONE SUMMER, curious about how roadies load in a rock concert, I visited the sports arena in downtown Washington. It was Saturday morning, before dawn. High above the cement floor, crew members called upriggers had started hanging lights and other equipment for the Jennifer Lopez concert that evening.

On a catwalk one hundred feet up in the air, the abyss rose all around me.[4] The only thing between me and the concrete far below was an open metal handrail on either side of what felt like a footbridge to a heart attack.

But the upriggers, trussed up in harnesses that stretched around their hips, traversed the bridge and walked out onto the narrow beams with forbidding ease. Up in that smoky air, grace was pretty much what kept them alive.

As I stood clinging to the rail, my insides gurgling in fright, a man the size of a linebacker strolled jauntily across the catwalk as if he were ambling down the street on the happiest day of his life. No hesitation, nothing tentative, just joy. He was draped in coils of rope, and the harness around his crotch forced his legs wide, which gave him a bouncing, rolling motion, as if he were a plus-size rodeo cowboy who'd just hopped off a bull. He had Jackie Gleason's lightness, a tightrope walker's balance, and a power lifter's strength, and he plowed all these qualities into a series of graceful steps that propelled him over the handrail onto one of the beams.

Other upriggers dotted the beams with the equanimity of birds on wires. One man, straddling his beam with his tattooed calves and work boots dangling freely, stretched out in one smooth taffylike motion to grab a length of cable rising up to him on a pulley. He was part Peter Pan, part aerial gymnast—with no net.

The men up there—along with one quietly focused, ponytailed woman—didn't just rely on might. There was a smooth, elastic quality of movement, and a delicacy of footwork that's necessary where the stakes are so high. Though I couldn't bear to, they had to look down, for each uprigger was in a push-pull tango with a down-rigger on the arena floor, as hanging motors, cables, and chains made their ascents. But my eye was on the upriggers, for their acrobatic grace and also—surprisingly, considering how perilous their job looks to mere mortals—their grace of mind. Serenity mingled with their minutely calibrated coordination.

There was even sweet hospitality. "You're not leaving the best office in the city, are you?" a man lugging armfuls of rope called out to me as I groped my way along the handrail of the catwalk toward the safety of the elevator. He looked me in the eye, smiled reassuringly, and went bounding by, into thin air and cigarette smoke, glancing back to toss me another welcoming grin (or was it understanding, mixed with pity for the landlubber?).

Through the grace of these superheroes in cargo shorts, I met danger and peace at the same moment. My fear was soothed by the jolly example they set, and it turned to wonder, all the more exhilarating given the risk.

CHAPTER 7

GRACE IN ART:

THE SCULPTOR WHO SET THE BODY FREE

Grace is the beauty of form under the influence of freedom.

—FRIEDRICH SCHILLER

AN AUTUMN RAINSTORM makes a sloppy, dreary mess of my drive to the Walters Art Museum in Baltimore. Mist engulfs the streets and darkens the morning to twilight; after I park and dash into the museum, I am chilled to the bone.

But when I get to the museum's second floor it feels like May, all radiant warmth and sun. I'm standing in a room of Greek art, looking at a Satyr Pouring Wine, or most of him, at least.

He's been cut off at the knees and his arms are missing, but with the cheery look on his face, the gentle bend in his waist, and the relaxed *contrapposto* swing of his boyish hips, he is the very image of grace. This marble is an ancient Roman copy of a piece by the magnificent Greek sculptor Praxiteles. Working in the fourth century BC, Praxiteles was the first to free grace from stone.

A Roman copy of Praxiteles's Satyr Pouring Wine. This charming goat-eared youth was a follower of Dionysus, god of good times.

Not much is left of his work. Most classical bronzes were melted down long ago, and though Praxiteles also worked in marble, few of his originals have survived the centuries. But so revered was this ancient Greek that generations of sculptors made studious copies of his works, and even the ones completely lost to us live on in rapturous written descriptions.

It's easy to see why. The fragments and copies of his art show a passionate belief in the world of feeling. The soft contours and personalities of his subjects are grounded in emotion, not just physicality, and this is what distinguishes Praxiteles from the artists who came before him.

Since inventing the nude as an art form a couple centuries before, Greek sculptors had been puzzling out how best to get their hands around the human anatomy, with its vexing mix of protuberances and lengths and its imperfect geometry.[1] Emotional expression was not a priority—far from it. As the physical form was perfected, movement crept in. You see this in the Kritios Boy, the landmark fifth-century nude that is the oldest we know of to display that leaning-into-one-hip *contrapposto* stance, which is crucial to bringing sexy nonchalance into stone. (Think of Michaelangelo's temperature raising *David*.) The Kritios Boy is quite nice-looking, built like a god, with an air of pampered smugness. But he lacks warmth; he stares past his observers like a movie star who doesn't want to be accosted. Such was the state of the nude before Praxiteles came along: heroic, perfect, and aloof.

Praxiteles changes that. Not only do his stone subjects appear to move, their movements are connected in a way that we instantly recognize as pleasing. His sculptures are wonderfully approachable. Praxiteles leaps beyond his predecessors not only to loosen up the human form but—and this is essential to his genius—to release an inner life as well, and to draw us into it. His art combines beauty with a sentient mind. This is why his figures feel so immediate and familiar to us; they close the gap of two millennia with an inviting dip in the hip, a humble ducking of the chin, and a play of mirth on the lips that is natural and alluring. Graceful. His works depict our softer side, the sensuality, vulnerability, and emotional truth that the body can express.

Also, Praxiteles was no snob. Working at the height of the Classical era, when carving the loftiest gods was the fashion, Praxiteles turned to the lower ranks. The goat-eared teenager I'm looking at isn't a god at all. He's a nature boy, a follower of Dionysus, a kind of rustic busboy of revelry.

To further distance his subject from the prevailing cult of perfection, Praxiteles doesn't give his satyr the bodybuilder's torso of Athenian athletes and Olympians. His is the soft, undeveloped physique of a boy. This is part of his charm: the ordinary becomes extraordinary. Judging from the sweetness of his pose—the flowing rhythm in his torso—he would have been a delight to chat with as he topped up your wine. (The jug he should be carrying is missing, but from the upraised angle of his right shoulder and the encouraging way he's gazing down at an imaginary drinker, you can well imagine him keeping the booze flowing.)

And that smile: he's clearly enjoying the act of service. Maybe he would have flirted a little. Maybe he would have brought over an extra drinking cup for himself and hung around, like Cary Grant, to make sure you were having a good time.

Praxiteles's most famous sculpture—indeed, one of the most renowned in all antiquity—is the Aphrodite of Knidos, a few ancient copies of which also stand in the Walters. Back in 350 BC or so, the original created such a sensation that a story spread of immortal Aphrodite's own astonished reaction: "When did Praxiteles see me naked?" For here is an intimate view of the venerated goddess of love, her posture relaxed; her weight sways luxuriously onto one leg, as if we're seeing her just as she stepped out of her bath, feeling warmed and renewed. It's an inviting stance, at once demure and seductive. Showgirls have been adopting it ever since.

Slightly plump, this Aphrodite is all curves and softness. In the full-length version, the most faithful copies of which are held in

A Roman copy of Praxiteles's Aphrodite of Knidos, one of the most famous sculptures in antiquity, which endowed the goddess of love with beguiling curves and an approachable human warmth

the Vatican's collection and in Munich, even her downward gaze is dreamy, full of secret thoughts. Praxiteles played with the Greek code of virtue and honor with his Aphrodite; he simultaneously unclothed her and veiled her in feeling. We see a sentient mind animating the body. Above all, this is what makes the sculpture graceful.

Like the satyr, this Aphrodite conveys something tender. If her regard is a bit inscrutable, it is fully human. The Romans found it very chic to install faux-Greek statuary in their courtyards, exposing them to the elements, and this may be why the marble surface of the Walters statuette is pitted and scarred. But its sensuality is palpable. Perhaps that's an echo of true feeling transcending even a Roman copyist's hands. Praxiteles's model is said to have been a celebrated prostitute named Phryne; the artist was one of her lovers.

Was it lust, love, or the Mediterranean sun that inspired Praxiteles to coax warmth and movement from marble?

His work was groundbreaking, but its source was the deep-rooted Greek fixation on the human body, through which the Greeks endeavored to realize even the most intangible things. They had anthropomorphic deities for everything. Including grace.

The Charites of Greek mythology—goddesses of joy and happiness—were to the Romans Gratiae, the origin of the word *grace*. In Homer's *Iliad*, one of the Charites is married to Hephaestus, the god of blacksmiths who was known as "the divine artist." This is an early link between grace and the highest works of art.

Writing around the same time as Homer, the poet Hesiod describes "three fair-cheeked Charites" whose eyes projected "love that unnerves the limbs."

The Charites were usually depicted naked and gently touching one another, all sweetness and tranquility, in the full flower of youth and vitality. Their pose conveys the uplifting and reassuring effects of human connection. There is something so charming, lovable, and profoundly meaningful about this visual signature that it has survived intact through the ages.

One of the most famous depictions of the Three Graces is by Botticelli, in a detail from his late-fifteenth-century *Primavera*, in which the physical aspect of grace is especially clear: these women are dancing, holding hands like girls playing Ring Around the Rosy, their circling steps emphasized by the flowing lines of their spectac-

Part angels, part Renaissance bombshells, the Three Graces of Botticelli's Primavera *embody both the spiritually invigorating nature of grace and its sensual delight.*

While Botticelli's Graces dance amid lush springy growth, Raphael places his sisterly trio in a barren field. The only life is in their hands.

ularly peekaboo gowns. Part angels, part Renaissance bombshells, they embody both the spiritually invigorating nature of grace and its sensual delight. Several years later, Raphael's fleshy, honey-toned painting of the three women holding fruit depicts the earthy, natural side of grace. Both of these works inherit their suppleness and bending, swaying postures of the body from Praxiteles's Aphrodite (and she, in turn, from his mistress). And they make this clear: grace is about being comfortable in your own skin. It is what the French describe so perfectly as *bien dans sa peau*, with ease, warmth, sensuousness.

Exalted as they have been by the Western world's great artists, the Charites were minor goddesses. Though they are most often described as daughters of the mighty Aphrodite, they were in service to other divinities. Yet their labor was a light one: to enhance the pleasures of life through joy, beauty, and abundance. Like Praxiteles's Satyr Pouring Wine, the Charites smoothed and lubricated social gatherings. Just as grace notes exist in music as a kind of perfume, a light adornment of the melody, the Charites were a delightful embellishment to whatever entertainment was already underway. This, I find, is an especially beautiful notion: grace exists where we forget ourselves and aim instead to bring pleasure to others.

PART THREE

Grace in Action

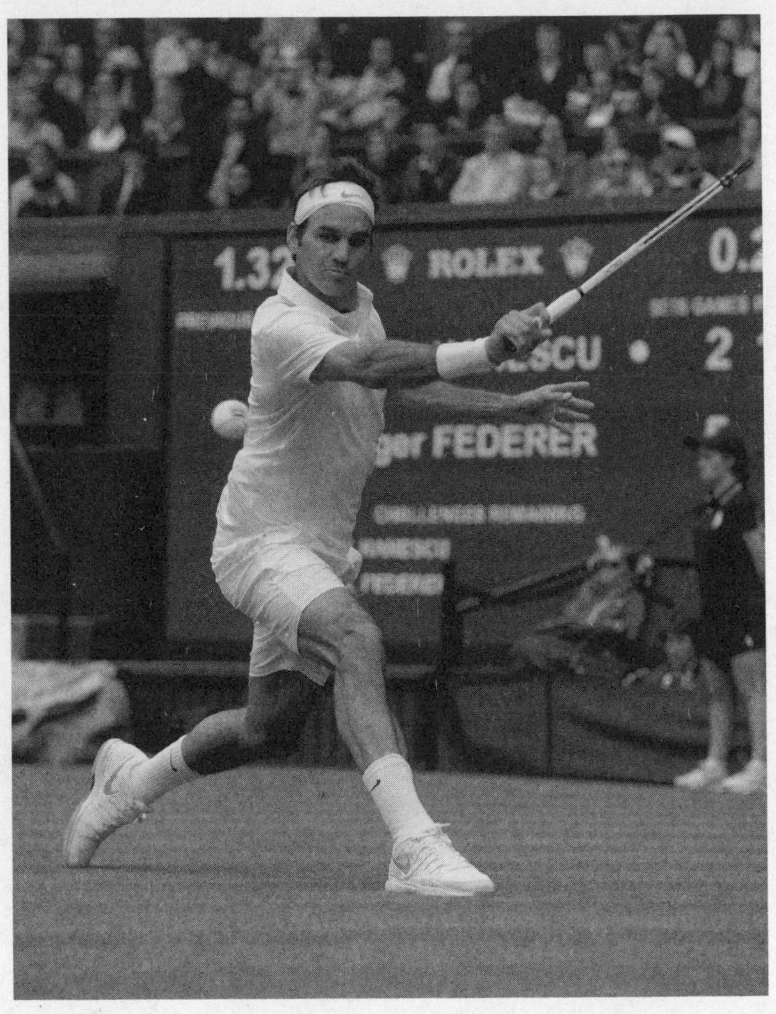

Elegant lines, rhythmic motion, agile equilibrium. Roger Federer is a prince among tennis players.

CHAPTER 8

ATHLETES:

ROGER FEDERER, OLGA KORBUT, AND OTHERS WHO PLAY WITH EASE

Have faith in the Yankees my son. Think of the great DiMaggio.

—ERNEST HEMINGWAY, *The Old Man and the Sea*

JULY 8, 2012. Wimbledon, England.

Clouds hang over the men's final at Centre Court, where Roger Federer is handily trouncing Andy Murray.

The Swiss tennis star's dominance is painful for Britain. Murray, a Scotsman, was the sentimental favorite of the crowd at the All England Club, where the Wimbledon Championships are held in an atmosphere of high civility. It's not men and women who play here, but "ladies" and "gentlemen"; Gentlemen's Final is the official designation of this match. Such was the degree of hope for the first home champion in seventy-six years that royals and rock stars were in the seats, among them the Duchess of Cambridge and Rolling Stones guitarist Ron Wood.

But even in their disappointment, spectators were awed by what unspooled on the grass court: Federer's flowing game, undulating and continuous. Federer sprinting full-tilt to the net to make a point; Federer skating backward to unfurl his forehand; Federer bouncing spongily side to side as if he were inside a moon bounce, gravity touching him as lightly as the laws of nature.

To read about it, this was no ordinary athletic triumph brought about through strength and suffering. Sportswriters didn't credit the outcome to muscular power, nor to aggressiveness or iron will. They described it in transcendent terms, calling Federer's win "artistic," "increasingly miraculous," an "impossible display of perfection." And on sports pages on both sides of the Atlantic, one word recurred, as it has throughout Federer's career: *grace*.[1]

The debate on Federer's place in the history of tennis greats is far from settled. But this much is certain: his gracefulness—in his form, his movement, and the quality of his game—is unmatched.

The shapes he creates in space are organic and full; you see this in his arching jump with toes pointed, in his oceanic surge forward, and in the winged sweep of his forehand. The way he moves is almost lyrical, with a fluid, continuous motion and rhythm. He centers his weight right over his feet, racing with ease in those crablike sidesteps despite the change in the game's tempo. Wide straddle, plant the legs, then stop! His arrested motion registers clean and crisp—we can see his position before he moves on, just the way a dance captain would want it—but it's never finite. However sharp his stops and his skittering footwork, the motor impulse is continuous. He links into his next move so swiftly that the pause is swept into the overall rhythm, like a bright dash of mezzo forte in a piano arpeggio. He bounds through it and on to his next step, offering up an aesthetically interesting range of dynamics but not a choppy, random stop-start.

Are his ankles bionic? They seem to have gas pedals inside. They accelerate no matter what stress Federer puts on them. Maybe it's no stress. There is no shock to his actions, but rather a springy resistance. Explosiveness is subtly cushioned and slowed, his equilibrium regained as he launches another combination of skimming, dancing steps.

"This is delicious," marvels a television commentator as Federer reins in his power for a precise half-speed poke that sends the ball to drop just over the net.

Federer's style of tennis is often likened to Swiss watchmaking precision, but there's nothing mechanistic about it. He is lively and unpredictable. His game is like one of the hundreds of keyboard sonatas that poured out of the baroque genius Domenico Scarlatti: rippling and delightful, with an occasional hearty folk-dance inflection. Federer's play has a rhythmic emphasis that gives it a rolling, buoyant flow.

By contrast, Rafael Nadal and Novak Djokovic, arguably the top tennis players in the world, cannot be considered graceful, despite their many extraordinary qualities. Nadal, the domineering Spaniard, is weighty, earthy; he doesn't have Federer's airy mobility. He charges to the net with the side-to-side body tilt of a linebacker, and with his fist-pumping reactions he conveys a howling, aggressive release rather than the self-possession of grace. Djokovic may be the more consistent competitor, but he lacks Federer's velvety finish. There's no easy flow into his next move. The force of his forehand sends his arm slapping across his torso like a rope; his body jerks with the recoil of his racket. As the wiry Serb lunges sideways for the ball, his trailing foot often kicks up, flexed, like a vaudeville clown knocked off balance.

I'd rather move like Federer. I'd like to move like him when I'm swatting a fly or racing to switch off the blender when I've left a spoon inside it. To be so responsive and smooth at top speed! I can confidently say these are not my habitual traits, but watching Federer makes me believe in possibility. He makes me feel better about the whole human race.

Athletics is a celebration of the body at its best, and if grace is the sweetest, most pleasing aspect of the body, it is in athletes where we ought to find it most prevalent. An athlete stands a good chance of being more graceful than the rest of us because his body works at a high level and he has put it through a great deal of repetition. A sound body and lots of practice are fundamental to the premier forms of physical grace. But an athlete is also engaged in a kind of warfare, and combat isn't usually graceful. Grinding, ball-crushing Serena Williams, for instance, is not graceful on the tennis court. (Few of the top female players are anymore, as gym-pumped power has overtaken their ranks.) With most athletes, you hear the grunts, see the labor, the struggle. Yet what marks the graceful athlete, what makes him almost godlike, is the absence of all struggle. The struggle may fascinate us, but its absence produces awe: How on earth does he make it look so easy?

That is the art of the graceful athlete. He is a living art object, poetry in motion. So many competitors train themselves into heavy muscular hulks, but the graceful athlete is honed according to principles of art. In his body, as in his performance, you find pleasing proportions, balance, and a sense of organized movement, with a lively and exciting rhythm. Yet his play has a feeling of harmony and unity, which creates a picture of wholeness.

For me, the most graceful athletes evoke a means of escape. With their beauty of form and the way they bound and float, as if invisibly winged, they mix the ordinary and the extraordinary. Graceful athletes gain flight on the same air the rest of us breathe, within a physical frame so like our own. We watch them for their inexpressible beauty, and the hope that they'll soar and take us with them.

Whether we call them men and women or ladies and gentlemen, we want to feel the exertions of our perfected surrogates; we attach our egos to their play and lose ourselves in excitement, anxiety, and nameless slip-sliding emotions as goals are blocked and putts pull left and a sprinter succumbs to a pair of big thighs hammering past, driven forward by an even bigger heart.

The ferociously competitive ancient Greeks idealized athletes as the highest rank of winners. Today, as then, we rely on our heroes of turf and track to give us a vicarious release from whatever weighs us down. Everyday life can feel just as competitive as the stadium, just as unpredictable, just as open to hazards and hostilities. *(Gonna lock horns with Blatherman, make him see it my way. . . . Gotta make sure ol' Turfpincher keeps her mitts off my accounts. . . .)* Risks and uncertainties are ever-present, and whether they stress us out or feel exhilarating, it's a rush when we overcome them. Sports offer a parallel universe, with rules: they show us our own agonistic lives in a more measurable, understandable form.

This is where the graceful athletes pull ahead, in our appreciation, even if they are losing. The wonder of them! They are free from whatever trips up the others, either mentally or physically. They can even seem free from gravity. They are light and easy and beautiful to watch—these Olga Korbuts, Nadia Comanecis, Lynn Swanns—and in the beauty of their display, they transcend the game. They pull us into a direct and instant involvement with a divine dimension of humanness.

On the ceiling of the Sistine Chapel, Michelangelo painted twenty Ignudi, naked athletes in the company of God Himself. Sensuously modeled, their bodies muscular and enlivened yet balanced in equilibrium, they are fleshly wonders, at ease in the realm of the spirit.

Why are they there? The Ignudi are not biblical figures. Perhaps they are angels. No one knows for sure. What's clear is that in Michelangelo's eyes, graceful bodies are next to godliness. He knew there is nothing more inspiring than a beautiful jock.

Ease versus Friction

Is there a single feature of athletic performance that constitutes grace? In sports, as everywhere, the judgment of grace is underpinned by ease. But there are shadings and variations of ease from sport to sport.

I watch for a sense that the body is being carried along by an unseen force, that it is weightless and frictionless, like running water or drifting smoke. Look at the way Germany's Mario Götze scored the lone goal to win the 2014 World Cup final against Argentina. A teammate sent him an airborne pass, and it seemed Götze flew out of nowhere to bat the ball down with his chest, step lightly, and in one smooth motion whirl his leg around to sling the ball past the goalkeeper. What exquisite coordination: jump, chest-bump, twist, and shoot. Was gravity caught napping? The ball hung perfectly in the air as Götze slowed time, spinning and curling like a leaping trout.

"He had three pieces of magic there," raved a television commentator, meaning the cross, the chest-bounce, and the volley.

Defying gravity isn't the only path to grace. There's also the cool, slippery defeat of friction. In this, French cyclist Richard Virenque was an ace, a man who stood out even in an especially artful sport. Man and exquisitely simple machine were inseparable, a wispy body paired with sleek engineering, a yin and yang of form geared to function. Bike and rider combined to create a unit of propulsive agility.

No one tops Virenque for finesse on wheels. The domineering mountain climber known for his long, lone breakaway rides was incomparably smooth, even in moments of intense effort. On a punishing Alpine climb, leg muscles pushing against the fulcrum of his back, he glided up the road like a sail in the wind, all elegance, not an ounce of wasted effort. An avid downhill skier, he understood the fine transfers of weight needed to shoot swiftly and efficiently down a mountain descent on a bike. Watching him swish by, as I did on many occasions when I followed the Tour de France in 2004,[2] I could imagine the moment set to music.

Virenque displayed his grace in other ways. One day in that Tour, he hung back to help a suffering Thomas Voeckler, a fellow Frenchman who was on a different team and was wearing the leader's yellow jersey. With the veteran Virenque riding in front, easing Voeckler's battle against the wind, the younger rider was able to rejoin the peloton, as the main pack is called, and to finish in time to hold on to the leader's position for another day. Maybe Virenque sensed that, over the three-week span of the race, Voeckler wouldn't ultimately keep the advantage. It was still a generous thing to do. A Tour commentator hailed Virenque that day as a "*bon* Samaritan."

The Tour de France has nothing in common with the American taste for spectacle or with a broad-shouldered conception of masculinity. Yet it is, for the French, the common man's Super Bowl. No ticket is needed to watch the racers go by; you simply stake out a spot along the course route. For the most part, other than at the start or finish, you can get as close to the speeding cyclists as your conscience and nerve allow. Trust in human decency is the chief form of security.

The French respond to such freedom with remarkable self-regulation. Interference is rare. Families make a day of the eternal wait for the blur of the peloton. But these are no rowdy tailgate parties; even on the most unaccommodating mountain roads, the gatherings are gracious affairs. Folks unfold tables alongside the ravines, set out food and wine as if they're dining on a terrace. They recline in lawn chairs in the shade of their RVs or beneath beach umbrellas, listening to the race reports on their car radios. They read books and newspapers.

The athletes themselves are surprisingly accessible. They sign autographs and chat with fans before the race starts each day, an expression of humility and connection that is all too rare in competitive sports.

Grace is not elitist or above it all; it is revealed in the common touch.

The Problem of Joe DiMaggio

Some athletes have great physical gifts but uneasy personalities. Or they are simply more comfortable on the field of play than off.

A graceful body can contain awkward inconsistencies. Fame can amplify them. Can a hero be graceful? Or does grace require a certain softness and vulnerability that a hero won't allow in himself? This was Joe DiMaggio's dilemma.

The legendary Yankees center fielder was conspicuously graceful in his movements. He was handsome and lithe, with impeccable grooming. Like Cary Grant, DiMaggio dressed elegantly, with never a slicked-down hair out of place. His walk was an extension of his appearance and his unearthly athleticism; he floated atop a long, loose stride.

"It seemed as if he was walking on air," said Maury Allen, one of his biographers. "He would glide through the stadium. He would glide through a restaurant."[3]

When DiMaggio came up to bat, his swing was an element of the impossible: energy going in two directions at once. Legs forward, upper body moving backward, all in a smooth orbit around the explosion of wood and leather. After the corkscrew twist of his torso, he'd unfurl like silk and stream to first base—no hesitation, no awkward reset. From the great amplitude of his swing, he redirected himself cleanly into linear force.

That same effortless flight sped him in the outfield toward hard drives and fly balls, covering huge territory, making running overhead catches. Wrote the English-born novelist and baseball fan Wilfred Sheed, "In dreams I can still see him gliding after fly balls as if he were skimming the surface of the moon."

Everything he did looked easy, even to the appraising eyes of his competitors. "DiMaggio even looks good striking out," said his chief rival, the great Boston Red Sox hitter Ted Williams. Williams was as rumpled, rowdy, and human as the Yankee Clipper was majestic.

DiMaggio's physical elegance was so pronounced it gave rise to emotions wholly apart from partisan passions and visceral thrill. He was worshipped as a hero. Of course, he was as winning an athlete as he was a graceful one. He helped the Yankees win ten pennants and nine World Series, and his 1941 hitting streak that ended at fifty-six games became a national obsession. But fueling the fascination was the sheer wonder that his seemingly miraculous grace inspired.

The way the public perceived DiMaggio's manner of playing ball spilled over into a way of seeing him as a man, even as something more than a man. DiMaggio respected this—perhaps was haunted by it—but he responded with icy reserve. He was shy and hated publicity. He kept himself always at a formal distance.

Some time ago my father encountered him in Atlantic City, in the lobby of a hotel. Growing up in New York in the 1930s and '40s, my father and his brother had often watched DiMaggio play in Yankee Stadium. Once they saw him hit a triple in each game of a double-header. Triples! Years later, suddenly there he was, standing off to the side by himself. Close enough to speak to. My father approached him and said hi, DiMaggio said hi back, looked away, and that was that.

"I always wished I had engaged him in talk, but I was shy, too," Dad told me. "I mean, there he was, Joe DiMaggio."

The ballplayer's first wife said weeks could go by without him speaking to her. Marilyn Monroe, his second wife, described his dark moods, how he would tell her to leave him alone. Their marriage lasted only nine months. Later DiMaggio grieved over the actress's suicide in a way that seemed like remorse for his aloofness: he took control of her funeral, decided who could and couldn't attend, sent roses to her crypt for the next twenty years. This man was more tightly wound than the innards of a baseball. He chain-smoked and suffered from ulcers. He was at ease with the game of baseball but not with his own imagination, where innumerable threats and foes lurked. He was ever poised to defend himself, guarding his hero status nervously, stipulating how he was to be addressed at events, when and where he could be seen.

DiMaggio was caught in a bind. His physical grace drew people to him; the resulting attention sucked it away.

He could be a champion, an icon, a god. But here was his struggle: for Joe DiMaggio, being human was hardest of all.

Stretchy versus Tight

Here is a nice point that Raymond Bayer, the French philosopher, made in his 1933 opus on grace, *L'esthétique de la grâce*. If we think of the internal motions of our own organism—the stretch and recoil of our arteries, the subtle pace of the heart with its contraction and release, the rise and fall of breath—the optimal functioning is elastic rather than abrupt.

It follows, Bayer continued, that we recognize smooth and springy motions as natural and appealing, even life-affirming. Graceful.

Yet that doesn't make graceful athletes any more comprehen-

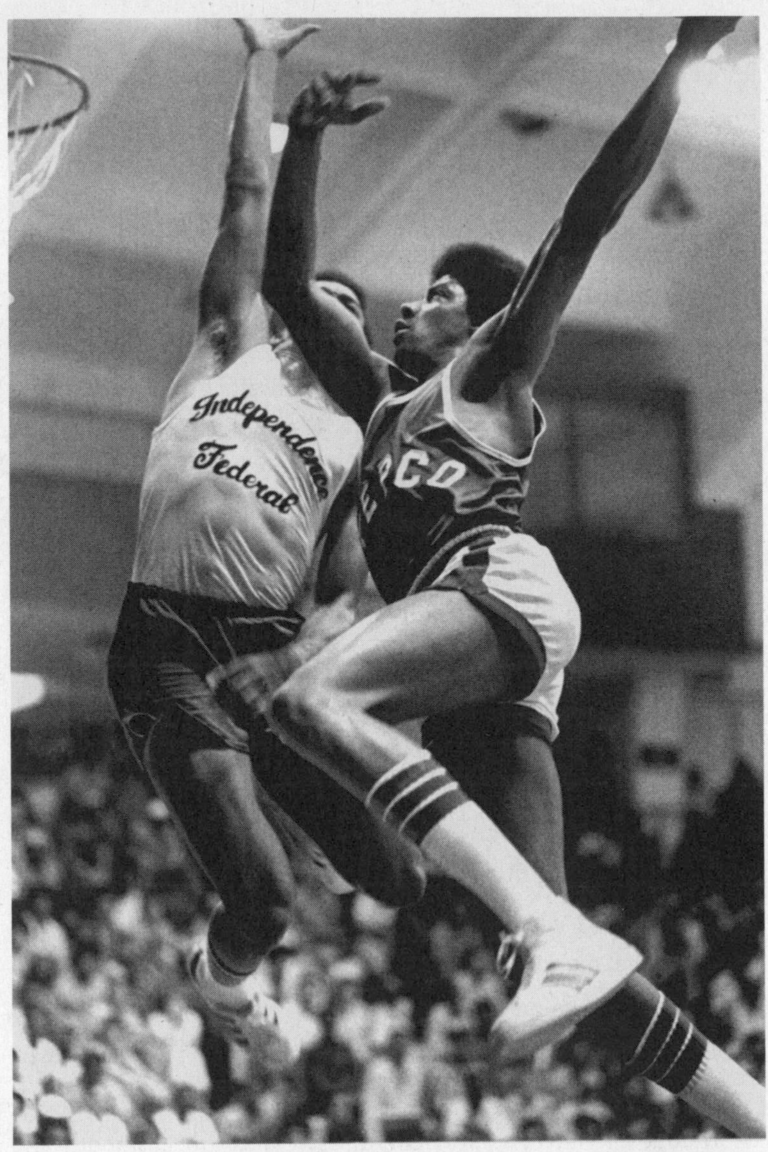

With his streamlined, airy ease, Julius Erving—"Dr. J"—offered an antidote for life's encumbrances.

sible. With the easygoing elasticity and adjustability that graceful athletes possess, I wonder: where do they hide their power?

In basketball, massive strength can intimidate opponents and excite the fans—just ask LeBron James—but the airy moves of Julius Erving are more delightful to watch. Erving crossed the court like a skipping stone bouncing on water. His soaring flights to the rim, smooth rotations in the air, and the gestural finesse that ran from his arms all the way to his fingertips elevated what he did to an art. He didn't hurtle pell-mell to the basket in a show of force; he seemed to rise up inevitably on an invisible wave. How? Springs in his ankles, exquisite coordination, control of his weight—who can say? He made his moves look easy. In a crowd of bulky giants, he was limber and light. He brought a balletic elegance to his slam dunks.

Erving's elastic grace in the 1970s and '80s has never been equaled in basketball. But even now, as power has come to dominate the sport, some younger players are winning notice for their grace. Rising star Stephen Curry has been rightfully dubbed "the sweetest jumper in the league" for his effortless leaps.

David Gower, captain of England's cricket team in the 1980s, had a similar loose, light-spirited elegance. Cricket is already such an intrinsically gracious sport, with its players dressed like Jay Gatsby out for a stroll, its leisurely, days-long games, and its intervals for lunch and tea. It seems so very *comme il faut*. Yet even in such a civilized setting, Gower stood apart as a man of natural class. His blond curls and faraway eyes gave him a Byronesque air. His swing was an extension of his romantic looks, though it was bolstered by hands of steel. You'd never know that from the batsman's silky ease. Gower didn't whack balls; he stroked them and scooped them and swept them effortlessly into flight.

Gower brought to bat the fine proportion of balance, muscle, and timing that eludes the power hitters, the way a dancer who is perfectly centered can float around easily in her pirouettes, rather than grinding out spins with wound-up force.

Evonne Goolagong, a leading Australian tennis player in the 1970s and early '80s and a three-time Wimbledon champion (twice in singles, once in doubles), skimmed the court like a Frisbee in a skirt. Her skipping, light-footed moves seemed to reflect a light-hearted spirit. With her willowy frame, she betrayed none of the coiled intensity of her rivals.

She'd be eaten alive today.

Light versus Heavy

The finish of a movement is crucial in athletic grace, as it is with dancers. Our eye follows the arc of a gesture and we want it to be infinite, to hint at flight and carry us with it. We are drawn to smooth, continuous motion, to birds wheeling overhead and the gait of a cantering horse and the sweep of gibbons in a zoo as they swing from branch to branch—especially to that. After all, we once swung, too. On a primal, subconscious level, flowing motion feels good.

Efficiency is part of grace. Neither wasted movement nor excessive movement, nothing baroque or embellished. You don't often see Federer chase after a ball and miss it or give up halfway there. He gauges in advance of a run whether he can get to it or not, and if not, he doesn't waste his energy. But efficiency in itself doesn't produce grace. John McEnroe had a remarkably efficient serve, but he didn't combine it with smoothness. His moves were quick but abrupt. His jumps were popcorn bursts, sudden and startling. He lacked finish. In terms of energy expenditure, it may well be more economical to keep the body quiet between jumps or a burst of steps, as McEnroe did, as opposed to the continuous motion you see in Federer.

The graceful athlete embodies our aspirations to be, if not the best, then the best-looking. Raw athletic superiority is simply beyond reach for all but a few; you need the genes and you have to kill yourself with drills. But grace? That looks more attainable, even for the spectator. That's part of its appeal, to draw us close. Arthur Ashe's classy demeanor and finesse on the tennis court made him seem more approachable, and more of a role model, than ornery Jimmy Connors. The skills of grace seem transferable, in the imagination if not in fact, from the sports arena to daily life. It would be crazy for me to think I could ever dunk like LeBron James, but I could at least ponder the possibility of regaining my balance with Federer's agility, of greeting people with the guileless cheer of gymnast Olga Korbut, of responding under pressure with the poise of soccer's Mario Götze, or of baseball's Sandy Koufax.

Koufax, the lefty pitcher of the Brooklyn and Los Angeles Dodgers in the 1960s, had a clean, elegant style. He propelled himself through space like an arcing fishing line. But his smoothness concealed devastating speed. Even Mickey Mantle was shut down by Koufax's famous curveball, elusive as a soap bubble. Koufax was elusive himself, capable of astonishing restraint. He matter-of-factly refused to pitch on the opening game of the 1965 World Series because it fell on Yom Kippur, the holiest Jewish holiday, and Koufax is Jewish. With the same quiet self-control, he returned to help win the series. A year later, he abruptly retired at 30, revealing that the cost of those sweet-looking pitches was an elbow nearly crippled by arthritis. Wanting simply to live his life with a healthy body, and having no hunger for celebrity, he bowed out of the game as gracefully as he had dominated it.

Does grace convey a competitive advantage? Or is the graceful athlete simply more beautiful to look at? In terms of practical results—the game won, the record set—the graceful athlete is not always superior. Federer can succumb to an opponent's greater power and attack; he has subsequently fallen to Murray, who is fast and strong but not especially graceful. In 2014 Federer lost his chance at a record eighth Wimbledon title to Djokovic.

But watching Federer hit his stride is simply more delightful than watching any other tennis player. His unique quality of movement stands out even to career beauty-watchers. Peter Martins, the Danish-born ballet master in chief of the New York City Ballet, and a former ballet star, told me that for him Federer is the supreme example of grace.

"I've followed tennis my whole life. I'm a huge fan of Bjorn Borg—that's how far back I go," Martins said. "But nobody comes even close to what Federer produces. I can't think of another person, and that includes every ballet dancer I've ever known. He is seemingly effortless. It is awe-inspiring to watch him play."

This is the advantage of grace. Athletes whose prowess lies strictly in what is measurable—height jumped, goals scored, runs batted in—are doomed to be eclipsed. Those numbers will be surpassed. Charles Barkley's career points scored in the National Basketball Association were overtaken by Shaquille O'Neal, and Shaq's were bested by Kobe Bryant. But Julius Erving, who doesn't figure among the NBA's top twenty-five points leaders, is the one whose play is remembered with a particular awe.

It is the graceful athlete who ends up mythologized, because while statistics are forgotten, we remember the luxuriant flow of grace. It stays with us, just as we store and cherish all manifestations of beauty.

Soft versus Hard

Some graceful athletes pair their physical ease with the joy of a child at play, and watching them, our pleasure is magnified. Olga Korbut, the Belarusian gymnast and multiple gold medalist in the 1972 and 1976 Olympics, was this kind of creature. She brought a

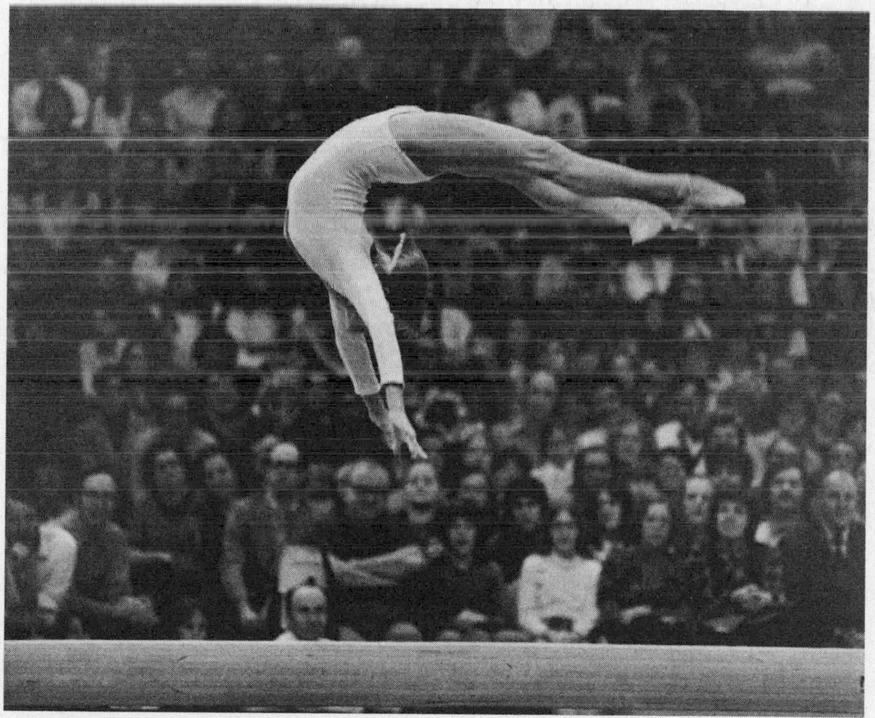

Olga Korbut, in command of herself and the forces of gravity.

fearless daring to her gymnastics, plunging so near to disaster you caught your breath, then swooping to safety with ease—and with that pouchy-eyed smile. Such goofy glee, at breakneck speed. And in her buoyancy, the way she sustained her leaps and flips, breathing the air high above before touching down and rebounding even higher, she demonstrated the soul of an artist.

How different Korbut was from gymnasts today. They're gunnery girls, stiff-spirited, cold-eyed fireplugs who charge at their apparatus but show no expression other than, perhaps, a choreographed smile and wave; otherwise, they look like tiny automatons. They hit the beam, the vault, the mat—bam!—like a bag of bricks.

A steroid aesthetic has taken over the sport. I'm not saying the gymnasts are doping—maybe they are, maybe they're not—but their stubby frames rocket through space with the aggressiveness and punch of football players. Power, endurance, and explosiveness are the coveted qualities. Mary Lou Retton, the first American to win the women's All-Around gymnastics gold medal in the 1984 Olympics, was called a powerhouse for good reason. She was all tight, compressed muscle, weighted firmly on her feet, keeping up a sharp, staccato beat as she hammered through her moves. She put on her game face to compete and didn't waste time breathing, or at least she didn't seem to. Watching her, we tightened up, too, and held our breath. There was joy in watching Retton, to be sure: it came from her sudden, smiling release, upon landing, of all that balled-up tension. But there was no prolonged sense of ease. That was banished to the past. Retton ushered in a new era of muscle on the mat. Grace didn't stand a chance against her.

By contrast, Korbut was gentle as well as lionlike. She was part hotdog, part poet. Her 1972 routines still look like miracles, not feats of power but of light, dancing grace that obscures the technical achievement. (Her back flip on the highest of the uneven bars was of a difficulty never seen before and is now banned in competition.) Korbut starts her floor exercise with a giant jump; like Hemingway's marlin breaking the surface in *The Old Man and the Sea,* she hovers motionless in the air for a moment, suspended in a swan dive, before she whirls into a somersault. She has a dancer's finesse, moving with measured care and ease, varying her dynamics. You see this on the other apparatuses too. In a back walkover on the balance beam, she wheels her legs slowly, grandly overhead in a cascading effect, giving us a good, long look at them. In a split handstand, she finds a still point and luxuriates in the quiet of it. She's simply breathing, upside down, legs sharp as surgical tools, spine a supple curve as she balances on a narrow slice of heaven.

Showmanship? Absolutely. What she was showing off was her ease in that realm of danger, and her love of it. The air, the beam, the bars were her bliss. She expressed that through her buoyant body language and her artless smile. It was a smile that dissolved borders. We were supposed to disdain the Soviets, but we were helpless, worldwide, when it came to the grace of Olga Korbut.

It wasn't only her smile that endeared her to the public. Competing for the All-Around title, Korbut screwed up on the uneven bars—stubbing her toe on the mat, missing a couple of moves—which cost her a gold medal that had seemed preordained. Still, she completed her routine, nailed her landing, and strode to her seat with a soldier's bearing.

Then she did what no one thought a product of the Soviet state would ever do: she crumpled up and sobbed into her warmup jacket. I was a child at the time, watching a world away on late-night TV, and she was mirroring my own feelings. I remember my surprise: that's what I would do! She was a kid, she made mistakes, she cared. She was human.

Perfection came and went that night, but grace never left her. It's the softness we respond to most, and she gave that to us. She also took care of every one of her fans by pulling back from the brink of tragedy: later that night she finished her Olympics with flawless, joyful routines on the beam and floor.

"I just felt like I was seven years old and I [was] dancing just on the grass outside," Korbut said in an interview years later, by way of explaining her graceful recovery from disaster.[4]

Korbut's disguised toughness and effortless grace was matched four years later by the young Romanian Nadia Comaneci. Just fourteen, she possessed a cool, noble elegance. She stepped up to the mat with those long dancer's legs and a magnificent sense of occasion. Such grandeur! And such beauty of motion: the harmonious lines, the airy, unhurried control, the sweeping rhythms.

The luxurious experience Comaneci gave us came at a terrible cost, however. She didn't have Korbut's sunniness. Comaneci's touch of melancholy lent her performances an added poignance, especially when it later came to light how brutally difficult her training was, how dark and harsh her life. She finally fled the country that had virtually imprisoned her. It's tempting to think that as a child she found some measure of freedom in the competition arena, whirling to a blur on the bars. What's clear is that her ability to compete with poise and grace demonstrates a subtle strength—a spiritual strength—of which we saw only a fraction at the Olympics. In her sport as in her life, resilience defined Comaneci and saved her.

Warm versus Cold

Grace on ice is one of the most miraculous feats a human can pull off. That unforgiving, inhospitable surface, those sharp steel blades—who but the most marvelous freak of nature could find a home there?

Among the great thrills of the winter Olympics are those televised shots of a skater's winged freedom on the ice, one leg raised in arabesque, a clipper ship cutting through high seas. Yet in skating as in gymnastics and so many other sports, the emphasis increasingly

The peerless English ice dancers Jayne Torvill and Christopher Dean, rehearsing just before winning gold at the 1984 Sarajevo Winter Olympics. With their uninterrupted fluidity, musical sensitivity, and refinement of line, they elevated the possibilities for grace on ice.

is on power, crowding out grace. A deliberate musical and legato presentation will tend to be graceful, but the sport has sadly sacrificed those qualities of subtle splendor to the easy-to-spot thrills of acrobatics.

Dorothy Hamill, the 1976 Olympic gold medalist, had an extraordinary warm, soft quality to her skating that was still apparent more than twenty years later when I saw her in a skating show at Washington's John F. Kennedy Center for the Performing Arts. She had such a light, spongy way of moving on the ice that she seemed to float, conveying flight and freedom but also tranquility. She was easy with being alone out there, didn't push herself on us, glided in her own world, but peacefully so. Her fluid, silken trails across the ice, even in that constricted space (the rather shallow Eisenhower Theater stage had been Zambonied), were so pleasant to watch that you couldn't take your eyes off her. To this day, when I call her skating to mind, I also recall the delight that I felt in response.

IN *ROCKY III*, a journalist asks Mr. T's character: What's your prediction for the fight?

"Prediction?" says Mr. T, who plays the boxing rival of Sylvester Stallone. He delivers his answer directly to the camera: "Pain."

Is there grace in a sport whose goal is to deliver pain?

The aggressiveness of sports is most overt in boxing, where blood spills easily. Even ancient amphorae depict boxers (heroically) with streams of red running from their noses. Yet the slipperiness of grace can be an advantage, as it was for Sugar Ray Leonard, for instance, who danced in the ring.

A dance quality in boxing is crucial. I got interested in boxing when I was taking a sports-reporting class in graduate school in Chicago. While my classmates flocked to the Cubs, I covered amateur boxing. I had a passing familiarity with the sport, having watched my uncle, the veteran HBO boxing analyst Larry Merchant, interview heaving fighters in the ring after their bouts. (He always said the losers were more interesting, more introspective, a bit of journalistic truth I've carried with me.) A deaf boxer I knew was at a continuous disadvantage because he had no rhythm to his movements, no inner musical guide.

Consider the oiled ease of Muhammad Ali. You'd never think such a big man could move so fast, and then his gloves would blur. Yet where was the effort? Hidden somewhere under that velvet skin. There was a smooth resistance in his moves, like they were slowed down and pushing against something. He carried himself in the ring with a lifted posture—not ducking in self-protection—and it was both defiant and dignified. He balanced those qualities throughout his career. He was an unapologetic diva—"I am the greatest!"—yet his shining self-pride seemed rightful, rather than bristly and defensive, and we shared in it. There was something delightful about Ali. Watching him, you felt pumped up, too. Instead of setting himself apart with off-putting arrogance and cold condescension, in the manner of, say, disgraced cyclist Lance Armstrong, Ali swept us into his delight, in good measure because he was so graceful in expressing it, graceful in living out his ideals—he tirelessly promoted racial and religious respect—and graceful in the ring.

Football is the uglier sport.[5] Unlike boxing or tennis, it is not a game of studious, calculating loners. It has none of baseball's tranquility and patience, nor soccer's fluidity, nor basketball's popcorn aerials. Football lurches and galumphs; it traffics in confusion, time pressure, and pileup after brutal pileup. But this is why the rare graceful football players give me such a thrill. In their finest moments, elegance can exist alongside the brutality.

Pittsburgh Steelers Hall of Famer Lynn Swann was the Mikhail Baryshnikov of football, a wide receiver who, in the 1970s, had the quicksilver body control and the ability to adjust to the ball while he was in the air that caused grown men to grow misty-eyed with rapture.

Could a lyric poet have dreamed up a better name for the man famed for his avian abilities, his flying, his darting? Swann had studied dance before he became a football player. He was dragged to classes as a child by his mother. Later, a hundred yards of turf became his stage.

Dance training "gave me another dimension," he told me in an interview a few years ago. "A comfort level in terms of my technique, timing, and sense of rhythm to the game." His tap teacher taught him that "the end of one move is the beginning of the next move. You had to be balanced in order to make that transition. There's a timing and rhythm to every play."

What it often came down to, he said, was "having the dance background in your head and having the rhythm, and rehearsing it over and over."

He spoke about football patterns and their steps as if he were a Broadway dance captain. Dance steps, he said, have long been part of the training drills. Players study grapevines, the sideways crossover step that's a folk-dance staple, as well as jazz-dance ball changes and something called a karaoke drill, lifting one foot over the other with a hip swivel. "You see guys making those moves all the time. If you're running and you've planted one foot and you're in control, how simple it is to plant it right and shift from the right to the left and change directions. Or if you're on the left foot, how about putting the right foot behind you, and bringing the left over. That's a grapevine."

If you had two left feet and you were covering Swann and his ilk, you were beat. Pure and simple.

"John Stallworth and I were watching film one day, getting ready for a Cowboys game," he said. "There was one defensive back who had terrible footwork. He just had a hard time with his footwork. The worst thing to do would be to run straight at him because he'd just backpedal." Make him weave, though, pull him right and then left, tie his feet up, and you're home free. "You cause him to turn his shoulders and his feet, and at some point in time we knew he would fall down. And he did." Ouch! To see a side of beef outdanced by a slim, fleet receiver is one of the game's glories.

Is it any wonder that a few well-coordinated football players have done so well on *Dancing with the Stars*? That tap-dance quickness they practice, the control and balance they need for their game, can translate into sensational displays on the dance floor. Emmitt Smith waltzed off with the mirror-ball trophy in season three; Jerry Rice, Jason Taylor, and even three-hundred-pounder Warren Sapp have also swapped shoulder pads for sparkly tuxes and ballroom steps. Sapp, a retired defensive tackle, was as silky and light on his feet as Jackie Gleason.

Dancers have long been attracted to the improbable grace of select football players. Gene Kelly put Baltimore Colts quarterback Johnny Unitas in his 1958 TV special "Dancing: A Man's Game." Choreographer Twyla Tharp paired New York City Ballet's Peter Martins with Swann in her 1980 TV special, "Dance Is a Man's

Sport, Too." (The "manly" grace among the most macho of athletes, and the machismo of the most graceful of dancers, was the theme of both shows.) Swann even outdanced Martins, who was then at the height of fame in the ballet world. During rehearsal, the football player was catching more air than the tall Dane. Choreographer George Balanchine, Martins's boss, was watching, and he called out to his star dancer that "he should jump a little higher," Swann said, "'cause the little fellow was jumping up higher."

Tharp, too, remembers Swann's jump, and more. "He was so unbelievably elegant," she told me. "He had an extraordinary elevation, and he had a capacity to hang in the air. His stamina was unending, his speed, his flexibility, his maneuverability to get around a corner very fast. . . . I've never worked with any other gentleman of that caliber."

Some players can be so creative on the field, they ought to consider a post-retirement life in the theater. Take the former Baltimore Ravens defensive standout Ed Reed, a free safety whose acting ability was Oscar-worthy. Time and again, his moves told opposing quarterbacks the same story: La-dee-dah, I'm going over here, so it's safe to throw the ball over there. . . . And over and over, they fell for his fiction and tossed him a big, fat interception.

It was part fakery, part footwork. With a dancer's versatility, Reed shifted seamlessly from defense to offense. Snagging a pass in the end zone in a game against the Philadelphia Eagles, he slipped into the role of a receiver for a 107-yard return that was a feat of elusiveness the haughtiest ballerina would envy. Linemen bore down on him, but he danced away from hit after hit, slipping past would-be claimants, pivoting on those flexible ankles, skating by with a stride as long as it was fast. Straight into the NFL record books.

Grace isn't always part of the wideout's performance. Players have become notorious for their bad manners and worse: the fisticuffs, the end-zone celebrations, the adrenaline-fueled taunts. The trend in recent years is to put power hitters in receiver positions—bulky men like Terrell Owens and Chad "Ochocinco" Johnson—who are muscular and massive enough to break tackles without having to slip away from defenders like darting fish. They are playmakers, for sure, but they do it without grace.

"IF I AM TO BE DESCRIBED AS A DIVER," said Greg Louganis, "one thing I would hope would stick out in people's minds is that I was strong, and I was graceful."[6]

No one reconciled the dichotomies of sport as simply and directly as Louganis, the four-time Olympic champion, greatest diver in history, icon of grace. He showed us how to be powerful and soft. His form was immaculate but not rigid, and the supple way he moved through the air, each shape emerging seamlessly from the last and foretelling the next, was a kind of silent music.

Louganis was an embodiment of the ancient Greek notion of *kalokagathia*, a word that combines *kalos*, "beautiful," and *agathos*, "good." It expressed an ideal extolled in philosophy, art, literature, and ethics. For *kalokagathia* describes the Cary Grantish person, living at the balance point of competing forces: a harmony of outer appearance and inner nobility. Beauty is as beauty does. In his silent meditations as he readied himself at the top of the diving platform, Louganis demonstrated the grace of repose. Well-being of mind alongside the well-being of body.

About that body: did Michelangelo design it? Surely the sensuously sculpted Louganis would have a place among the Sistine Chapel's Ignudi.

Like them, the diver was perfectly poised between the realms of flesh and spirit. Louganis standing on the platform delivered an erotic charge to inspire yards of ancient odes and an army of bronze nudes. Yet when he left the edge to fall through the air, his movements escaped the world of the body. He became a magnificent abstraction, a series of geometric ideals—sphere, spiral, line—and then a single, refined purpose. Slipping into the water, he escaped our world entirely, disappearing past sight and sound.

"I don't view my diving as a mechanical thing," he said. "It's more like a choreographed dance."

A dance the angels must envy.

Because he's one of us.

CHAPTER 9

DANCERS:

THE GRACE OF TRANSCENDENCE

Grace is a changeable beauty: a beauty of its subject which can come to be and just as well cease to be.

—FRIEDRICH SCHILLER

IN DANCE, it has become very chic to distort the body and stretch it to extremes. This has pushed grace out of the picture.

The artistic trend in the latest ballets (and in many new accounts of old ones) is toward a hard-edged, instant-gratification, rock-concert sensibility. Dancers whip and whirl, drill and dive, as though they could bore through metal. Sometimes their bodies look like they're being blown apart, joint by joint, as in the finale of a work called *Double Evil*, by the popular Finnish-born choreographer Jorma Elo: the leading ballerina dashed off a volley of pirouettes and vaulted toward her partner, who flip-flopped her over his shoulder. She landed on her back with legs splayed open, crotch to the skies. In most works, including this one, the ballerina is a stand-in for ideal womanhood in one way or another. But here, in her final moments, she was subverted, deconstructed down to her underpants. No longer the queen of the ballet, she was reduced to a scribble of lines and arcs, drawn by a cruel compass. Elo's aesthetic is broken, jagged, abrupt, ironic. This is not to say his work isn't artful or alluring in many ways. A discordant and disturbing style can also yield beauty; think of Picasso's cubist paintings and Stravinsky's pounding composition *The Rite of Spring,* which incited a scandal at its Paris premiere but is now considered revolutionary. These are clearly works of art. But they are not works of grace.

In recent years—reflecting a desperate bid for audiences, or to mimic the razzle-dazzle of televised reality dance shows, or as a consequence of the ballet competitions popping up around the world—ballet has become obsessed with distortions. You see dancers screwing themselves up to "snap a skill," as they say in cheerleading, whether it be a swift string of turns or a leap in which the dancer seems to fly apart in the air—whatever it takes to make audiences gasp.

In ballet training, the focus is on technique—the mechanics of the steps—rather than style, which is personal and takes longer to discover and nurture.

The emphasis on technique, and on pushing it and pulling it apart, has produced a fragmented quality. Many contemporary choreographers, inspired perhaps by the jerky, disconnected aesthetic of modern art and some modern dance, prefer this over fluid seamlessness and long, connected phrases of movement. Grace has become old-fashioned. New ballets are typically about a series of clever moves rather than poetry, storytelling and transcendence.

The explosiveness that results can feel exhilarating to watch, but after a while you tire of having your system jarred.

What has been lost among so many of today's dancers is exactly what made people fall in love with ballet hundreds of years ago: its harmony of the body, its balance and ease. Its grace. "Ballet is all that is left us of the combined movement of the Greeks," Edgar Degas once said, explaining why he painted dancers;[1] he knew more than a little about the refined athleticism and sensuous allure of ballet. His painterly obsession with the art form reflects the dancers' smooth, rhythmic sensuality, and the vicarious delight that it offers.

When I leave the Kennedy Center after a good dance program, I feel like launching myself into the air; one of these days I'm bound to get so carried away that I'll probably smack right into the giant bust of John F. Kennedy that's planted outside the Opera House. I get a fluttery feeling inside when I see a dancer soar lightly across the stage, and I feel like I'm being carried along with them as dancers glide through difficult moves with ease and pleasure. Graceful dancing is about a sustained performance, rather than individual tricks. Athletic moves and fast footwork can be part of this. But even in soaring nearly to the lighting grid or in turning half a dozen pirouettes, a great star like Mikhail Baryshnikov never showed strain, and he always stayed in character. He gave himself entirely to the performance, to the choreographer's intention, to us, without self-flattering mannerisms (the *ta-da!* flips of the wrists, for instance, which have been spreading through male performance).

Then there is the emotional connection that we feel with the graceful dancer. Of course, dancers can startle and overpower audiences to great effect. But graceful dancers connect with our sympathies. They convey a sense of being one of us, of dancing for us, of going through the experience onstage in our place. This is because their way of moving is on a human scale, and this is what we are most comfortable with, whether we are watching dancers or visiting someone's home or walking into a building. The graceful dancers' unostentatious ease corresponds with our own experience of living in our bodies. We feel their movement, sympathetically, as pleasurable, and we see it as in scale with our own bodies. Because of this human scale, graceful dancing draws the audience into a more private, intimate experience. It's the principle of less is more. No strenuous acrobatics are necessary. The graceful dancer can evoke emotion through the simplest of means.

Margot Fonteyn, for example, did it through standing still.

I didn't know anything about scale or proportion when I first encountered Fonteyn. I fell in love with her through a photograph. It was on the cover of an album of Tchaikovsky's *Sleeping Beauty* that my father gave me when, at age twelve or thirteen, I became a serious ballet student. Dressed in a white tutu as Princess Aurora on the day of her wedding, Fonteyn was captured in a pose of perfect stillness, her head slightly inclined as if she were listening to the very music that the photo invites you to enjoy. When I finally saw her dance—on film, as my ticket-buying days arrived too late to see her live—it was again that sense of alert tranquility that I found most wonderful about her.

That photo of Fonteyn will forever exemplify a ballerina for me. She is shot from behind, silhouetted in a sunlit doorway with her arms stretched above her like wings. Her fingertips rest on the curve of the arch that frames her. The eye travels down the line of her arms as if it is following a stream of water, taking in the slope of her back and waist, her gently twisting torso, and her leg stretched out behind her. The line from head to toe is rhythmic and unbroken. The dominant feeling is one of ease.

What is touching about this photo is its human-scale grace. She faces the landscape that you see through the doorway, spread out in front of her. Her pose assures you she could step across

Serene self-possession was Margot Fonteyn's gift.

the threshold and be at home in the outside world no matter what befell her.

I wasn't alone in my awe of this image. Many years later, I was surprised to find the same album cover in a collection of items that the artist Joseph Cornell, famous for his boxed assemblages, had gathered in his workshop.

How can a woman so personify grace in just one pose? This was Fonteyn's particular magic, and it arose from her essence as a dancer. Serene self-possession was Fonteyn's gift. What set her apart, in the early decades of the twentieth century and throughout her long career, was simply this: a soft, easy, and musical way of moving.

She was never a bravura performer. Her physical gifts were far from perfect, by ballet standards. She had blocky feet (choreographer Frederick Ashton called them "pats of butter"), a rather inelastic waist and spine, and limited flexibility in her legs. With the quiet focus that would characterize her long career, Fonteyn turned her limitations into a style. The low line of her arabesque was of a piece with her natural reserve and understatement; the modest curve of her feet was a repudiation of overworked vanity. Indeed, those feet and legs—resilient and firm—gave her the kind of grace that comes from strength, from being able to sustain balances and to move serenely in a continuous stream of motion.

In 1949, Fonteyn unleashed a frenzy with her ability to defy gravity. The Sadler's Wells Ballet—precursor to the Royal Ballet—had arrived in New York from a London still deep in recovery from World War II. No one expected greatness from these spunky youngsters making their American debut with *The Sleeping Beauty*. No one expected it, until Fonteyn ran onstage.

She had none of the affectations of a grand ballerina. She expressed only joy, Princess Aurora's joy, all the pretty zest of a sixteen-year-old royal on her birthday. In the Rose Adagio section of the first act, Aurora dances with four suitors, taking each by the hand and then letting go of the support to balance alone in a high, full-sail arabesque on one leg. The ballerina takes four unassisted balances on pointe, after dancing a taxing solo: it is a tremendous feat. Fonteyn delivered each one as if she were spun sugar, suspended on air. She even held her final pose for a few extra beats. That last arabesque, by a young ballerina carrying the weight of Britain's postwar aspirations on her shoulders, was a triumph of grace under pressure. And more.

"In that miraculous balance," said Robert Helpmann, one of Fonteyn's dance partners, "the entire reputation of the English ballet was formed."[2]

A documentary about Fonteyn shows her standing in front of a mirror in a dance studio, so close she nearly touches it. She's studying the way her arms move as she turns, sweeping them one at a time across her body and up again as she rotates, working out the way to keep their motion fluid and ongoing as she shifts positions. She is concentrating on the continuity of their curving lines—their gracefulness—the way Degas must have studied hands in order to capture their gestures so expressively. As the British critic Richard Buckle wrote, Fonteyn thought herself into becoming a great dancer.[3]

This thinking led to dancing that was clean, neat, and clear. Her unadorned style recalled life's simple pleasures: a picnic on the lawn, a well-tended garden, afternoon tea. Her dancing followed the classic design principles of harmony, proportion, balance, and rhythm.

She could linger in a smooth legato and then quick as lightning—her two feet like little rabbit teeth taking neat, sharp bites of air—she'd run and arrive at the other side of the stage perfectly in time with the music.

Many dancers overlook the expressive power in their upper bodies, but this was Fonteyn's chief asset. The way she inclined her head and flashed her eyes lent color and charm to her dancing. You never lost sight of the woman above the legs and feet, the human being living the experience onstage. Whether by serendipity or design, this was a smart focus. From an audience point of view, the head and arms are the most relatable parts of a dancer. They are what we respond to most emotionally, because while most of us will never have a dancer's range of motion in our legs, we can well imagine moving our own arms and heads with a dancer's grace.

Fonteyn's intelligent, methodical way of working in harmony with her body, rather than yanking it about and risking damage, accounts for her uncommon longevity onstage. Fonteyn was in her forties and thinking of retirement when Rudolf Nureyev landed in the West from Russia; their famed partnership gave her another twenty years of dancing. Fonteyn's simplicity, sparkling gaiety, and polish were the perfect foil for Nureyev's messy exuberance and heat. Theirs was the opposite of the Fred Astaire–Ginger Rogers chemistry: Fonteyn gave Nureyev class, and he gave her sex appeal. Crucially, he also gave her pointers on technique from his Russian training. Fonteyn, world-famous and the unrivaled queen of a company stamped with her style, was not above accepting his tips. This, too, is why she would dance into her sixties. She had the grace to continue learning and adapting, to be open to new ideas, to rethink roles she had long mastered. She had the grace to enter into a true partnership with a young newcomer and to treat him as her equal.

Every time Fonteyn and Nureyev stepped onstage together, their complete sympathy and responsiveness to each other offered further lessons in grace. You see this in their 1966 film *Romeo and Juliet*. The balcony scene is an embodied conversation of understanding. It begins with fearful hesitation—Fonteyn divided as she approaches Nureyev's Romeo, her head and feet inclined toward him, her midsection drawing back. It ends with her stage-skimming delight. Interestingly, Fonteyn makes this clearest in her shoulders. When her Juliet is anxious, argumentative, urging Romeo to listen, they push forward; when she submits to her fate, and to Romeo, they slide back and her arms fall loosely—gracefully—in surrender.

One of the essential tenets of grace is making people feel good, and this was precisely Fonteyn's effect. Lincoln Kirstein, the impresario who brought choreographer George Balanchine to this country and founded New York City Ballet with him, once remarked, "Of all the century's ballerinas, Margot Fonteyn most embodied the art of pleasing." So many of today's dancers are mistaken in how to win over an audience; they believe it is done by maximum effort. The cheerleader mentality underlying their exertions—the high kicks; the infinite agility, more rubber band than human—pushes us away. They're not one of us, and we fear they'll fly apart. They show us the work, but not the joy.

Fonteyn never revealed the labor behind her dancing. She offered the ease and delight of it. With her recognizable humanity, her spirited eyes and skimming steps, she pulled us onto her plane to share the joy with her.

She was graceful offstage as well as on. Like Cary Grant and Joe DiMaggio, Fonteyn dressed immaculately, echoing the principles that governed her art: simple, spotless, elegant. Even before she was clothed by Yves Saint Laurent and Dior, she was known for her impeccable grooming, hair fastened in a bun, the seams of her stockings ruler-straight.

So she was perfect onstage, offstage, in every sector of life—right? Not at all. Fonteyn's personal life was a mess. She fell into a pattern of bad romances, the worst of which was her marriage to a Panamanian diplomat named Roberto Arias. He had a roving eye, and according to her biography, Fonteyn was preparing to divorce him when Arias fell victim to a failed assassination attempt, which left him paralyzed from the neck down.[4]

Fonteyn became his nursemaid. She fed, dressed, and cared for him with staggering devotion, drawing on her ballet discipline and her old-school upbringing. For better or for ill, she remained graceful, uncomplaining, and dutiful to the end.

As Fonteyn became an aged icon, she made public appearances in those old Dior gowns to raise money for Arias's medical bills and to support his extended family. Worn out by cancer, nearly penniless from debt, she died two years after he did. She was seventy-one.

Fonteyn deserved better, but presumably she didn't dwell on that.

THE TURBULENCE of Fonteyn's personal life revealed her gracefulness as a core value, not just an aspect of performance. The defining characteristic of her brand of grace was serenity, in her unflappable cheerfulness, in her fluid motion and airy stillnesses onstage, and in her workmanlike ability to make the best of things, whether it was the limited limberness of her body or her marriage. In doing so, she transcended her difficulties.

Difficulties exist to be surmounted, wrote Ralph Waldo Emerson, and the great heart doesn't complain about them: "A strenuous soul hates cheap successes." Within many a graceful person—dancer, athlete, whomever—beats a large and uncomplaining heart.

Russian ballerina Natalia Makarova has one of those. Her quality of movement was not like Fonteyn's—Makarova ran hotter, more impassioned and free—but the two ballerinas shared what all graceful dancers possess: the ability to move effortlessly and to transfer that ease to us as we watch them. To lift us spiritually beyond their steps, beyond the stage, beyond any easy form of description.

As serenity was the foundation of Fonteyn's gracefulness, Makarova's openheartedness and generosity are what make her graceful. Her giving nature arose paradoxically from the strictest austerity.

She was born in 1940. Her childhood was defined by the Siege of Leningrad, three years of hell when the Nazis encircled the city, choking off supplies. Nearly a million inhabitants died.

Her father was killed in combat. In the postwar privation, Makarova once lost her family's monthly ration cards and was beaten by her stepfather. If her grades fell, there were more beatings. Afterward, her mother would command her to ask for forgiveness.

"No way," Makarova told me one fall afternoon in her mountainside estate in California's Napa Valley, overlooking vineyards turning gold.[5] Seventy-two at the time, she still had translucent skin, lightly careworn; her blue eyes shone as she grinned toothily.

"I would never ask. I'd rather suffer." She rolled her Rs luxuriously in the rumbling accent of her native land.

Makarova started ballet training late, enrolling at the renowned Vaganova Academy at thirteen, and fought to keep up with younger classmates. Life was a strain, but it was also exquisitely simple: nothing but dance, art, books.

"What's good about Russia: we had our own freedom, actually," she said. "It was free from frivolous things. This whole Soviet world, without food, without entertainment, without nonsense, it's kind of pure. And you concentrate on the real treasure. That's why it built the spirituality and the substance, at the same time."

Makarova realized that her greatest gifts were contradictory: strong self-discipline and fearless spontaneity, stemming from her natural physical coordination and spirited personality. These qualities produced in her a distinctly luscious, free-flowing, effortless-seeming grace that made her stand out from the technique-driven stars in the West, after she defected in 1970.

A finger strayed to one of her gold hoop earrings as she described her sudden impulse at twenty-nine to make one of the most important moves of her life. She was on tour with the Kirov Ballet in London. She had made it to the top rank of the company but was tired of losing parts to lesser dancers with Party ties. She was bored with her repertoire of the classics and newer Communist drivel with names like *Russian Boat Coming to Port*.

Most of all, Makarova feared that her prized spontaneity onstage would evaporate. So she swallowed her tears and told the English friends she was visiting to call the police.

In one decisive moment, in the thick of the Cold War, Makarova became the first ballerina to defect from the Soviet Union.

"Being spontaneous, it's what saved me," she said.

When she eventually landed at American Ballet Theatre and,

later, joined the Royal Ballet, Makarova's generosity onstage—her big-hearted dancing, expansive and full of feeling—made her an instant sensation. Audiences reacted passionately to the musical responsiveness of her upper body and arms, the bend and sway of her torso, and her living reactions to the dancers around her. ABT, for example, already had technicians, and Makarova wasn't one of them; she had a long struggle with the mechanics of ballet due to her late start. But no one in the company had seen such interpretive grace before. It was not about distortion. It was not about hiking her foot up to her ear. And it was certainly not about steps.

"Her arms were just unbelievable," said Amanda McKerrow, who was a young dancer in ABT during the Makarova years. "She had this freedom of her chest. The freedom and expressiveness of her arms and back were just amazing, and unique to her."

"She had the ability to never look rushed," said Cynthia Harvey, a Makarova protégé. "Her movement quality had such a smoothness that she almost looked like she was doing legato movement even when she was doing allegro movement. She never looked awkward."

In the graveyard scene of *Giselle,* when the heroine of the title appears as a ghost, Makarova made you believe she had entered an otherworldly state from her first steps, rolling through her feet as if she were treading on mist rather than solid ground. This was an unusually nuanced touch, for a dancer to change the way she works the little bones in her feet. But Makarova didn't stop there. She altered her breathing and the focus of her eyes, to give the appearance of being in a trance.

Dramatic roles were her strength—the desperate romantics of Frederick Ashton's *A Month in the Country* or John Cranko's *Onegin,* both inspired by Russian love stories. Jerome Robbins created *Other*

Casual grandeur. Natalia Makarova and Mikhail Baryshnikov in Jerome Robbins's Other Dances, *in 1980.*

Dances for her and Mikhail Baryshnikov, accompanied by Chopin piano mazurkas; this rich character study, crafted in the style of a sophisticated folk dance with clicking heels and high, proud arms, captured Makarova's grandeur and Slavic earthiness, and the swimming, liquid quality of her dancing.

Makarova's dancing felt like the human dream life made visible. She brought this about through qualities of gracefulness—a generous use of the full body and a sense of natural ease in connecting steps and passing through them fluidly rather than drawing attention to any single pose, which together with her dramatic ability suggested intangible qualities of yearning and escape.

"She didn't look like anybody else," Baryshnikov told me. He knew Makarova in Saint Petersburg and was a member of the Kirov Ballet, a few years behind her, when she defected. "She had that mystery, and extraordinary coordination and freedom and total transparency."

Makarova was free and transparent—and generous—not only in her dancing. She was all of those things offstage too. She was generous in passing on her knowledge to other dancers: she taught the Americans to dance like Russians, resculpting a generation of dancers inside and out, showing them how to dance larger and more confidently. She also gave ABT a ballet, *La Bayadère*, a nineteenth-century tale of love and murder set amid opium smoke and Indian royalty. It was created by Marius Petipa, choreographer of *Swan Lake* and *The Sleeping Beauty*, but *La Bayadère* was little known in the States. Makarova staged it from her memories of the Kirov production, with its mesmerizing chain of twenty-four ghostly women crisscrossing the stage with ethereal ease. Its success had critics hailing ABT's once-unremarkable corps as second to none.

Bear in mind that ballerinas don't take on this kind of mammoth directorial headache in their peak dancing years—if ever. But Makarova felt she had gained immeasurably from the variety of dancing she had learned at ABT, particularly the expressionistic, sucked-in physicality of British-born choreographer Antony Tudor, one of ballet's great modernizers. She wanted to give back.

"I am different because I have better schooling, better understanding of the line, gesture, how feet working, positions," she told me, mounding her hands to suggest properly trained arches. "They taught me modern things . . . and I wanted to give what I had: my schooling."

And when her friend Baryshnikov followed her example and defected in 1974, Makarova was the first to get in touch with him. She made sure the twenty-six-year-old didn't have to job-hunt on his own, as she had done four years earlier. She arranged his debut with her in *Giselle* at ABT. For that, he said, "I will be grateful for the rest of my life."

GRATITUDE: I learned about it from a stripper.

I was with a friend in a basement bar in New York's East Village that was known as an insider's rock club. This was not where you would expect a revelation. The narrow room was dark and hot, with a sticky cement floor and a beery, frat-house smell. The band we'd come to hear, Bambi Kino, specializes in songs the early Beatles covered. The music had a warm nostalgic pull; it was upbeat and strummy, but no one had ventured onto the dance floor. All you saw were hard edges everywhere.

Until the strippers swept in.

There were three of them, hired for the evening from an upscale burlesque club. They were all smiles and good cheer: the Three Graces of the Dive Bar. But the one I remember most is Miss Ekaterina. A platinum blonde trailing white chiffon and feathers, she lit up the room like moonlight. She had eyes for everyone in the joint, though I don't think many of us returned the favor, riveted as we were by her twinkly pair of pasties and all that unbound flesh.

The chiffon slid to the floor as she whirled through her maneuvers: back walkovers, six o'clock kicks and impeccable balances with her foot by her ear. Ekaterina was quite the contortionist. She even managed to bend the whole nature of the scene. Hers was not a vulgar striptease; there was no exaggerated lolling or thrusting, and her G-string stayed modestly—miraculously—in place. She had a friendly air, with the relaxed warmth of a Modigliani nude, and it was this directness that suggested a lovely bit of romance. She wasn't "acting," in the empty-eyed, remote self-armor of those at the raunch end of the stripping spectrum. Ekaterina was completely at ease, in her element, and her aim was to include as well as to tantalize. She wasn't content to be the center of attention. She wanted us to move, too.

The show channeled the spirit of the Beatles' early years in Hamburg's red-light district. That's why the strippers were there. When the musicians launched into one of their gentler songs—the pleading melancholy of "Bésame Mucho," with its surf-guitar twang and spy-movie groove—Ekaterina began coaxing folks to the dance floor.

As the rockers crooned, she swiveled her hips and locked eyes with us one by one, punctuating her invitation with a persuasive little shake of the pasties. If you looked amenable, she'd extend a hand

and lead you into a jiggly duet. If in some way you signaled you weren't entirely comfy with the come-on, she'd smile soothingly and move on. No pressure.

Ekaterina worked the room with one principle: everyone is welcome to the party. By the time she'd made her way around, that underground bunker felt like the sweetest place on earth. The whole atmosphere had softened. Was it the bare skin? The velvety way she moved? It was both, and the fact that, naked and exposed, she was unafraid to weave among us. She wanted to mix with us.

Matter of fact, this beautiful creature seemed to think quite highly of the motley crowd before her. Ekaterina spun an invisible web around everybody there, joining us together in what, strange as it may sound, had become an elevating experience.

Those who had accepted her offer were noodling around on the dance floor. Others were leaning against the brick walls clutching plastic cups of booze, clearly enjoying what had become a really lovely show. Was it just a basement burlesque, or a big tent for the battered egos in all of us?

Even the band members seemed awed by the strippers' gentle magic. They had adopted a studious head-down posture, but every now and again they'd steal shy peeks at the ladies, not wanting to gawk or appear disrespectful.

Before the striptease got rolling, I was a little nervous about it. Given the macho, biker-bar vibe of the place, I was bracing for drunken rock snobs to turn into slobbering morons. And I harbored just the teensiest shadow of a worry that there might be some insistence, that in some way I might be called on to participate and the bathroom door would be yanked open on all my creaky uncoolness.

Instead, in that loud, impersonal enclosure, I felt the glow of welcome. I didn't ask for it, didn't expect it, yet there was Ekaterina shimmying her breasts at me with her encouraging smile that said, "Why, hey there! Yeah, you—the chick who feels like an invisible, unfunky, post-ingenue mom whose roots are showing—you absolutely rock!"

Strippers, you see, have a kind of wisdom to offer. They are not self-conscious. They are not snobs. They know it's not having a "perfect" body that counts, but how you use it—and your attitude. The best of them approach a social setting with the goal of pleasing everyone there, without seeking to dominate, intimidate, or overcompensate in some jerky way for their insecurities. They're basically up for anything, within legal limits. In shucking their clothes and, if you like, curling up in your lap, they open a window onto a world without boundaries, of infinite possibility.

If the three women in that club could be graceful in such a hard-edged environment, couldn't we all?

At one point, as one of the strippers twirled past the band, an errant feather from her boa wafted onto the drummer's T-shirt and hung there like a blown kiss. It was a metaphor for what had happened. The hard edges had melted away, and something sexy and a bit retro-cheesy, but also redemptive, had flown in.

CHAPTER 10

WALKING WITH GRACE:

CATWALKS, CROSSWALKS, AND PRESIDENTIAL BEARING

But the expression of a well-made man appears not only in his face . . .
It is in his walk, the carriage of his neck, the flex of his waist and knees, dress does not hide him,
The strong sweet quality he has strikes through the cotton and broadcloth,
To see him pass conveys as much as the best poem, perhaps more,
You linger to see his back, and the back of his neck and shoulderside.

—Walt Whitman, *"I Sing the Body Electric"*

I LEARNED AN AWKWARD TRUTH at Fashion Week: most runway models can't walk.

Granted, you send a dance critic to Fashion Week and you're not going to get a nuanced analysis of tailoring trends and pleating quality. I was looking at performance. But so were the detail-driven designers. Their shows are like rock concerts, with aggressive lighting and pounding music. The models march at a swift pace to boost excitement. Inasmuch as fashion trades on feelings, fashion shows are all about high-pitched emotion, even sensory overload.

But if the models don't move well, the clothes lose their power. Minus a great walk, the spectacle fails.

Grace is not easy to spot among the models, most of whom resemble Giacomettis come to life. Many of the young women are emaciated, abstractions of the female form, all exaggerated lines and angles. Hipbones jut from praying mantis legs, thin and sharp. Tender fabrics can take on hard edges when worn by the average runway model.

The biggest problem is their stride. "Walk like you have three men walking behind you," advised the late designer Oscar de la Renta. Well, the average runway model clumps rigidly along, glassy-eyed, as if those three men are zombies and she is their stone-cold queen, still stiff from the grave.

But Karlie Kloss is different.[1] She has a way of moving—at once soft and powerful—that goes beyond simple locomotion. When I first saw her, in a silk gown by Carolina Herrera, the six-foot-tall Kloss prompted thoughts of the *Cutty Sark*, with the hem of her dress billowing in her wake as she sailed down the runway.

Kloss has the grace to know why she's there: to promote the clothes, to capture the imagination, to draw spectators in with her warmth, allure, and the sense that she's putting on a show just for you—and to take a good picture. She offers a show to the photographers as well. She eased up just as she approached the bank of cameras dead ahead; she stopped and took in their zooms with hungry eyes and a roll of her shoulders that echoed down into her liquid hips. Then—and this is what the photographers love about her—she gave them another pose to snap, keeping her gaze focused on the cameras even as she started to make her U-turn.

Like a dancer locked onto her visual point of reference in a pirouette, Kloss's eyes lingered on the cameras before she turned her head to look where she was going, up the other side of the runway, where she finally drifted out of sight.

What made Kloss stand out on the runway was not just her ease of movement, but the mood she projected. No bored stare, no I-could-care-less dust-off. Kloss had a knowingness in her eyes as she strode forth; she tucked her chin slightly so the light danced off her cheekbones, and she aimed for the flashbulbs with the focus of a panther on the prowl.

"I love the way she shows," Herrera gushed to me backstage, when I asked her about Kloss. "She moves like a cat. I love the way she walks. For me, it's more important than beauty."

WALKS ARE PERSONAL, a movement signature, and they tell us a lot.

In the *Aeneid*, Virgil writes that when Venus appeared in disguise to speak to her son Aeneas, he was completely fooled. Score one for crafty moms! That is, until she walked away:

Thus having said, she turn'd, and made appear
Her neck refulgent, and dishevel'd hair,
Which, flowing from her shoulders, reach'd the ground.
And widely spread ambrosial scents around:
In length of train descends her sweeping gown;
And, by her graceful walk, the Queen of Love is known.[2]

Clever Venus could alter her attire and even her voice, but there was no masking the way she moved. Virgil, the greatest of poets, is silent on the details; he leaves it all to our imagination. And yet he prompts delicious contemplation: What would the goddess's immortal tread look like?

It would have to be more regal and more bewitching than that of any other woman. The kind that turns your head clear around. Maybe it would look like the mysterious, floating glide down a castle corridor that the beautiful Belle exhibits in Jean Cocteau's 1946 film *Beauty and the Beast*, in a stark black-and-white scene so magically rendered it feels full of Vermeer light and unearthly air.

Perhaps Venus possessed the hypnotic majesty of Dolores, a former model (back when runway models were all about elegance, not attitude), who in 1917 had the most mesmerizing walk of all the Ziegfeld Follies showgirls. She stood more than six feet tall. In a Follies show, after a parade of other girls had gone by, Dolores would saunter across the bare stage in a peacock costume that fanned around her like a full-body halo. This has been called the most spectacular single effect of all of Ziegfeld's shows, which were a riot of spectacular effects. They could run four hours long with exotic dancers and staircases and even, patriotically, advancing battleships. But Dolores stood out for her simple grace: that of a self-possessed woman, in a killer outfit, with a good, slow walk.

Her footsteps have echoed through showbiz history. More than half a century later, ghostly peacock-crested visions of Dolores and her walk appeared in Stephen Sondheim's 1971 musical *Follies*.[3]

A PERSON'S WALK is so telltale that for Paul Taylor, one of the world's greatest modern-dance choreographers, walking is the first thing he asks dancers to do at his auditions.

"I can eliminate half of them by how they walk," he told me with a casual wave of his cigarette, as we sat in his studio headquarters on New York's Lower East Side.[4] "They're either too self-assured or not assured enough, or they're just weird. You can tell an awful lot."

His eye for honesty in the hips gave rise to *Banquet of Vultures*, a 2005 work that centered on a devastatingly sadistic portrayal of former president George W. Bush, complete with red tie.

"It was George Bush's walk that gave him away," Taylor said, stabbing the air. "It was a pseudomilitaristic thing that he had no experience with. A total phony."

Bush's walk was stiff and self-conscious. Someone must have told him to swing his arms more, because that's what you noticed, those two canoe paddles rotating rhythmically into view with too much force.

A graceful walk brings the body into natural balance. The weight glides forward over solid footing. There is power in the midsection and buoyancy in the upper body. The arms shouldn't draw attention to themselves.

Why is all that important? Because grace inspires trust. Harmonious movement is the physical manifestation of ease and confidence, whether you're Cary Grant at a party or a president walking across the White House lawn. Be graceful and put doubts about your abilities to rest. Yet Bush was so uneasy with the complexities of basic locomotion, could you trust him with the fate of the nation? He often looked like he was playing the role of a president, rather than embodying the office in the fullest sense. And the act started in his walk. That tough-guy swagger was edged in effort, as if he had a splinter in his drawers. (And a splinter of doubt in his mind, or some niggling deceit.)

The most compelling communicators look composed as well as

confident. They appear comfortable with themselves. Take John Wayne. The actor's languid nonchalance was essential to his allure of toughness. It suggested he wasn't looking for a fight but if *you* were, you'd be sorry.

Wayne knew about the perils of a false persona. He regretted playing a fur-hatted, mustachioed Genghis Khan in a flop called *The Conqueror*, remarking that the lesson learned was "not to make an ass of yourself trying to play parts you're not suited for."[5]

Would George Washington have become the father of our country if he hadn't had such a studly walk? In his day, with the American colonies gaining confidence, people had a growing interest in the art of civility, and with that came an appreciation of how one moved. Washington had an extraordinary physical magnetism: not only was he tall and good-looking, but he moved well. "His movements and gestures are graceful, his walk is majestic," wrote a fellow officer of the twenty-six-year-old Washington.[6]

His body would have attracted attention no matter how he used it, for at six feet tall, Washington towered in an age of much shorter men. Great height isn't always easy to carry around, as Abraham Lincoln, six foot four, would discover. In her clear-eyed history *Team of Rivals*, Doris Kearns Goodwin describes Lincoln's stooped posture and awkward gait as giving "the impression that his long, gaunt frame needed oiling. . . . He lifted his whole foot at once rather than lifting from the toes and then thrust the whole foot down on the ground rather than landing on his heel."[7] But Washington was well-coordinated and athletic, and he held himself high. His statuesque presence, combined with the fluid physicality that came from a mastery of horsemanship and fencing, made a powerful impression. Thomas Jefferson said he was "the best horseman of his age, and the most graceful figure that could be seen on horseback."[8] In a letter written eight years after Washington's death, and tinged with envy and more than a little sarcasm, John Adams listed reasons why the former president was considered a hero by the American public, among them Washington's "elegant form" and "graceful Attitudes and Movement" (especially coveted, you can imagine, by the heavier, hot-tempered Adams), along with his "great Self Command" and "So much Equanimity."[9]

These qualities weren't just impressive. They held symbolic, moral, and political importance. A nation governed by its people needed a leader who exemplified self-governance. How right Adams was to spotlight Washington's self-command, evident in the way he mastered his emotions, his interactions with others, and most especially his body. The first president's elegant posture and dignified bearing, his air of thoughtfulness and calm, his way of looking at people "full in the face" with those engaging blue eyes, as one admirer noted—all of this gracefulness served to inspire and encourage a generation of rebels and nation builders. England would gladly have hung him, yet he acquired *through his own efforts* a regal character and bearing to outshine that country's blue-blood sovereign. Washington was bodily proof of democracy's advantage.

Even before attaining the presidency, Washington was famed for his courtly etiquette. To most colonial Americans, good manners meant good morals, and Washington's dedication to the guiding maxims he'd copied out by hand from a Jesuit manual was not unusual for his day. The first of his 110 *Rules of Civility and Decent Behaviour* was "Every action done in company ought to be done with some sign of respect to those that are present." And another: "The gestures of the body must be suited to the discourse you are upon." Presumably, he took these words to heart, adding this age-old wisdom to the discipline he'd gained from a farming life—he was known as a hard worker on his family's Virginia plantation—and, later, his military service. In 1775, Benjamin Rush, one of the future signers of the Declaration of Independence, wrote that Washington "has so much martial dignity in his deportment that you would distinguish him to be a general and a soldier from among 10,000 people. There is not a king in Europe that would not look like a valet de chambre by his side."[10]

Washington didn't have to act out the role of leader of men.

Barack Obama entered office more smoothly, more gracefully, than George W. Bush did. He has the gently loping walk of an athlete, and certainly at first he carried himself with self-possessed dignity. His solipsism got everyone's attention, as a strong stage presence will do. He still has the slow walk, though his posture is less upright; his ambling gait looks heavy, and more tired than relaxed. In recent years, he's become more strained, more aloof, more distant—and less graceful. Watch him when he speaks to a crowd, or in those staged encounters with people in diners and lunchrooms; as much as these interactions are all about communicating, the president often has trouble with the nuances. Though he may keep up the chatter at one of these mealtime events, you can tell he's holding himself back when he avoids looking people in the eye. After a brief, perfunctory glance around, his lids drop, he'll look away, down at his plate, into the middle distance, while he stays on message. Verbally, at least.

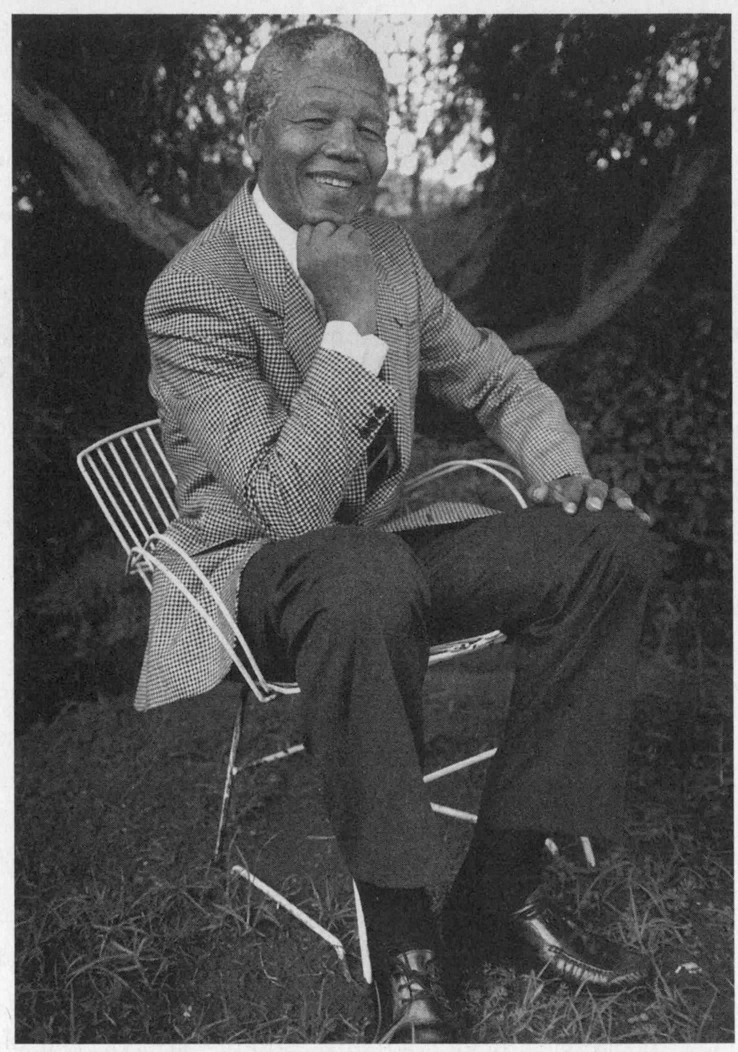

South African President Nelson Mandela was the embodiment of joyful equanimity. After twenty-seven years in prison, he had every reason to feel bitter, yet he put the past behind him to lead South Africa into peace and democracy. Here, the humble humanitarian and descendant of royalty playfully poses on an antithrone.

Gloves, pearls, and poise. Canny politician Margaret Thatcher was keenly aware of her self-presentation, and she wasn't afraid of femininity. At a Pentagon ceremony in her honor, the British prime minister's graceful appearance and air of genuine interest stand out against the bolt-upright military and the self-conscious awkwardness of U.S. Defense Secretary Caspar Weinberger.

It is the habit of a man in a bubble. A man who doesn't truly want to engage, in the way that the irrepressible Bill Clinton did. Being approachable brings risk; it's far easier to stick to a script, to a teleprompter. But smoothly managing the unexpected gives people the sense that you're in calm control. Obama needs to realize that his efforts to avoid mistakes make him rigid, dull, less able to connect with the public.

Admitting mistakes reveals your humanness. It's more graceful to acknowledge messing up than to shield yourself behind a mask of perfection. This is something Joe DiMaggio might have reckoned with as well. Flaws can be charming. We love a flawed hero, as long as he or she is more hero than flaw. (Babe Ruth got the proportions right. Lance Armstrong got them wrong.)

Perfection is boring. Being human is interesting.

"OF COURSE, carriage is all-important," Rita Moreno told me over lunch, the same one in which she'd done her marvelous banquette dance. As an example, she brought up George Chakiris, who played her *West Side Story* boyfriend, Bernardo.

"Ach!" Moreno cries, pushing away unseen other guys with poor carriage. "He was the only dancer who could compete with Astaire in one way: he had such elegance. When I see the movie, I only look at George. Talk about gliding! It's like he never touched the floor. George is doing something beyond acting. He's being."

(He's now in Los Angeles, making jewelry; she sees him now and then. "That skinny old fart still goes to ballet class almost every day," she said.)

When she played opera diva Maria Callas in *Master Class* at Berkeley Rep a decade ago, Moreno said, "I had to find a way for her to move. I was not familiar at all with that kind of woman who is always on display. It has a great deal to do with carriage, and the chin and the neck up high." She lengthened her small frame upward, her neck a long-stemmed rose.

Moreno studied films of Callas to get her physicality just right. To show me what she meant, she held herself formally, swiveling elegantly like a queen. "Her posture was always perfect. When she'd bend down, she'd bend with her whole torso.

"That's the way a dancer moves also; the entire upper torso moves," she said. "There's never a collapse. They never sink, ever. Even when they're exhausted."

WATCHING PEOPLE WALK is a favorite pastime; it appeals to the dance critic and the writer in me. I watch a neighbor amble by and wonder, what story is she telling? Every day at dawn I head up the street to the local swimming pool (not my most graceful moment; undoubtedly, my own stride at that hour says: Not a morning person! Gotta force myself to do this). On my way, I usually see a young woman with her aging St. Bernard. He walks slowly, head down, tongue out, the picture of doggy melancholy. She matches him with her own languid legato and the same head-down posture, because her eyes are glued to her iPhone.

Our cell phones are changing our bodies in ungraceful ways. They're killing our posture, flattening the natural curve of the neck. Folks on their phones aren't just walking into one another and everything else in their path; they're shut off from one another. But this woman and her dog make a graceful couple. They have tuned in to each other's snail-level energy; they move to the same beat, swaying together in cross-species harmony.

I LIVE IN THE SUBURBS, so I find myself driving around a lot on short jaunts to the market, my kids' schools, the post office. I'm always in a hurry. (Who isn't?) Increasingly, the stumbling blocks along my path aren't lights and traffic jams but crosswalk confrontations.

Grace matters here.

The other day I was pulling into a shopping center when an elderly man suddenly lurched out from between two parked cars, poised to cross in front of me. His face, rutted and weathered, was framed in fluffy white hair; he wore a bulging backpack and clutched a ski pole in each hand. He was an extraordinary sight in the middle of the day, miles from any nature trail.

I slammed on my brakes, and as we caught each other's eye, we began a nervy duet of uncertainty. I waved him on, he waved me on, I waved him on again, and with a courtly nod and a smile as bright as his head of hair, he finally took the lead. Carrying himself with spindly grandeur, he looked like a giant daddy longlegs as he picked his way across the shopping center driveway, touching his poles to the asphalt. When he had passed my car, he revolved in a smooth quarter turn to give me another smile and a salute. Oh! I especially loved that little salute at the end, so gentlemanly and so witty. The whole graceful exchange gave me a lift.

As urban planners paint our roadways with more crosswalks—a good thing—cars and pedestrians are just starting to figure out this dance. As a driver, you never want to be the jerk in the crosswalk, but sometimes you are, and it's a gift to be forgiven.

"Don't block the crosswalk," sang out a soft voice from a street corner in my neighborhood one day, as my husband and I rolled up to a red light in our car.

The source of the song wasn't exactly a surprise. We live in a very pro-clothesline town, where inside creatively color-schemed Victorian houses dwell decidedly un-Victorian thinkers. It has long been a haven for writers, artists, alternative anyones, and assorted quirky types. One of these was standing on the sidewalk as we idled in front of the food co-op. Frumpy, bald, and pudgy, he was wearing a white undershirt, white gym shorts, and leather sandals with white tube socks pulled up to his knees. He clutched a stack of papers firmly to his chest and stared past us with the faraway gaze of someone who'd dropped a little too much acid some decades ago.

Indeed, we were over the white line. Heeding the man's gently sung admonition, John backed up the car. "Sorry, dude," he called out amiably.

"That's okay-ay," the fellow sang back, still avoiding eye contact. But he thanked us in a lovely way, reaching his hands around his bundle of papers to clasp them palm to palm in a yogi salute. He waved them toward us as he crossed in front of our car with a loose, bobbing stride. His prayer hands and sandaled feet were in perfect nodding rhythm. With his gentle voice and soft physicality, he looked like a suburban Buddha, blocking negative energy, sending out light.

He could have glowered at us, he could have barked out some sarcasm or slapped the hood as he strode past; maybe we'd have backed up anyway, maybe not. But if he'd acted like that, we would have all been left feeling pretty bitter about our chance encounter. Instead, that little crosswalk cha-cha was a sweet moment because the guy with a grievance handled it with grace. And we followed his lead.

It's worth paying attention to crosswalks: they make us stop and wait and can prompt us to look around, to take time to reflect and notice things. They're a good spot for grace to happen.

A San Francisco singer, storyteller, and choreographer named Joe Goode once told me about a moment of grace he experienced at a crosswalk, as he stood waiting for the light to change. It was at a time when the bottom had dropped out of his world, yet something carried him forward. He was somehow able to find possibility.

Or rather, it found him.

Goode had been trying to launch his dance career in New York. It wasn't going very well. The arts scene was competitive, and Goode, who wanted to bring humor and songwriting into his work at a time when dark irony was in vogue, didn't feel he fit in. He grew depressed.

It was just an ordinary street corner, but he'll tell you it took on mythological tones, as a place where two worlds met: the sloppy present and a shining future. As Goode stood on Bleecker Street waiting for the light to change on a wet, bitter day in January 1979, feeling like the very embodiment of the name—miserable, hopeless, bleak—his mind lit up with a new thought.

"Suddenly I had this idea: I could drive away," he told me. "Those words just called out to me. I was struck by the concept that I didn't have to stay there, that I was able to take action."

He acted fast. He got one of those driveaway cars, from an outfit where you arrange to deliver someone's car to another part of the country, and drove it to the guy, who had moved to Key West. Then he stayed on the island for a while with friends. Goode eventually moved on, heading as far from New York as he could go. Finally landing in San Francisco, he found a welcome for his renegade spirit.

A few years ago, Goode choreographed a dance-theater piece inspired by his Bleecker Street epiphany. The piece is titled *Grace,* and it's a meditation on the extraordinary arising from the seemingly ordinary, with a luscious, slippery style of dancing mixed in with funny anecdotes told by the dancers. At the end, an assortment of kitchen chairs floats up to the lighting grid. You watch them and think: the ease and wonder of grace, right in my kitchen? Why not?

Goode is a big man, with the round, kindly face of a country doctor, and he speaks softly, in a faint drawl, a vestige of his native Virginia. When I spoke with him before he headed into a rehearsal at the American Dance Institute in a Maryland suburb, he cradled a nervy little dachshund against the folds of his flannel shirt. She goes everywhere with him.

As his thoughts returned to the sudden revelation of that wet winter day, that bit of grace that had changed his life, a calm came over Goode. His dog and I felt it, too. The dog nuzzled her head in the crook of his elbow, closed her eyes, and began to snore.

"I was so grateful in that moment, to have that opening," Goode said, absentmindedly stroking his dog's ear. "I remember the details, but also I remember the feeling, that I can take a left turn. That felt very graceful to me."

PART FOUR

Grace under Pressure

CHAPTER 11

THE PRATFALL EFFECT:

STUMBLING INTO GRACE

Very little grows on jagged rock. Be ground.

Be crumbled, so wildflowers will come up where you are.

—RUMI, *"A Necessary Autumn inside Each"*

"AND THE OSCAR GOES TO . . . Jennifer Lawrence!" The stunned twenty-two-year old, wearing a strapless confection of pink silk, looked authentically shocked, which made us really like her.

Then she tripped and fell on her way to the stage, face-planting in her magnificent gown, which made us really love her.

The audience at the 2013 Academy Awards gave her a standing ovation.

"You guys are just standing up 'cause you feel bad that I fell, and that's really embarrassing. But thank you," Lawrence gasped into the microphone once she'd reached it, after what must have felt like the longest journey of her life. But with impeccable poise and the ability to laugh at herself, she transformed her fall into a screwy-sophisticated Cary Grant kind of moment.

Grace is an act of transformation, making an ordinary moment into something extraordinary. And nowhere is that more visible than when we fall and the veils of composure drop away. But must they? Whether we're talking about a physical stumble or some event that brings us to our knees emotionally, grace can help us meet life as it comes with ease, equanimity, and courage.

I find Jennifer Lawrence's fall fascinating and inspiring. It's terrific theater, starting with her open-mouthed, socked-in-the-gut reaction to hearing her name announced, and the little upward tug she gives the neckline of her bodice, to make sure that, you know, she's not going to experience some kind of wardrobe malfunction on live television.

And then she does. I love the moment of stasis when, after she trips, she lies utterly flattened on the steps, and time stops. She sinks into the carpet, seems to give up under an oppressive weight. Her shoulder blades wiggle and collapse. She draws a hand to her face, and just looking at the back of her head you can feel her gasp.

But then she gathers herself—you see it in her back, where there's a little muscular rebound as resolve settles into her spine and goes to work. She's the drowning Ophelia in reverse: that many-tiered dress may have pulled her underwater, but then it seems to bear her back to the surface. Lawrence rises and moves onward to the stage—talk about grace under pressure—and the dress is no longer an anchor but a sail.

Here is the yoga of grace, the practice, not the perfect.

Falls elicit an emotional reaction, which is why choreographers like to use them. They see in them both the vulnerability and the courage of the fallen. Mark Morris, one of the world's leading modern dance choreographers, created a work called "Falling Down Stairs" for an Emmy Award–winning film, with Yo-Yo Ma playing Johann Sebastian Bach's Unaccompanied Cello Suite no. 3. It has one of the most dramatic and graceful openings you'll ever see in a dance: the whole cast tumbles down a flight of stairs and spills onto the stage, like water rushing over rocks. Their velvet gowns fly up behind them.

I have seen those gowns backstage; designed by Isaac Mizrahi, they resemble loose choir robes of the softest, richest puppy's-ear velvet I've ever felt. They're cut to reveal the body in motion, especially the hindquarters. It seems to me that Morris envisioned his dancers as earthy angels, falling and soaring, flaunting their big round bottoms, their seats of power, the essence of their humanity—which is to say, the divine.

In any fall—in any humbling moment—there's an arc between death and rebirth. "Pride goeth before a fall," as the proverb tells us. Pride slips away, all right, and in its place is something new. In the most graceful recoveries, there is clarity, resolve, and a deep dip into the well of self-discipline.

I once saw a ballet that unspooled so carefully, with such deliberate perfection, it nearly put me to sleep. In her central solo, the leading ballerina wasn't dancing so much as demonstrating her steps, blandly preoccupied with her technique. Then for some reason—maybe she'd finally warmed up to being onstage, maybe her opening-night jitters had vanished—she seemed to wake up. She flew into a turn with enthusiasm, missed her mark, and crashed to the stage like felled timber. After scrambling back to her feet before the rest of us could exhale, she went on to give the performance of her life.

Even the best dancers slip and fall periodically, but with this one I feared bloodshed. I haven't seen such a spectacular spill since I witnessed a middle-aged man fall unconscious while standing and plummet with dead weight onto a subway platform. Adrenaline must have returned the ballerina to her feet, but also, I suspect, a blazing sense of duty. She was humbled by her fall, and humbled by the enormous challenge of making up for it. And, like Jennifer Lawrence, she sucked it up and got back to work.

If anyone should think ballerinas are delicate and fussy, think again: this one reacted like it was fourth and goal with six seconds on the clock and not a blooming thing was going to stand in her way.

She fell because she put a little too much juice into that turn. She took a risk and soared through the consequences with grace. That's a moment you remember.

Tripping and falling, admitting failure and weaknesses: these things endear us to people. Psychologists call it the pratfall effect. John F. Kennedy experienced it after he fell off his pedestal by botching the Bay of Pigs invasion in 1961.[1] What started as a plan to overthrow Cuban leader Fidel Castro ended in disaster, with missed air strikes, sunken ships, downed planes, and more than one hundred dead. The failure left a stain on his administration, but Kennedy had the grace to admit his mistakes and take responsibility for them. The result: his popularity increased. People liked him more when he showed the world that he was fallible, and that he could shoulder the blame. He ceased to be a figure of overwhelming awe (and maybe even resentment, as we can tend to hold a person's über-competence against him) and became a person to whom folks could relate.

. . .

MARTHA REEVES FELL during a performance recently, and it was Maxine Powell's lessons in grace from nearly fifty years ago that got the singer up on her feet again.

"She taught us how to relax your body, and not tense up, because you'll break something that way," the seventy-three-year-old Reeves told me. "I was able to fall and not damage myself, because of Mrs. Powell's training."

She was appearing in a benefit performance in New York, singing "Dancing in the Street," the song that had made Martha and the Vandellas famous and became an anthem of the free-loving 1960s. Reeves, in a sparkling evening gown, was shimmying to the instrumental break, banging a silver tambourine on one hip, when she took a few steps along the thrust stage and tripped on an electrical cord. She stumbled, rolled, and landed flat on her back.

"You're gonna fall, there's no doubt about it," the veteran performer said. "But being taught how to fall, it all came to my mind and it kept me from feeling embarrassed."

Someone recorded the episode and posted it on YouTube. Despite the tumble, Reeves held on to her microphone. "I'll keep right on moving—nothing's gonna stop me now," Reeves said into the microphone, with remarkable composure, as she was helped to her feet by her backup dancers.

"When you fall down—" she continued, and paused for a perfect four-count measure, "you gotta get back up." And she did get back up, brandishing her tambourine like a laughing full moon. She found her walk, and found her way back into her song. She seemed even lighter on her feet then. As she continued to strut down the stage, beaming, she jiggled her hips like a kid.

CHAPTER 12

WORKING AT GRACE:

LESSONS FROM VAUDEVILLE

Everyone knows the difficulty of things that are exquisite and well done—so to have facility in such things gives rise to the greatest wonder.

—BALDESAR CASTIGLIONE, *The Book of the Courtier*

WALK INTO our own national temple of classical culture, and you'll see that the balancing act of grace—skill without apparent effort—is built into the depiction of grace displayed on its walls. I'm standing under the portraits of the Three Graces that hang in the Library of Congress, just under the ceiling in the art-filled Great Hall.

The first time I noticed these renditions of prim young ladies in chignons and long gowns staring down at me from above, I felt strongly that they were out of place. Painted by the American artist Frank Weston Benson in the 1890s, when Benson was known for his portraits of genteel northeasterners, they give off a slightly uptight vibe.

Unlike their ancient counterparts, they are not naked, smiling, or touching. They aren't even together. Each is sealed up in her own frame. Chastely attired in white, these long, lean priestesses of purity look down on me with the chilly appraisal of New England debutantes.

As if they didn't look high-minded enough, Benson added a Puritan touch. Alongside her sisters Music, with a lyre, and Beauty, with a hand mirror, the third of the Graces brandishes a shepherd's crook, symbolizing a good, solid work ethic—Husbandry, as the library's guidebook tells me, a word with overtones of thrift and self-discipline. No hedonistic layabout, she.

I think about this. While the more prudish and censuring aspects of Puritanism chafe against my view of grace as easygoing and broad-minded, a strong work ethic makes perfect sense as one of its pillars. In fact, hard work explains a lot about Cary Grant.

I've come to the Library of Congress to puzzle out how Grant came by his gracefulness, and what I've begun to realize is that however much some of it may have been innate—good physical coordination, reflexes—much of it was deeply worked on. I leave the echoing Great Hall and make my way through a labyrinth of corridors to the hushed, cathedral-like Main Reading Room, with its marble dome ringed with angels, alluding to celestial realms.

I've got something more down-to-earth in mind, and soon one of the librarians delivers it: a well-thumbed, slightly crumbling copy of *How to Enter Vaudeville: A Complete Illustrated Course of Instruction*. It was published in 1913 by Frederic La Delle, a thirty-year veteran of the stage, whose illusionist act, he informs us, was "a culmination of years of experience comprising originality—cleverness—versatility—showmanship." Comprising dignity, too,

I gather, as the through-and-through decency of his profession is what he is most interested in conveying here. His book is an encyclopedia of vaudeville acts (sharpshooters, barrel jumpers), but it is also a conduct book about how to be in that world. How to comport yourself onstage and off, in rehearsals, on the road, throughout your career. How to live with yourself and others in a fast-paced, competitive, always-on-the-go arena where material rewards are fleeting, but joy is—or can be—abundant.

La Delle's manual for vaudevillians is a guidebook for life.

I have no idea if Grant consulted such a book, but it's fair to say that within its pages lies the philosophy of the craft he stumbled into in his early teens, at a time when progress through the entertainment business wasn't about one's needs as an artist. Success came through disciplined, unceasing work.

"Special talent is not required for acting any more than it is for any other profession," La Delle announces on the first page, opposite a drawing of himself in a high collar, cravat, and three-piece suit. What is required: practice, and the drive to "do something better" than the competition. Also, sweat. Any reward—and La Delle charmingly frames that as a kind of joyful, transformative grace—will come only with time and toil: "In the theatrical profession, whatever you contribute to human happiness as well as your own, will be paid for liberally."[1]

What this master illusionist reveals is that there is no magic to his business. Being alert to the moment, paying attention to others, performing with ease and naturalness: these tricks of the trade are also fundamental principles of grace. Vaudevillians learned them—lived them—through rehearsal, revisions, and then reacting on the fly. Figuring out how to make an act work when it was dying (hello, grace under pressure) took a kind of creative energy that came from being fully present. No wandering thoughts. A moment-to-moment slalom skiers' Zen of responsiveness.

As the *How to Enter Vaudeville* manual puts it: learn to make every move in a perfectly natural manner.

Live theater works different muscles in actors, and survival in that world is one reason that performers such as Grant, Ginger Rogers, Fred Astaire, and other greats from Hollywood's Golden Age still seem so alive today, so warmly three-dimensional.

Watch Rogers gaze at Astaire in *Top Hat* as he woos her with Irving Berlin's gently bouncy song "Isn't This a Lovely Day (To Be Caught in the Rain)?" How Rogers's eyes consume him, how her face brightens by degrees! Rogers is one of the most graceful creatures of any category. She danced with an emotional responsiveness you rarely see in any dancer, film or otherwise. This is what made her the perfect foil for Astaire, the cool perfectionist. Rogers deepened the drama as she danced, with the way she reacted to him with her body and her eyes. That responsiveness is also there in the scenes where she is simply listening. But she not only learned how to dance, sing, and act on the vaudeville circuit, she developed an enduring levelheadedness and work ethic that carried her through seventy-three films and were justly prized in a Hollywood of fragile egos and high-maintenance insecurities. That's grace, too, because it makes things easier for everybody else.

There was no time to be a diva when, at the end of an engagement, vaudeville players had to cram into railcars as the caravan of nomads sped onward to the next gig, next audience, next screwy set of variables and random calamities.

Unlike Hollywood today or Broadway or pop stardom, the

vaudeville existence concentrated and distilled all the challenges and stickiness of life. Vaudeville acts were physical; a pretty face wasn't as important as what you did with your body. The players had to be able to move, and in concert with others; they developed rhythm and timing, action and reaction, and the ability to tune in to the entire theater while staying tuned to each other. They had to think on their feet, go onstage no matter what, fill in at a moment's notice, improvise in a pinch, put up with schedule changes, travel from town to town doing their laundry in hotel sinks and checking their egos at the door.

Toward the back of La Delle's book is a chapter titled "How to Make a Success in Vaudeville." Its placement at the end implies that success comes well after one's act is learned, and only when the social graces are mastered. His words could apply today, to Amtrak's Quiet Car, to the subway, to the office:

> There is nothing so disgusting as to see some performers enter a railroad station or car and at once try to attract attention, loudly commence to talk show business and tell how they killed them in Schenectady, etc., seeking by this means to call the attention of the other occupants of the car, that they are actors. . . . Let your conduct at all times and in all places be that of ladies and gentlemen. This same suggestion holds good while you are around the theatre, as managers know everything that goes on back of the curtain, even if they never come back there, and I know of

a good many acts of just fair ability to get by
nicely owing to their gentlemanly and lady-
like conduct.

GRANT ALWAYS HAD HIS ANTENNAE OUT, one on his costar, one on us. That sensitivity for others, for making them feel understood, supported, and cared for, can be traced right back to his acrobat's attentiveness and reflexes. To his vaudevillian toil.

CHAPTER 13

"TO BECOME UNSTUCK": FINDING GRACE DESPITE PHYSICAL DIFFICULTIES

All things are doubly fair
If patience fashion them
And care—

—Théophile Gautier, *Art, translated by George Santayana*

The pianist is pounding out "Tradition," from *Fiddler on the Roof*, and all around the room legs are kicking.

Once a week at the headquarters of the Mark Morris Dance Group, one of the country's busiest and most acclaimed modern-dance companies, a dance class engages people with Parkinson's disease. Though many of the students in this class are elderly, and some arrived using canes, walkers, or motorized scooters, the lesson follows the routines of any dance class. We start small, warming up the joints. (I thought I'd be just an observer, but here I was in my socks, trying to keep up. The rule for this class is, if you're here, you're gonna dance.) Everyone sits in a circle on folding chairs or in wheelchairs. In the middle sit the two instructors, facing each other so that we all have a good view of the movements we're supposed to copy.

First we write our names in the air, hands high, jabbing and slashing in space, to music by Bach. We add punctuation, making broader slashes and big loops, singing along as the pianist plays "My Bonnie Lies over the Ocean." Now, as the beat grows faster and faster in the thundering anthem of pride from *Fiddler on the Roof,* our arms and legs are sweeping around together in a seated folk dance that's as punchy and defiant as if we were a community of modern-day Tevyes celebrating our heritage in a little Russian village.

Well, almost.

One leggy, delicately built woman can't stay seated; she weaves and bobs lightly around the room. A few can move either their legs or their arms, but not both. One man is listing slightly to one side and not moving much, but his eyes follow the others, shining with obvious delight. Everyone is pretty spirited, in fact. A hunched elderly woman who is swallowed up by her wheelchair and hasn't responded to much in the class so far is holding up her trembling hands; every now and then she keeps time on her armrests. We progress to larger and larger movements, and finally we're swirling across the floor in wobbly full-body improvisations, like waves of jelly.

"If we think of grace as a magical combination of phrasing, fluidity, musicality, suspension, the sense that one movement leads into the next—all that goes away with Parkinson's," David Leventhal, one of the instructors, told me after the class as we chatted in an empty studio. "The idea is to get some of it back."

Parkinson's affects the production of the neurotransmitter dopamine, a chemical in the brain. Dopamine regulates movement and emotional responses by making it possible for different parts of the brain to communicate with one another, coordinating the body's actions and making them smooth and controlled. When people don't get enough dopamine, control is replaced by shaking, stiffness, loss of balance, slowness, and often apathy and depression.

Leventhal, a former dancer in Morris's company, is the program director of Dance for PD, a course of free weekly instruction for Parkinson's patients. He has a gentle, soothing voice, pale blue eyes in a boyishly open face, and a lanky build. Most of all, he has lots of patience, and a kind of quiet studiousness. These qualities made him a perfect candidate when, in 2001, the leader of a local Parkinson's support group came to the newly opened dance center looking for someone to teach dancers' secrets of mobility to patients.

The project started as an experiment. Leventhal and fellow dancer John Heginbotham had six students of varying abilities. One student used a cane, another a walker; they all moved slowly and had trouble remembering steps. With lots of repetition—perhaps the chief secret of dancers—the two men taught them to glide and circle around the studio in a way that was musical and expressive and engaged the participants' brains through complicated patterns and awareness of space. This is where Leventhal's classes differ from therapy exercises that target strength and endurance but may not have the smoothness and fluidity of grace as a goal. Now, dozens of patients take his class each week, and Dance for PD has spread to thirty-eight states and twelve other countries.[1] A fascinating 2014 documentary on the program, titled *Capturing Grace*, chronicles the Brooklyn students' preparations for their first public performance of excerpts from Mark Morris's weighty, playful choreography. Directed by PBS correspondent Dave Iverson, who also has Parkinson's, the documentary has been screening at film festivals around the world. In it, Leventhal notes that "our society tells us again and again that there are people who can dance, and people who should not even bother. And I think that's such a tragedy."

Defined by their loss of movement, people with Parkinson's may feel that because of their symptoms, they dwell outside the human experience, that they are cut off from the basic pleasures of moving and belonging to a group. But the Dance for PD classes make a powerful case that grace is everybody's right. Anyone can dance. The human spirit will find a way to dance, and grace can dwell in any body.

Leventhal begins with the basics. "Lots of these people go to physical therapy, where they work on symptoms," he told me. "But to be able to move musically is very satisfying, and so here we try to keep the essence of the art as pure as possible. We get them to think about balance as dancers do, as a dynamic action of opposing forces: my weight is going down into the floor as I move up. That's an elementary technique that dancers use all the time." Thinking about the quality of movement—how you want your way of walking to look and feel, as opposed to focusing on the mechanics of taking steps—is what dancers work on a lot. It's an aesthetic goal rather than a functional goal. So Leventhal and his coteacher, a chipper young woman named Janelle Barry, ask their students to move their arms like swans' wings, as if they're fluttering onstage in *Swan Lake*. Suggesting an image that is easy to conjure instantly in the mind's eye gets around the movement blocks that arise if you just ask someone with Parkinson's to lift an arm, Leventhal said.

The music also helps. Judy, the tiny woman in the wheelchair, has advanced Parkinson's and dementia, he said. "For her to start clapping with the music is a huge positive thing. It doesn't matter if she's not doing the choreography; she's right there."

The effects are palpable. By the end of the class, the students are smiling and chattering together with the glow of an exhilarating workout amid good company. Even those with more limited expression have a softness about them.

I asked Ron, one of the participants, what he got out of it. "A chance to move in ways that you never would before," he said in a gentle, slightly halting voice. "And trying to attain gracefulness is very special."

A woman named Carol told me, "I'm really comfortable here. I feel very included, and connected to people."

For the participants, the instructors, and the researchers who are interested in this program, the uplifting connection to others in the room that Carol mentioned is as much of a benefit as the loosening and strengthening of muscles. You can just feel it in the room. But these effects are difficult to quantify. What are the data points for grace?

"The intangibles are very important, but they're harder to quantify and write about," said Joseph DeSouza, a professor of neuroscience at York University in Toronto. I called him after hearing him speak about Parkinson's and dance in a live-streamed discussion about the Dance for PD program. He specializes in movement research and has begun studying the alleviation of symptoms in Parkinson's patients who take weekly dance classes at Canada's National Ballet School.

The benefits for patients are so pronounced, DeSouza says, that he would like to see dance classes prescribed, like medicine, for all those with Parkinson's. But that will take winning over the medical community with hard evidence. "How does this help people's self-image change? We're trying to come up with quantitative measurements for this," said DeSouza. "But it's down the road."

What is clear, he says, is that the Parkinson's dance program "is the first experience I've come across in my career that people love to do. You get almost no dropouts. People come no matter what. Now, to write papers on that is very hard. It's personal. But if we could get people off the couch and into a community center or a school where they can actually see and feel these intangibles, so many more would benefit."

Rachel Bar is helping DeSouza with his research. Having graduated from Canada's National Ballet School and danced with the English National Ballet and Israel Ballet, she is working toward a doctorate in psychology. "It amazes me how dance is able to get people to become unstuck from the disease," she said. "I've seen people who want to move and can't put a foot forward. And the musical cues work every time. It seems so simple. They say, 'Let me just wait for the music to start,' and then they're off. It blows my mind."

The infectious pulse of music (it's not for nothing that many Dance for PD classes feature Broadway show tunes), its inviting pull, the communal activity of dancing—these all beckon to a deep-rooted delight in play and creativity. The classes become a realm of freedom, free of judgment, where the reward is simply the beauty and glory of doing something joyous. It's the reward of making art.

Susan Braden excelled in any sport she took on: tennis, squash, running. She traveled around the world as a foreign-policy expert; she helped get Estonia into NATO, she was knighted in Poland, she was a senior adviser to Hillary Clinton at the State Department. She had her eye on a climb up Mount Kilimanjaro.

That aspiration changed the day she ran a race with one of her three children and suddenly couldn't finish it. "My legs felt like boards," she told me. "It was so bizarre; I couldn't bend my knees." Braden, fifty-two at the time, was diagnosed with multiple sclerosis, a chronic disease of the nervous system that can cause fatigue, muscle weakness, spasticity, and pain. Its cause is not known and, as with Parkinson's, symptoms vary widely among patients.

For Braden, the disease, by its nature, forced her to slow down and focus on the present—literally—for the first time in her life. Any lapse of attention and she'd fall. She developed tingling sensations in her skin, like red ants biting her all over. She discovered that stress made the symptoms worse. MS, she told me, can also make her anxiety-prone, depressed, "bitter and whiny."

"On one level it's devastating," said Braden, who is now fifty-nine. "On another, it's been incredibly liberating and freeing, and has given me a whole new outlook on life that is much richer than I could ever imagine it could be." She looks like a jock: trim, tanned physique; no makeup; short, fluffy hair; and a warm smile. She gets around with care and a walking stick in each hand. Sports are no longer possible, so she has turned to yoga and meditation. The slowed, inward focus has allowed her to separate herself from her pain. But the spiritual benefits are even greater, she said. For the first time in her on-the-go life, she has allowed herself to do something soothing for her body and her spirit, just for the peace it offers. She quit her job; now she spends her days gardening, going to art galleries, occasionally swimming, and spending unhurried time in nature. And finding grace.

"There is no grace at work," she said. "All the bureaucracy, the infighting of people and garbage that surrounds work—you carry it with you. I was an analyst; it was my way or the highway. My whole job was to convince other people about what I thought. Now I realize there are a thousand ways of looking at things."

"Grace is knowing yourself," she continued, "and translating that into how you relate with the outside world. The disease made me do that whether I wanted to or not."

To help others achieve some measure of the calm she has found, Braden assists her yoga instructor, Maria Hamburger, with a class for MS patients. One frigid February afternoon when snow and ice cover the ground and the temperature is in the single digits, I join the class, a roomful of cheerful if slow-moving yogis at Georgetown University Medical Center. A few have climbed out of their wheelchairs, with Braden's help, to join their classmates on candy-colored mats.

Hamburger is a petite, powerfully built woman who has an authoritative but patient approach, like a cosmic midwife crossed with a personal trainer. Folks are so bubbly at the start of her class that she has to quiet them down like schoolchildren. "Let's just land," she says, urging us to close our eyes and breathe deeply.

"Yoga meets us where we are," she tells us as we stretch into tentative downward-facing dogs, rear ends in the air, hands and feet on the mat. "This is today's pose—not what you could do, but what you can do. It's bright and it's beautiful."

We sit cross-legged and rotate our shoulders. "Yesterday I did this and lifted my butt off the ground," cracks a man named Billy, the class clown with mischievous eyes and a trickster's grin. "Yes, I was hovering!"

"Stop meditating, Billy," the woman next to him says good-naturedly, the way you'd rib your little brother.

After the class, Billy, who is unable to walk much, slides back into his scooter as he tells me about the chronic pain he suffers. It's difficult to believe; his lighthearted wisecracks had the class chuckling all the way through—a grace for the rest of us, if not for him. Kristie, who is sixty-six and walks with a cane, tells me the more yoga she does, the less clunky she feels. On recent hikes through the red rocks and canyons of Sedona, Arizona, she has been able to increase her mileage.

Braden finds it difficult to walk around the block some days. But, she says, "when your world is more confined, what you *can* do becomes all the more precious."

Hamburger agrees.

"It's not whether you have it all together or not," she says. "Grace comes through the challenge, the longing, the courage. It's when people put their vulnerability out there.

"Life can be shitty and hard," she adds. "Grace is to see both sides."

Like any good dancer, Amy Purdy has a great pair of legs, but there is far more to her talent than what she does with them.

Still, the legs grab your attention. Purdy is a double amputee, and her prosthetic limbs carried her with deceptive ease through a recent season of competition on ABC's *Dancing with the Stars*.[2] She and her partner, Derek Hough, finished second, just behind the unsurprising winner, Olympic gold-medalist ice dancer Meryl Davis.

"We have Wonder Woman in this room, I'm telling you!" gushed Bruno Tonioli, one of the show's judges, after Purdy and

Amy Purdy lost her legs to meningitis, then went on to competitive snowboarding, dancing, and appearances with Oprah Winfrey's The Life You Want Weekend *tour. After getting her prosthetics, she said, "I made it a goal to walk as gracefully as possible. It was important to me because I still wanted to be looked at as Amy, not as 'Oh, that girl with prosthetic legs.'"*

Hough had entwined themselves in more ways than you'd think possible throughout a steamy, ingeniously choreographed cha-cha on the season's first episode. The twisting hips and tight, fast footwork posed no problem for Purdy, a competitive snowboarder who won a bronze medal at the 2014 Paralympics in Sochi, Russia.

Tonioli was right. Purdy is a natural superhero, with all the required muscle power and retro-glamour. And those legs: peeking out of her adorable gold-fringed cha-cha pants, gleaming metal rods led to flesh-toned plastic feet—part Terminator, part department-store mannequin. Purdy's bionic limbs give her a fascinating fembot-bombshell look. (She may be too modest to consider herself a bombshell, but "fembot" is a label Purdy proudly embraces in her motivational speeches and her blog, Through the Eyes of a Fembot.)

Purdy is, without question, an inspirational performer. She survived bacterial meningitis in 1999, at age nineteen, which robbed her of her legs, kidney function, the hearing in one ear, and very nearly her life. Seven months after receiving her prosthetics, she was back on her snowboard, regaining the moment-to-moment responsiveness, core strength, and sense of balance that make her a sensation on the dance floor.

"And what have you done with your day?" the show's cohost Erin Andrews deadpanned to the camera, after Purdy described how she had won her medal, flown to Los Angeles, rehearsed, and danced—all in little more than a weekend. Yet what is most extraordinary about her is the sheer beauty—and grace—of her dancing.

You expect to see skin on *Dancing with the Stars,* and glitzy getups and snappy footwork. But for most of the contestants, conveying feeling is the toughest part. Most never get there. Purdy and Hough shade their dancing with emotion without making it forced and schmaltzy. Looks pass between them as if they are sharing secrets. Purdy is all slow burn, swaying her hips like a merengue queen. She isn't the least bit self-conscious or afraid; there's no tension in her shoulders. Even with those mechanical limbs, she has more honest expression and grace in her body than the other contestants have with their full complement of fleshly parts.

In Hough, an Emmy-winning choreographer and previous champion of the show, she has a gifted partner who makes her look good. But he has been transformed by her as well. Perhaps he's wary of upsetting Purdy's balance; perhaps her unflappable equanimity has touched him. What's clear is that Hough has brought his physical expression in line with hers, so it is warmer, more grounded. He doesn't mug outrageously for the judges. He is fully attentive to his partner. Hough appears more human because of the bionic woman in his arms.

There's a Zen saying, "When the shoe fits, we forget the foot." Watching Purdy dance, we forget her disability. It doesn't even seem right to use the word *disability* when the poignancy, emotion, and grace of her dancing can leave you breathless.

On week 3, the contestants were tasked with commemorating the most memorable year of their lives. Purdy chose the year her father gave one of his kidneys to her. A family video from that period shows her in her hospital room, dancing with her dad, twirling under his arm on her new prosthetics before she has mastered walking in them.

"If I can dance, I can walk. And if I can walk, I can snowboard. And I can live a great life," she reasoned at the time, recounting the moment on camera.

The dance that she and Hough performed that week was remarkable, full of images of falling and soaring. At one heart-catching moment, she melted into Hough's arms and he swept her around his back as if she were weightless. As if she were swimming through air.

"I am not my legs," says Purdy.

"We are such stuff as dreams are made on," wrote Shakespeare.

Bodies are temporary; dreams don't have to be.

One day, exoskeletons with electrodes wired into the wearer's brain might enable a paralyzed person to dance, by neurally commanding the limbs. Hugh Herr, head of the Biomechatronics Group at MIT, told me that with such a device, "a person can think, fire their own biological muscles, and the exoskeleton can respond appropriately.

"They could help us learn a new task, like dancing, or playing piano and golf," Herr said. "They could wrap around our bodies and teach us." Like our own personal Derek Hough.

Herr watched *Dancing with the Stars* with interest because he knows Purdy. She has come to MIT to speak with him about collaborating on a better set of limbs for snowboarding, with the limb integrated into the board, he says. Like Purdy, Herr is a double amputee and an athlete, having lost his legs to frostbite while rock climbing in 1982. He has been able to climb better after his accident than before, he says, using specially designed prosthetic limbs.

And unlike flesh and bone, his legs are upgradable.

Dance is a new frontier. Herr recently unveiled a bionic leg specially made for dancing. He designed it for Adrianne Haslet-Davis, a ballroom dance instructor who lost a leg in the Boston Marathon bombing in 2013. That bionic leg was able to return her grace to her: a year later, she danced for the first time since the bombing, padding softly through a brief rumba with a partner at a TED conference in Vancouver.

Inside Haslet-Davis's titanium-and-carbon dancing leg are a motor, wires, tiny computers, and springs that mimic tendons. Unlike the conventional, "passive" prosthesis, this leg "can act like a gas pedal, can thrust," says Herr.

"There is no disability," Herr says. "There is only poor design."

The most meaningful application of grace is to connect us more deeply with one another, even (or perhaps especially?) in the smallest moments, as I experienced in an encounter one year at my town's Fourth of July parade.

Having watched our three children marching by with the swim team, John and I decided we'd cut away from the parade early and avoid the day's rising heat. We were hurrying down the sidewalk toward home when, in my peripheral vision, I saw a man in a wheelchair, stationed on a grassy rise. He had a patch over one eye. His crooked mouth was trying to form words that didn't come, and he was leaning to one side—toward me?—with a feebly lifted arm.

All this I perceived, even as I kept walking, turning over his physical display in my mind. Though his appearance was unusual, there was something cheerful in his good eye, something friendly and familiar in the way he was reaching out. I couldn't shake the vision of his crumpled face and that extended arm, and a few steps later it hit me with a shock: I knew him. His daughter and my eldest son had been in grade school together. The tall, athletic man I'd known from birthday parties and school assemblies was surely suffering the effects of a stroke.

Chagrined that we hadn't recognized him immediately, but

drawn in by his enthusiasm, John and I swung back to where he was sitting. His wife and daughter were next to him. They greeted us warmly, and we spoke for several minutes—small talk about the parade and our kids' college plans. It was clear that the father couldn't speak. But that didn't stop him from joining in, nodding and smiling as best he could. His one eye sparkled. He looked supremely happy to be sitting in the shade with his family. I think he was also pleased that he'd managed to flag down an acquaintance he hadn't seen in years.

He'd done it through grace, pure and simple: welcoming gestures, a kind look and listening attitude, eloquent fillips that connected with a passerby—and rescued her from indifference.

PART FIVE

Understanding Grace:

THEORIES AND PRACTICE

CHAPTER 14

THE SCIENCE OF GRACE:

SURVIVAL OF THE GRACEFUL

What a piece of work is a man! . . . In form and moving how express and admirable!

—William Shakespeare, *Hamlet*

After Roger Federer's Wimbledon win in 2012, data crunchers tabulated his 78 percent success rate at the net, where more than a third of his overall points were won. They counted how many shots he hit from behind the baseline and from inside it, and the percentage of points he won on his first versus his second serves.

But math can't explain what Federer does in tennis.

Science can't fully explain it either, though this much is certain: his flowing tap dance on the tennis court is the result of an exquisitely wired and perfectly functioning brain. With every step, his motor cortex, basal ganglia, and cerebellum are performing feats of hidden harmony, conversing through intricate circuitry to determine Federer's position in space, plan a course of action, finesse the speed and timing, contract the right muscles, and keep his body balanced.

Yet just how Federer's brain accomplishes all its physics and engineering calculations during a single set—even during a single serve—remains a puzzle. Laboratory tools can tell us even less about what sets an extraordinary mover like Federer apart from his peers. How does he receive information through the same neural processes as his opponents and yet respond with such grace? Research can't tell us what gives him his superb awareness, rhythm, and ease—what gives him his qualities of art. Science has no answers for why a fortunate few are more graceful than the rest of us.

Where grace is concerned, the focus in science has been on why some people lack it altogether—that is, why motor system disorders such as Parkinson's rob people of basic, smoothly coordinated movement.

What scientists do know about grace is that it depends on a neural miracle: the intactness of one hundred billion cells in the brain, all working together. Those who study the brain's diseases as well as its flawless operations measure grace in the everyday actions that the rest of us take for granted: the simple act of walking, or lifting a glass of water to the lips.

Apostolos Georgopoulos is a neuroscientist who directs both the Center for Cognitive Sciences at the University of Minnesota and the Brain Sciences Center at the Minneapolis Veterans Affairs Medical Center. The brain mechanisms of movement are his specialty—for example, how we sequence actions and how we process information to increase the speed of movements without affecting accuracy. He speaks with reverence about how brain cells organize themselves for a single, straightforward action such as reaching for a cup of coffee.

"But walking on a tightrope, gymnastics, or even the elegance of a slam dunk in basketball, for that part we know nothing," he told me. "Of the higher levels of coordination, we have no idea."

The reason is that in sophisticated, large-scale actions, many parts of the brain are involved. And that's where you run into the problem of how to measure the systems without affecting them. Given the available technology, neuroscientists can only look at a small part of the brain at any given time. Wireless telemetric devices can record the brain's electrical activity to capture, for instance, abnormal waves that can indicate epilepsy. But capturing the whole-brain activity of a person who is dancing or fencing or leaping on a balance beam remains out of reach.

"Trying to record the brain in a graceful act, we have to intrude on the act," says Georgopoulos. If there was such a thing as telemetric whole-brain assessment, a portable device to allow scientists to look at the entire brain at work, "we could make great strides."

To make matters more complicated, our actions are not purely "motor" in origin. They are sensorimotor, driven by visual input, hearing, bits of news picked up by the muscles and the skin. A number of brain structures take that information and adjust the contractions of various muscles to produce a coherent whole that we consider aesthetically graceful.

How would one begin to pick all that apart?

Scientists know relatively little about the parts of the brain that contribute to smooth motor functioning. Conversely, they know quite a lot about what happens when those parts don't work. Very small problems in the brain's motor structures will show up as tremors, unsteadiness, or other movement deficits. A common first sign of Parkinson's, for example, is trembling in a hand or a finger, which signals a problem in the basal ganglia, a group of structures deep inside the brain that help regulate movement.

But there is an important fact that science can tell us about grace: as long as your brain is intact, you can be as graceful as you want to be. It is simply a matter of practice.

"You and I, if we were trained from our early childhood on graceful motor coordination, we could become as graceful as Nadia Comaneci," says Georgopoulos. "Probably everyone has that capacity. And the earlier you start, the better."

Call it the Georgopoulos Theory of Grace: Practice makes graceful.

What looks like poetry on the tennis court to us is mostly a matter of reflexes and practiced strategies to Roger Federer. It is unceasing practice that allows his brain to engage and activate spontaneously without him thinking too much about it. Repetition produces easier and smoother action as his brain cells fire repeatedly in a certain pattern, which strengthens the connections between the cells. Neurons that fire together wire together, as they say in the brain business. With enough practice, these connections get stronger and stronger, and performance grows easier and easier. Grace becomes habit.

Georgopoulos compares acquiring grace to learning a language. As expressing yourself in a foreign tongue becomes more automatic and fluent with practice, so does easeful moving, even if it is something as relatively small-scale as refining your posture so you have a lighter, more balanced and fluid stride. As in all things, learning is easier if you start young, but the potential is there for all of us.

In fact, our brains want us to get busy with this.

Here's why: the reason that we have a brain is to plan and execute movement. This is what our brains have evolved to do. We are equipped with a brain so we can move and eat and procreate and not get eaten. Maybe you thought we have a brain for thinking? That's just a tiny part of the package.

About 99 percent of our brain is a motor system, and the remaining one percent is there to help the motor system. To boil it down further, the brain is mostly concerned with muscle contraction. It's through muscle contraction that our organism breathes and circulates oxygen, and muscle contraction is how we move our skeleton so we can obtain food, avoid predators, and create relationships and keep them.

Now consider how strange it is—mindless, in fact—that we tend to trivialize our bodies. We hold up the mind, the intellect, as the superior and far more interesting entity. So many of us view our bodies as incidental, inconvenient, disappointing, embarrassing, better to be ignored. We may see the body as an object for adornment or judicious pruning to fit a cultural ideal, rather than as an organism of myriad capabilities whose value lies in its uniqueness, and is deserving of care. We focus most of our efforts and sense of pride on what we accomplish in a contained space with minimal bodily involvement—with our intellect alone. The life of the mind reigns over matters of the flesh. We have, in large part, eradicated activity from our daily lives and replaced it with sedentary habits and the belief that the height of human expression is "using your head," that is to say, perfecting thought and reasoning.

This is not so.

The brain is part of a dynamic system. It fires up the body, and the body, in turn, fires back. It is through the body's experiences, what it relays to the brain, that we apprehend the world. This is what the growing field of embodied cognition is exploring: the idea that just as the mind is tied to the body, so the body influences the mind.

Think about how physically rooted our language is. We describe abstract concepts and feelings in bodily terms: the future lies ahead; the past is behind us. We say someone "leaves us cold" or "looks hot"; we feel "up" when we're perky and "down" when we're fatigued, depressed, and slump-shouldered.

The body comes first. Understanding our moving, physical selves and valuing not only surface beauty but the movement ideal—the graceful—enriches our appreciation of humanity in general. The mystery of movement is part of its enchantment. Think about it: nobody truly understands how we move. Even for neurologists, complete understanding is a long way off. The mechanisms by which our brains orchestrate our movements, getting our bodies out into the world, which is at the very core of our evolutionary mandate, remain obscure.

Neuroscientists turn awestruck when they talk about the secret choreography of those hundred billion brain cells, all working together to produce graceful motion. "It's all amazing," says Georgopoulos, describing the wonders of the neural dance. "Until you start looking at the brain and you're even more amazed. How does all of that work so flawlessly?"

Consider some of the most graceful physical displays: Olga Korbut's joyful Olympic floor routine, say. Controlling the body while it sails through the many actions involved, calibrating the force and speed of all the muscles and connective tissues, harnessing and extending the joints, adjusting blood flow and breathing, maintaining balance and spatial awareness: what a production! What the brain has to accomplish to put us in motion is much more impressive than what goes on during the thinking process. Especially when we're sitting down and thinking, which is what most of us do all day, which means that while we may believe we're being high-minded (to use an embodied term) while we're stationed at our desks, we are in effect sending a good portion of our gray matter out to lunch.

On some level, you already know this. You know that some of your best ideas come to you while you're out for a run or a walk. (Albert Einstein reportedly thought up the theory of relativity while riding his bike.) You return from the gym, the pool, or a run more clear-headed than when you set out.

Our moving bodies literally shape our brains. Studies show exercise helps us think and learn by raising growth factor chemicals in the brain, which build new connections between the brain cells involved in learning.[1] The more complicated the physical coordination involved—such as in a dance class or a tennis match—the bigger the brain boost. Why? The brain is more challenged when the body tackles a complicated activity. Brain cells, like muscles, need a physical workout in order to grow.

German researchers found that after a complicated ten-minute fitness routine, high school students scored better on tasks demanding a high degree of attention than those who had pursued regular activity. Those who hadn't exercised at all did the worst.[2] Research suggests exercise may even stimulate the growth of neurons in brain regions damaged by depression.[3] And a Canadian study showed that in the elderly, mild activity such as walking slowed declines in memory and cognition, as compared with sedentary peers.[4]

Results of a study in China suggest that longtime practice of tai chi chuan, the graceful, slow-moving martial art that focuses on balance, coordination, and relaxation, may reshape the brain in the way aerobic exercise can; studies also show tai chi can improve memory and thinking.[5] Physical activity is so strongly connected to brain benefits, in fact, that the Alzheimer's Association promotes regular exercise as a way to lower the risk of getting the disease and other forms of dementia, and to slow their onset.[6]

But this is a book about grace, not an exercise manual. What does this have to do with being graceful? Let's return to the Georgopoulos Theory of Grace: it is all about doing. Practice moving—walking, playing tennis, dancing—and you will get better at it. Not only that, but you will get better at moving in general. You will move more gracefully by moving more, period.

Moving gracefully, with upright, lifted posture and smooth, coordinated movements, has benefits beyond our own aesthetic and sensual enjoyment. There are ripple effects to grace, which are felt by those around us. How we move affects others, because we are natural imitators. Our brains are oiled to copy motor patterns.

"You see children, how they pick up mannerisms from their peers? It is natural, innate, spontaneous," says Georgopoulos. "You don't have to teach anyone.

"You see it in monkeys. One will start something very, very gracefully, jumping from branch to branch, and all of a sudden the whole group will be doing it. It's very common. People are the same way: we mimic motor stuff. And if that motor stuff is graceful, that mimicry will become graceful."

Just picture it: You, walking around with the calm, graceful stride of Catherine Deneuve or Sidney Poitier, your body a glorious instrument of buoyancy, inspiring admirers and imitators at every turn. Spreading elegant moves and the good feelings that go with them. How you will be beautifying the world!

But you will not become more graceful contemplating the idea in a hammock. (Though, fellow hedonists, I am otherwise resolutely pro-hammock. Nothing declares your independence from domestic drudgery like a hammock.)

"Life is like riding a bicycle," wrote Albert Einstein to his son. "To keep your balance you must keep moving."[7] Our ability to sit and stew is really not so special. In fact, at least some of the human capacity to process data, calculate, hypothesize, and reason can be duplicated and even surpassed by machines. Look at Deep Blue, the computer that vanquished chess grandmaster Garry Kasparov. In 2011, its room-size successor, Watson, beat a pair of top-ranked human competitors in a contest with even more complicated rules than chess, the TV game show *Jeopardy!*[8]

Yet machines are a long way from replicating lifelike movement. Grace, in fact, is something robotics engineers have yet to achieve. Even the most realistic-looking androids produced by Japanese roboticists on the leading edge of bot technology fall far short of executing the smooth, nonjerky gestures of their human creators.[9]

Indeed, there are few creatures in the world (an octopus, for instance) that can top the range and complexity of the human body in motion.

"There is only one temple in the world and this is the human body," wrote the German romantic poet and philosopher Novalis, whose devotion to the flesh is all the more poignant because he died at age twenty-eight. "Nothing is holier than its sublime form. . . . One touches Heaven when one touches the body of man."

The lives of a Borneo orangutan and her baby depend on grace in the treetops.

. . .

KIKO'S LONG ARMS are soft and loose, like a rag doll's. His whole body looks relaxed and loose, no matter how he moves. He's a copper-colored Cary Grant, silkily at ease even when he's scaling a fifty-foot tower to reach the steel cables of the National Zoo's Orangutan Transport System.

This soaring network, called the O Line for short, is a jewel of Washington's zoo. It stretches high overhead from one primate building to another, letting orangutans like Kiko do what they love to do: swing freely through the air. It's the next best thing to a canopy of fruit trees.

It's also an immersion in graceful behaviors. Watching the fluid physicality of Kiko and his companions as they glide across the void, defying gravity, betraying no exertion whatsoever, is an utter delight. The orangs invariably attract a crowd when they're out in the open loping along the cables.

We cloddier earthbound primates can't resist our distant cousins. In fact, these shaggy orangs are the key to assembling a theory of grace.

In his poem "Eleanore," Alfred Lord Tennyson tells his sweetheart what he loves about her in a way that could be an index of grace. He writes of "full-flowing harmony" and the "luxuriant symmetry/of thy floating gracefulness" and adds:

For in thee
Is nothing sudden, nothing single;
Like two streams of incense free
From one censer in one shrine,
Thought and motion mingle,
Mingle ever. Motions flow
To one another, even as tho'
They were modulated so
To an unheard melody . . .

I love this poem for the way it highlights inner and outer grace—the one mirroring the other—and for Tennyson's entwining of Eleanore's wondrous movement quality with the intangibles of smoke and scented air. Such a creature seems a long way from earthy, hairy Kiko. Yet in crucial ways, the two are not so far apart. Our tree-dwelling ancestors diverged from Kiko's about thirteen million years ago, but we still share 97 percent of our DNA with orangutans. We're a notch closer to chimpanzees and bonobos, our closest primate relatives, from whom we split about six million years ago. According to the leading primatologist Frans de Waal, director of the Living Links Center at Emory University's Yerkes Primate National Research Center, evidence suggests that just a few million years ago, well after we had become bipedal, we were probably still climbing into trees at night to sleep and avoid predators.

Our tree history has been with us for a very long time, and it is still present in our brains and our bodies. We spent millions upon millions of years climbing and swinging through forest canopies, avoiding our enemies down below and feeding on the sweet fruits up above. We were beautifully adapted for this, with broad chests, upright backs, and lovely loose shoulders that rotated smoothly, allowing us to brachiate, or swing arm over arm. We still carry that physiology with us: our shoulders remain our most flexible joints, capable of movement in every direction, though twenty-first-century habits tend to tighten them up. Evolution didn't plan for purses, driving, keyboards, or the muscular crunch that comes from trying to hold the phone with your neck.

There was a lot at stake in how we moved through the meshwork of branches all those years ago. It was a wobbly, complicated environment, more air than surface. Locomotion was difficult up there. We had to bridge gaps in the canopy and stay balanced on curved, flexible tree limbs, and we had to do all that accurately and quietly. A missed handhold could be fatal. Crashing around noisily could rouse a predatory bird or a tree-climbing tiger. Agility was essential when outmaneuvering enemies or scoring a fig supper.

The complexity of the arboreal habitat "requires a lot of acrobatic moves," de Waal told me. Look at the rhythmic timing and the coordinated gripping and releasing that primates use in brachiating, he said. "They need to make smooth movements because if not, they'll fall. It is critical that they do this right." It's especially important for large primates, who are most at risk of death from falling. Kiko is a good example. Orangutan means "person of the forest" in Malay; with males often topping two hundred pounds, orangutans are the largest tree-dwelling animal. They brachiate with ease, but you'll never see one of them jump excitedly from tree to tree, as monkeys do. Orangutans are very deliberate—and much more graceful—in their movements, as Kiko demonstrated with his unhurried, exquisitely smooth bearing.

It's a safe bet that our ancestors would have noticed if one of their kind wasn't very good at swinging through trees. De Waal has observed chimps slowing down for a fellow chimp who limps. On the other hand, he has also seen males attack a limping male to take over its position in the chimp hierarchy. For our ancestors, too, we can assume that moving poorly would have had social consequences in addition to being a safety risk.

So how did we manage?

"We have been selected to be acrobatic, basically," said de Waal.

Our proto–Cirque du Soleil selves had to make constant body adjustments, for one thing. Primates have one of the largest movement vocabularies of all mammals, from the wide range of motion in the limbs to the delicate grasping abilities of the fingers.[10] Swooping from branch to branch like shaggy pendulums was swift and energy-efficient, allowing us to use gravity to travel along a smooth trajectory with a minimum of effort. It was almost like flying, as long as our transitions from branch to branch were steady, fluid, and unbroken.[11] Gibbons, a distant (and ultra-acrobatic) relative, can brachiate through trees at speeds up to thirty-five miles per hour. Among today's homo sapiens, however, it's mostly kindergarteners and CrossFit junkies who carry on the proud brachiating tradition. The rest of us have been out of practice too long and lack the upper-body muscle to support our adult weight.

Up in the trees, the looping, rhythmic grace of brachiating was important. It allowed us to avoid predators, search for food, and move about freely in an otherwise difficult habitat. We can see echoes of the primal, pendulum-type mechanics that we once lived by in many activities: in the waltz, with its swooping one-two-three rhythm; in our delight in the curving trajectories of figure skaters and ice dancers; and in the fluid, metronomic back-and-forth of a tennis volley.

The ease of motion, harmony, and flow that we admire today in graceful movers are all part of the primate repertoire. Looking at our evolutionary past, it's possible to arrive at a theory about one function of grace: it helped us flourish in the trees. What modern humans see as graceful behaviors would have contributed to moving safely through our primal environment.

If graceful movement was important to our ability to thrive, it makes sense that evolution would build in a positive response to it. One can venture to say that our ancestral brains recognized graceful behaviors as useful and worthy of imitating, and our emotional response developed in kind.

I spoke about this with Lawrence Parsons, a cognitive neuroscientist at the Centre de Neuroscience Cognitive in Bron, France, outside Lyon. He studies how the brain perceives music and dance. Though there is no way to test the idea that we're attracted to grace because our precursors may have lived by it, he said, it's a plausible guess.

"One theory of why we have emotions is that they're wired in to help us, in complicated situations, do the right thing," he said. "If I'm hanging around in trees, figuring out how to survive without getting eaten by hyenas and birds, I have to pay attention to how other primates move. I have to look at it, it feels good to look at it, and the more I look the more I learn about it."

Physical grace would have still mattered once we left the trees and started walking around on the African plain. Soft, silent locomotion, agility, and fine motor control would have helped us evade our enemies. Gracefulness also signaled the healthy workings of an intact brain, guiding a body that was able to feed itself and accomplish everything else needed to survive. Insofar as grace correlates with health, our graceful ancestors would likely have been prize catches, matewise.

As balladeers from Tennyson to James Taylor and the Beatles have reminded us, the way we move has long been key to landing lovers.

Emily Cross is a cognitive neuroscientist and senior lecturer at Bangor University in Wales, where she studies body coordination and learning by scanning the brains of dancers, gymnasts, and contortionists. She believes there is an argument to be made that easy, graceful movement factored into mate choice in our long-ago past. Scientists refer to such effortless-seeming movement as "efficient," since energy isn't wasted in uncoordinated, disorganized actions that can lead to fatigue and strain.

"From an evolutionary perspective, we want to spread genes

with people who move efficiently versus an individual who can't move efficiently," she said.

"Our evolution has selected for those who can move more smoothly and effectively and beautifully," she continued. "Those who have the utmost motor control and can make the body do exactly what they want, who can produce super-smooth, super-efficient movement, and make it look easy: that's what human biology is aiming to get to."

ANOTHER NEUROBIOLOGICAL piece of the grace puzzle is a phenomenon that we share not just with primates but with all mammals: empathy.

For centuries, philosophers have been theorizing about our sympathetic feeling for one another's experiences. Adam Smith touched on it in 1759 in his first book, *The Theory of Moral Sentiments*. The Scottish philosopher who would later champion self-interest as the key to prosperity in *The Wealth of Nations* looked at "fellow feeling" as a cerebral matter, an act of will and imagination.

Wrote Smith in *Moral Sentiments*: "Though our brother is on the rack, as long as we ourselves are at our ease, our senses will never inform us of what he suffers. They never did, and never can, carry us beyond our own person, and it is by the imagination only that we can form any conception of what are his sensations."[12]

In 1852, British philosopher and political thinker Herbert Spencer took a different view, applying the concept of sympathy to the idea of grace. Like his contemporary Charles Darwin, Spencer was an advocate of evolutionary theory. In fact, it was he, not Darwin, who coined the phrase "survival of the fittest." Spencer also had wide-ranging tastes. He was a connoisseur of dance, for one thing. Perhaps this is why he took up physical grace as a matter of philosophical inquiry. As a dance-goer, he would have been accustomed to the feeling of being swept away by the performers' musical whirlings, which may have been the source of his deeper understanding of our internal connections to others—something that was, apparently, beyond Smith's experience.

Indeed, Spencer's essay "Gracefulness" was inspired by a bad dancer. As he watched her, he wrote, he was "inwardly condemning her *tours de force* as barbarisms which would be hissed, were not people such cowards as to always applaud what they think it is the fashion to applaud."[13] (I've seen this phenomenon countless times, and you may have, too. Once one primate starts to react, it's natural for the rest to imitate. We are easily steered by the actions and emotions of our fellow apes. Even in the opera house.) Yet this dancer's overexertion helped illuminate for Spencer its opposite. What is essential to grace, he concluded, is economy of force. To move gracefully, one needs to minimize force rather than overdo it.

But why, Spencer asked, should the dancer's surplus of force be so distasteful to him? The answer must be that in watching her, he felt the strain of her efforts in his own body. "I may as well here venture the hypothesis, that the idea of Grace as displayed by other beings, has its subjective basis in Sympathy," he wrote.

> The same faculty which makes us shudder on seeing another in danger . . . gives us a vague participation in all the muscular sensations which those around us are experiencing. When their motions are violent or awkward,

> we feel in a slight degree the disagreeable sensations which we should have were they our own. When they are easy, we sympathize with the pleasant sensations they imply in those exhibiting them.[14]

According to this view, in some barely perceptible way, when we behold the flowing movements of the orangutans, or the apparent effortlessness of Federer's gliding serve and catlike landing, it's not just that we like the way they move aesthetically. We feel their gracefulness in our bodies, too.

In the nineteenth century, the Germans came up with the name *Einfühlung*, or "feeling into," for what we now know as empathy. Our feeling-into ability is a big reason why watching graceful movement is so pleasurable.

We identify closely with the bodies of others. We feel their motions—we fly along with trapeze artists and sprinters blazing down a track—and we also feel their emotions. Who didn't exult when Usain Bolt threw up his arms in victory after bounding over the finish line at the Beijing Olympics? We pick up the feelings of other people viscerally, without thinking about it.

Sensing these emotions isn't the same thing as mind reading. It's more like mind feeling. The word *emotion* derives from motion, after all. Its origin is in the Latin *e-* plus *movere*, or "moving out," in the sense of displacing and stirring up. Those who coined the word realized that our feelings are rooted in physical disruption. We sense them bodily before giving them cognitive meaning.

Your average dog and cat also have empathy, as anyone knows who's been sick in bed with his pets arrayed around him.

"All these empathy mechanisms go back to maternal care," de Waal told me. "That predisposes females especially to be sensitive to the emotions of offspring, because they needed to pay attention to hunger or danger. It's common to all mammals."

At times, this brain circuitry can be a little inconvenient. When my husband and I took our feverish eight-year-old son to the hospital and doctors drew blood from his arm, he winced—and I was the one who fainted. I didn't have time to think, "Gee, I bet that hurts him. It must feel really bad. Oww . . ." Just seeing the needle poke into his arm was enough to make me swoon.

I'm a wreck during my other son's wrestling matches, where I can scarcely breathe. My daughter won't go to them anymore; she finds them too stressful, and she means the physical, stomach-cramping stress we all experience to some degree or another when we feel into someone else's distress. Spectators recoil when a football play leaves athletes writhing on the field. A dancer's slip onstage is always accompanied by spontaneous gasps from the audience.

But it's not just pain that connects us empathetically to other people. It's pleasure as well. Greg Louganis's dives not only look good to us, they feel good to us, too. We feel into his gracefulness. We're swept into his slipstream, carried along by his silky spiraling and unfolding, and by the arrow's flight of his body as he pierces the water.

Neuroimaging studies bear out the human pull toward graceful movement, said Cross, the neuroscientist in Wales. She has seen this while studying how the brain engages with art. "The brains of perceivers are so strongly attracted to graceful movement—efficiency and smoothness of movement, as in athletes, dancers, and martial artists, all of these groups who have incredible control and kinesthetic awareness," she said. "We say, 'Yes, that's efficient, and yes, I want to watch that,' so the brain is more rewarded by watching that than by watching not-so-efficient movement."

Dancers and stage actors will tell you that they become so attuned to one another's movements and sensations that they can feel their colleagues' emotions pass right through them, even when their backs are turned. In a recent interview on NPR, Cate Blanchett spoke of feeling the degree to which her audience is paying attention when she performs live theater. "You know that someone is answering their mobile phone in Row G, and that someone else is opening a lolly wrapper in the back of the stalls," she said. "And so you have all of these awarenesses, and it makes you fearless, in a way. Because you can tell whether something is living or dying when you're on the stage, and you can do something about it."[15]

Similarly, movie actors such as Cary Grant, Christopher Walken, and Rita Moreno learned in their live performing experience a sensitivity and empathy that they could employ even on film. Able to communicate that living connection with their fellow performers and with the audience, they come across as especially three-dimensional, warm, and spontaneous—and graceful. Feeling into one another's energies is not New Agey mysticism, it's not a sci-fi supernatural force. The notion that you and I might feel each other's "muscular sensations" appears to be supported by science.

"WE HAVE THIS dedicated neural tissue that responds to other bodies in motion," explained Cross. "It's special circuitry that has evolved in a very specialized way in the human brain."

Studies suggest that there can be a flow of information from one brain to another, as we map other people's physical circumstances into our own sensorimotor system.[16]

"It's a key element to why humans are humans," said Lawrence Parsons, who has conducted numerous studies on how we identify with the orientation of another human body, and how we mentally simulate the actions of others. "One of the strengths of our species is we are so socially connected. So we have more skills and variable strategies through our collective intelligence than other creatures. We empathize so much with our fellow beings that even without language we pick up what they've experienced. We don't have to spend time explaining things. It allows us to build in our own mind what it would be like if it happened to us.

"These types of skills are grand strategies to keep ourselves alive," he continued. "If you want to know how to walk through a forest in a way that a lion won't hear you, you see others doing it, you think of yourself doing it, and then you do it. That empathy is a very important, highly powerful learning system, for the individual, the group and the species."

In primitive cultures, as Parsons points out, everybody danced and everybody made music and they all danced and sang together as a way to tell stories. Now we're specialized; some folks are performers but most of us are just observers. This ability we have to feel what others are doing and to replicate it internally to some extent gives us a way in to activities that used to be communal.

Most of us don't live acrobatic lives, either. Watching elite athletes and subtly triggering our own sensorimotor systems may be the only way we can stimulate our otherwise dormant athletic natures. When the activities we observe are graceful, so much the better. They leave their restorative traces in our nervous systems, and our pleasure buttons get a workout, too. (Of course, the system also works with other aspects of pleasure. Plenty of activities and art use dissonance and jerkiness and roughness, all of which can have a kind of beauty as well.)

Adam Smith didn't go far enough. It is not only through our imagination that we make a guess about what others are experiencing. It is also through our nervous systems. This is where empathy originates: feeling into others. Bodies talking to bodies, as de Waal describes it in his illuminating book on the subject, *The Age of Empathy: Nature's Lessons for a Kinder Society.* Mammals that we are, we unconsciously coordinate our movements with one another, starting from infancy. Babies synchronize their movements with adults. You know this if you've ever had an exchange of fish faces with an infant.

Yawns are notoriously contagious. So is the physicality of emotion. If a friend is describing her traffic woes, waving her arms about as she recalls all the bottlenecks and bad drivers, chances are your shoulders will tense up, too, and you'll nod in time with her agitated rhythm. When someone recounts something sad, you lean forward and tilt your head, and your eyes may moisten in sympathy.

An athlete knows to avoid nervous competitors and onlookers before a race because the tensions of others will tighten his muscles up, too. This is why you see skiers, cyclists, and runners preparing for their starts with eyes shut and headphones on.

But there is a positive side to bodily empathy. Our heat conked out this past winter just before Christmas, which meant the parts to fix it didn't come in until after New Year's. After the charm of walking around in blankets wore off, we endured a week of physical strain, the unconscious effect of hugging ourselves inward against a cold spell that electric heaters did little to ease. But on New Year's Eve, a couple of my teenage son's friends showed up. They had ridden their bikes over in the arctic weather (one was in shorts!), and to them, our house was a haven. They tumbled in, laughing, bright-faced and jolly. They possessed a kind of messy, energizing, effortless grace, and it inspired a complete change of atmosphere.

Board games came out, macaroni and cheese went in the oven; we ate in front of a corny video of a roaring fire. The change was physical, too. Feeding off the boys' high spirits, everyone loosened up, laughed, and felt uplifted, and the house grew warmer in a meaningful way.

We are made for socializing. Each of us has social cravings in varying degrees, some more, some less. But we are inherently social animals. This is why solitary confinement is the worst criminal punishment we can inflict, short of death. We are forever minding other people's business, and that is why it is important to recognize the mark that grace—just like awkwardness or abruptness—leaves on our bodies and emotions. We tune in to one another's movements, so graceful actions send out waves of pleasure. Thinking of grace this way, isn't it worthwhile to pause a few moments to hold the door for someone behind you, or to smooth your breathless haste into a calm and cheerful demeanor as you approach a meeting, or to welcome someone into your group who is standing uncertainly by the door? We feel a graceful act deep inside, and it feels good, even when someone else is performing it.

Bodily empathy is social glue. Group leaders have long intuited this; witness how many group endeavors, be they kids' summer camps or management retreats, begin with some kind of physical centering activity. When I was in sixth grade, my homeroom started every morning with a patriotic song, which we belted out while standing at our desks. I wish the tradition were still carried on, but sadly it was missing from my children's experience, though they were in the same school district I was. They don't know those vintage American folk songs my generation can sing in its sleep: "My Country 'Tis of Thee," "This Land Is Your Land," "It's a Grand Old Flag," and so on. Just as important, the act of producing music from within our bodies drew a bunch of rowdy prepubescents together as a group with a minimum of effort, and with widespread enjoyment. We all tuned in to that—physically as well as musically. The delight of singing brought about a graceful transition from arrival to schoolwork.

Think of grace as the artistic, empathetic side of an embodied language that humans have been speaking throughout time. Our actions speak louder than words, as the saying goes; why not soften them, round them, make them graceful?

The dance world has raised bodily empathy into an art form. One of choreographer Paul Taylor's most popular works is called *Esplanade*. It is accompanied by Bach's Violin Concerto in E Major and the Concerto for Two Violins in D Minor, music that can be delicate and unhurried but also urgent, like fireflies bearing momentous news. While you might expect these elegant string compositions to be matched with formal, dignified patterns of movement, Taylor's dance consists of rather ordinary walking, running, standing still, and devil-may-care sliding across the floor, all strung together with deceptive naturalness and exuberance. This is the ordinary raised to extraordinary, for in the last minutes the dance builds to an ecstatic outpouring of rolling and tumbling. Taylor says he was inspired by the sight of a girl running to catch a bus. Maybe he also saw her trip and fall, for here is a great big casserole of falls: dancers plunge forward and backward, spin and swan-dive to the stage.

But Taylor shows us that falling can lead to flying; it's all a matter of rhythm. The dancers' falls are part of an arcing pendulum trajectory: they swing through the air, fall, roll, and swing up again. Momentum carries the dancers onward and upward; thrillingly, they carry us with them. Soon the women are taking flying leaps into the arms of their partners, one after the other, bounding into the air to the beat of the Bach, and our spirits sail alongside. It's one of the most uplifting dances you can see, because you feel that uplift, too. For a few wonderful moments you feel as if you're whirling, spinning, and swinging, too, flying through the air as naturally as breathing.

Taylor likes to tuck in a dark side, shading every joy with the knowledge that it may not last. But here's the consolation offered in *Esplanade*, as in so many of his works, and as in life itself: in the end, it's the twin graces of movement and companionship that can pull us out of the depths. Science and art both prove it.

CHAPTER 15

AMAZING GRACE:

RELIGION WITHOUT JUDGMENT

Nothing else in the world matters but the kindness of grace,
God's gift to suffering mortals.

—Jack Kerouac

I DON'T REMEMBER the first time I ever heard the song "Amazing Grace." But I do remember the first time I noticed it.

I was sixteen and serving as a United States Senate page. We were grandiosely known as Democracy's Messengers, though really we were just pimply gofers in blue blazers, and when we weren't delivering packages and documents through the network of underground passageways between the congressional offices, we were planning things like how to get fake IDs so we could drink and dance at the discotheques in Georgetown. Sometimes we did a little homework. We attended school for a few hours before dawn in the attic of the Library of Congress, the small top layer of the ornate

Beaux Arts confection known as the Thomas Jefferson Building. Our school, just above the Great Hall, was as dusty and romantic as it sounds. We took a rickety elevator each morning to a warren of manual typewriters and antique microscopes; from its high windows we watched the Capitol dome across the street turn pink in the rising sun.

The cloakrooms adjacent to the Capitol's Senate chamber were a kind of clubhouse for us, where we sprawled on the long leather sofas when the Senate wasn't in session. Among the cloakroom staff on the Democratic side, where I worked, was a former page in his early twenties named David. We girl pages, and there were only a few of us, all had crushes on David. He was a rosy-cheeked Adonis out of Alabama, with a drawl as thick as pudding, a wicked sense of humor, and a head of glossy Pre-Raphaelite curls. (This was the late 1970s.) He could sweet-talk the most condescending congressional staffer, though many a phone call earned a chipper "Fuck you very much" from him, muttered under his breath after he'd hung up. His usual lunch was an oily indulgence of grilled cheese slathered in mayonnaise. Everything about him seemed decadent and wild, including this: he was getting his private pilot's license on the weekends.

One Monday morning we arrived in the cloakroom to discover that David had died in flames in a plane crash back home.

We pages liked to think of ourselves as quite adult and supremely distanced from the typical high school grind, but in many ways we were lost, unguarded children. Forget the dimly lit corridors and tunnels we prowled with our packages; the darker labyrinth we traveled each day was one of myriad adolescent anxieties, and we navigated it all on our own. Capitol Hill had no other young people. We were surrounded by crusty old congressmen hawking chaw into the cloakroom's brass spittoons, jowly scowlers whose heavy-hitting steps made folks scatter. David's death was incomprehensible any way you looked at it, but I was stuck on this: Of all the adults we saw every day—most of whom were remote, weighed down, and, to us, near death themselves—how could it be that our David, the buoyant free spirit, was the one who fell?

In the confusion that followed, I didn't have much interest in the memorial service that was hastily organized for the pages, and I attended it disconsolate, tuning out the speeches. Then a girl I knew stepped to the microphone onstage, a sweet, pretty House page from Mississippi. She had been a swimsuit model and gave facials in her dorm room; I knew she was a big believer in the benefits of olive oil and Jesus Christ. Unaccompanied, and in a clear, ringing alto, she began to sing "Amazing Grace." And everything changed.

The words distilled exactly my feelings at hearing them, feelings mingled with the weirdness of my first experience with death: *how sweet the sound / that saved a wretch like me / I once was lost / but now I'm found / was blind but now I see*. Wretched, lost: that was me. And I wasn't alone. It was a transformational moment, where the gloomy auditorium seemed suddenly boundless and all the scattered reactions pulling me in different directions dissolved, replaced by a calming sense of connection. I felt connected to the slow rising and falling of the tune, to the shining strength of the voice, and to everyone around me. At the same time I was released from self-pity; I entered a mode of wonder. The controlled emotion and sincerity of the song lifted us all up, I imagine; it lifted me up, anyway.

I'm not much of a religious person (my Jewish upbringing was, let's say, subtle), but at that time I felt the spiritual dimension of grace, as a comfort to the soul, a reminder of love, and a luminous portal to something beyond ourselves. "Amazing Grace," surely one of the best-known songs in the English-speaking world, has an uncannily graceful way of blending a verbal message of hope with the living sensation of it. You can't hear that song without feeling some stir of longing or resolve, and you most assuredly don't have to be Christian to identify with it. Part of its popularity is that it is nondenominational: in its long history it has spoken to those of many faiths, and to folk singers, pop stars, and protesters. It jumped from the Baptist hymnals of the white Southern plantation owners to the Sunday gatherings of their slaves, who were drawn to its message of liberation; from there it traveled through African-American history to become a staple of gospel singers and civil rights marchers.[1] It has been an anthem of the antiwar movement and, played on bagpipes, it became a chart-topping recording of the Royal Scots Dragoon Guards, a regiment of the British Army. It resounded through innumerable memorial services and gatherings after the attacks of September 11, 2001. It was sung by Germans at the opening of Berlin's Brandenburg Gate in 1989, an expression of optimism for a divided city and divided country on its way to unification.

Could the author of "Amazing Grace," the eighteenth-century English poet and clergyman John Newton, have known how powerful his words would be, and how universal they would become? They would not be put to the familiar tune until long after his death, but when he preached those verses at his small country church on New Year's Day, 1773, his focus was clear: to celebrate salvation through God's infinite and undeserved mercy. A former slave trader, Newton credited God for delivering him from an ocean storm, and as in Paul's conversion on the road to Damascus, the spiritual effects were lifelong. Newton renounced slavery and dedicated himself to preaching the gospel of love, gratitude, and grace.

But exactly what is the religious grace that "Amazing Grace" extols? Certainly, there are more ways than one to look at it, even for believers. While much of this book discusses gracefulness as a natural quality as well as a cultivated one, acquired through attention and practice, many religions view grace as a gift from the divine. For Christians, it's a gift in the purest sense: a total freebie, and you can't do anything to deserve or merit it. It comes to you no matter how screwed up you are. God simply pours it into you, from His heart to yours.

This action of pouring out, or offering, is embedded in the word for "grace" in the original Greek of the New Testament. The Greek word *charis,* which is the singular form of *charites,* is translated as "grace." But biblical scholars note that an early meaning is "favor," as in a gift or act of kindness that one person extends to another. *Charis* implies physically reaching out, inclining or leaning toward someone, in a gesture of offering. (This brings us back to the Charites of ancient mythology, the demigoddesses who reached out to others with their gifts of joy and pleasure.) *Charis* is a dynamic word. The way I see it, the *charis* of God is like the beginning of an irresistible dance, a cosmic cha-cha. He offers His hand, inviting you to join Him, promising to hold you up if you trip. In giving you the divine favor of grace, God, like a sensitive dance partner, is giving you Himself.

Grace "is God's own life, the very life of God, unmerited and unconditional. That's why it's important: it's a life source," said Michael K. Holleran, a Catholic priest at the Church of Notre Dame at New York's Columbia University, when I asked him about the meaning of grace.

"Grace can also be an aesthetic sense, whereby all our actions become graceful," he continued. "Our thoughts, words, and actions are transformed by it." Father Michael is also a Buddhist teacher who spent twenty-two years in the silent order of Carthusian monks. He's a passionate advocate of the contemplative tradition. Though it may seem paradoxical, the dynamism of grace is an important part of that tradition. The force of divine life and love flowing from the Almighty to us, who ideally pass it on, is fundamental to the mystery of God, and to our own mystery.

"For many years I have danced my morning prayer; I follow the inner motions of the psalms," he told me. "I just can't contain it. When I celebrate mass, it's also a dance, with all the gestures. There's a divine choreographer: our whole life can become a dance, sometimes graceful, sometimes more like a modern dance, but it's all grace, all divine movement."

We happened to be speaking on February 11, the Feast of Our Lady of Lourdes, which marks the day the Virgin Mary is believed to have revealed herself to a girl in the French town of Lourdes. We got to talking about the traditional Catholic prayer, the Hail Mary, whose opening line "Hail Mary, full of grace" refers to something more than how the mother of Jesus walked around the town of Nazareth.

"She has a superabundance of life and love. She's so completely full of grace, it can't go beyond," said Father Michael. "We believe that Mary is a channel, the purveyor of this divine love. She can be approached much as the Buddha is approached, for divine energy. Mary and Joseph pour it out to others, and we are called to do that, to pour grace out to others. It's dynamic. That's why the image of the dance is expressively so full."

It's not an easy task, pouring out unconditional love to others.

God's ability to do it provokes awe, as John Newton so movingly put into words: ". . . that saved a wretch like me." "It often takes the experience of failure to open us up," Father Michael continued. "You know, 'Boy, I made a complete mess of this, but here is God, filling me up with love.' That's why it's so amazing to us. As it should be. It's unmerited, which is what love should be, and it inspires us to treat others that way. That's how the whole world can be transformed."

James Martin, a Jesuit priest who was a regular on Comedy Central's *The Colbert Report* and wrote the best-selling *The Jesuit Guide to (Almost) Everything*, also sees grace as a reaching out, an offer to ease hardship with love. He calls it "God's self-communication to us."

"Grace means that we are given a taste of what God is like, and when we have an encounter with God we feel encouraged and lifted up and consoled," Martin said. "It's what helps us to really flourish. Not just get through life, but to shine and do more than you would think you could do." He gave the example of the funeral of a close friend that he led recently, from counseling the family to writing a homily and celebrating the Mass. "It was really draining. And I look back and say, 'How was I able to do that?' The answer is God's grace. How is it that people found what I said comforting? It's God's grace."

But though he sees grace every day, Martin finds the appreciation of it is missing. "It's not that people don't experience grace, it's that they're not given invitations to talk about it. They're not invited to think about it. We lead such hectic, nonreflective lives. . . . It's a question of noticing." The Middle Ages had its problems, but one aspect worth revisiting is that "noticing God was part of

For Christians, the Virgin Mary possesses a superabundance of life and love, and thus is a purveyor of grace. The Madonna, *by Martin Schongauer, c. 1490–91.*

daily life. The world was suffused with a sense of God's presence. Today, society encourages us to produce and keep busy." But what if we worked just as hard at recognizing the moments of grace around us? Martin offers a miniparable: Instead of pecking away at e-mails, you pause and pay attention to your kid when he comes home from school excited about acing a test. Imagine how he would feel! And how you would feel. That's all grace.

So is *any*thing—and everything—a form of grace? Yes, in Martin's view. "I think a saint is someone who sees every moment in life as grace-filled, every moment as an opportunity to encounter God." In other words, one who notices the beauty in the ordinary and sees life as miraculous.

"Not noticing: that's a tragedy," Martin said. "Grace is an experience, and the first way to experience something is to notice it. And as we Jesuits say, savor it."

When I asked Martin Marty about grace, the prominent Lutheran religious scholar and emeritus professor of the University of Chicago Divinity School quoted a poem by British Victorian poet and Jesuit priest Gerard Manley Hopkins. Titled "God's Grandeur," it describes the maternal sense of the Divine, endowing the world with beauty and grace through direct, palpable contact, just as a hen tends her eggs. The poem begins: "The world is charged with the grandeur of God," and it ends thus:

And though the last lights off the black West went
Oh, morning, at the brown brink eastward, springs—
Because the Holy Ghost over the bent
World broods with warm breast and with ah! bright wings.

In the Torah, the first mention of grace is in reference to Noah, whose moral righteousness was favored by God. Noah Leading the Animals into the Ark, *by Francois-Andre Vincent after Giovanni Benedetto Castiglione, 1774.*

This protective grace, Marty said, is also a power, at once ordering and freeing. Rather than being an abstraction, grace is visible in concrete human actions.

"The love of Christ controls us. Why? Because it's liberating," he said. "It turns you loose. You get to transcend boundaries." As an example, he cites Pope Francis's gesture of service to the poor during Easter Week, soon after he was elected. Traditionally, popes have observed Holy Thursday by ceremonially washing the feet of twelve priests chosen to represent Jesus's disciples. But Francis went further. He entered an Italian prison to bathe and also kiss the bare feet of a dozen inmates, including those of Muslims and women.

"That's grace," Marty said. "You have to reach beyond your boundaries. You break your bounds through grace."

In that, grace is like artistic inspiration. "What is every musician and composer doing? You're pushing up against normal limits. Why dance? Why not just walk? You break the bounds. For those who believe in divine grace, that's the whole show."

Reaching out to ease troubles with love, inspiring folks to go beyond their limits, to look out for and care for one another—these attributes of divine grace are not found only in Christianity. One rabbi I asked about the Jewish notion of grace boiled it down to this: God's graciousness allows us to act like mensches without too much trouble.

"Grace is a quality that engenders love," said Scott Perlo, the associate director of Jewish programming at Sixth & I, a historic Washington synagogue. "If you have grace, people will fall in love with you. There's something about you that's unusual, intangible, very difficult to define, and adds a special quality of beauty to your actions."

Take Noah, for example. The first time grace, or *chen* in Hebrew, is mentioned in the Torah, it is in reference to Noah. This makes sense: God really liked Noah, chose him to pilot the arc through the great flood. "Noah found grace in the eyes of God," said Rabbi Scott. "God essentially said there's something deeply meaningful about him. What was that thing? He was a righteous man, a morally righteous guy, and he found favor in God's eyes. And God just had unconditional love for him."

As in many things biblical, however, much is open to interpretation. "I was looking to see what famous rabbinic commentators have to say about this," said Rabbi Scott, pondering what exactly it meant that Noah found grace in God's eyes. "Some say that this is compassion. The Hebrew word for 'compassion' is related to the word for 'womb,' a love like a mother's love, beyond reason, which may be similar to a Christian idea of grace. But additionally there's a sense that Noah *did* something to cause that. There was something about Noah that makes God love him."

The rabbi explained it this way: "You know how there are people who, no matter what you do, you're never going to please them? And then there is somebody who allows himself to be pleased easily. That is a gracious person." That is perhaps how God saw Noah. It is, in any event, how God's graciousness operates, the rabbi said, by treating us in a way that makes us feel loved and wanted, and this makes us, in turn, behave with grace. Rabbi Scott's explanation reminds me of Father Michael's dynamic bucket brigade of grace. God pours grace into us, and we serve it forth to others.

"Being gracious," Rabbi Scott added, "is allowing other people to be or appear graceful." In other words, graciousness—your willingness to be easily pleased—is a gift; you are giving others the spotlight and then applauding like mad and tossing roses. The gracious person creates ease with his approval, rather than judgment. For example, suppose I was to meet my editor at the train station so that we could ride up to New York together for a big story. Also suppose I had a computer meltdown before I left home and then I couldn't find my keys or even my *purse*, and suppose there was a big delay on the subway and by the time I got to the gate at Union Station—humping up the stairs with my bags—suppose the waiting area was empty, because everyone had boarded already. But oh, there was Ned, Editor of Menschdom, stepping into view with a big smile and zero reproach, reaching gallantly for my bags and whisking us onto the train just in time. And let's just say, because this is all true, he seemed to think my breathless arrival as a hot mess of sweat and stress was a totally fine way to start a business trip.

That is graciousness.

"God is compassionate and gracious. That is what allows us to be graceful, favorable, and pleasing," said Rabbi Scott. "Grace, in the Torah, is a characteristic, a virtue of the character, and also something that you can gift to another person, by being gracious to them. Does it describe how to be gracious? It doesn't seem to. It's an elusive quality. But everybody sort of gets it."

As in Hebrew, the Arabic word for "compassion" is related to the word for "womb." And compassion, or *rahmah*, is the best interpretation of grace in the Islamic tradition, said Umeyye Isra Yazicioglu, an Islamic studies professor at Saint Joseph's University in Philadelphia, when I called to ask her about grace.

"God has ninety-nine beautiful names of perfect attributes, such as the forgiver, and the one who avenges for the innocent and the just," said Yazicioglu, author of *Understanding Qur'anic Miracle Stories in the Modern Age*. "But what is interesting to me is that 'God as the compassionate one' is the most mentioned attribute in the Qur'an. The idea is that the creation of the whole world, and humanity, is an act of compassion. That God has created the world through this breath of compassion, and God is continuously creating and sustaining."

As in the Christian and the Jewish perspectives, we get a taste of that infinite compassion and grace when we act gracefully toward others, Yazicioglu said. "Let's say I did an embarrassing thing in front of you and you kindly overlooked it. That is a graceful moment. When you act gracefully to me, you're opening up a glimpse of the Divine Being to me."

Yazicioglu has a lilting Turkish accent, and her voice rippled with purring sounds as she spoke with me. It's difficult to imagine that someone so charming could do anything embarrassing, but that is the point, she said with a little giggle. We are *all* fragile and sensitive, susceptible to harm. We may worry about strangers on the other side of the world; the distress of others can unnerve us when we see it on the news. Animals aren't affected in the same way. Being human can hurt. But this vulnerability, this need we have for comfort, and the longing for others to have it, too, is what makes the experience of grace so delicious, she said. If we didn't need grace, it wouldn't feel so good to receive. "We all need fellowship and love and forgiveness; we are all deeply vulnerable beings. That is very painful unless we realize we are *meant to enjoy grace,*" said Yazicioglu. "We can be open to all these different ways of feeling compassion, to enjoy things like healing and forgiveness, gratitude, safety."

I asked whether, in the Islamic tradition, a person can merit divine grace, and work to earn it. "In some sense yes, but also not quite yes," she said. "The world could run without me in the picture. But someone decided the world is missing something without Isra in it. I can't say I deserve this. It's just an act of pure compassion. But we have to be open to it and be willing to consciously reflect it to other people."

She offers this example: "There is a mystical story of God's grace as a hard rain coming down, pouring down. But the spiritual teacher adds that you need to turn up your bucket to receive the rain. If you want to fill up your bucket, there's an active part to it, in opening yourself up."

It all comes back to embracing human vulnerability, Yazicioglu said. "We tend to think in everyday life that we can only meet our needs at the expense of someone else's needs. It's part of our busy world. But in a different worldview, it's a world of abundance and everyone's needs can be met. And I have something at stake in *your* needs being met. I can't be fully at peace until I see you happy. That makes us more vulnerable, but we also have more opportunity to experience and reflect compassion."

To be sure, in any religion that has notions of a supreme being, human vulnerability is a central issue. The mortal flesh is weaker than the higher power. So the appeal of divine grace is logical. For the weaker, vulnerable human, receiving God's grace makes everything—getting through life, enduring other people—easier.

Not all religions have a tradition of grace, however. When I spoke with Edwin Bryant, professor of Hinduism at Rutgers University, he brought up the intense meditation practices of some Indian sects, which are "incredibly austere, where you're living in a forest and barely eating and barely breathing," he said. "Those are not grace traditions; they are coming from a place of willpower and mind control." But in the Bhagavad Gita, the ancient and best-known Hindu text, Lord Krishna speaks at a few key moments about his grace (*prasada* in Sanskrit) and specifically ties it to ease. In essence, Bryant said, Krishna, the supreme and absolute being, makes the case that *bhakti*, or devotion to Him in hopes of gaining His grace and compassion, is an easier path to enlightenment than the rule-bound ritualistic and meditation practices.

"Fixing thy heart on Me, thou shalt, by My grace, overcome all obstacles," the god tells Arjuna, the warrior prince who asks for Krishna's guidance on the eve of an epic battle. "O Arjuna, the Lord dwells in the hearts of all beings. . . . Through His grace thou shalt attain Supreme Peace and the Eternal Abode."[2]

"Thou shalt come unto Me," Krishna tells the worried prince.[3] Across the thousands of years since those words were inscribed, you can sense the relief they offer. And the grace.

"To me, grace doesn't have anything to do with religion," said Sally Quinn, founding editor of the website OnFaith. She describes herself as spiritual but not religious. For her, grace is most evident in acts of nurturing and loving, and in surprising moments of uplift.

Quinn told me she experienced grace when her husband was dying. He was the former *Washington Post* executive editor Ben Bradlee, who guided the paper for twenty-six years, through the Watergate coverage and on, becoming the most celebrated newspaper editor of his time. I knew him only slightly; he had retired before I came to the *Post*, but he still loped through the building's halls on occasion, beaming a great soft smile. A booster of features and arts coverage, he was a regular at the Style section's holiday parties. Yet the man famous for his charismatic charm and vibrancy began suffering from dementia, and during his last two years he slipped in and out of lucidity. The nights were the worst, Quinn said: Bradlee was plagued with hallucinations and psychotic episodes and would wake up screaming and thrashing. He couldn't be left alone.

"Taking care of him was a period of grace for me," Quinn said, as we sat in the book-lined study of their expansive Georgetown home two months after his death in October 2014. He was ninety-three, twenty years her senior. Quinn has nightly dreams about her husband, in which she asks him, are you feeling okay? Do you need anything? She misses the care.

"It gave me—well, *pleasure* is not the right word, because he was deteriorating," she said, "but it gave me enormous satisfaction. It was enriching as well as painful." Quinn dressed him each morning, and combing his hair was a special joy for both of them.

After Bradlee's funeral at Washington's National Cathedral, Quinn and her family drove to the cemetery where he was buried. One of the grandsons walked out of the chapel there to find an eight-point buck staring calmly up at him in the afternoon rain. A consolation, and a grace.

In my conversations with these spiritual people, I began to see more clearly how grace underlies so much of what we all hold dear, despite our different faiths, cultures, traditions, whether we are believers or nonbelievers, skeptics or seekers. Grace—its wonderment, its comfort, its ease—has woven through the human story in so many ways. I find the religious descriptions of grace beautiful and somehow familiar on a gut level, familiar because they mirror what I have intuited about grace for so long. Especially the idea that grace is a gift unmerited and freely given, in the way your love for your children or anyone else you cherish streams on despite the things about them that drive you nuts—despite, for instance, the time you were awakened by the police calling late at night because your kid's friend's sleepover had turned into a kegger and someone threw up and your kid went out to buy paper towels to help mop up the rug but the only drugstore open was across the state line where there was a curfew for minors and the cops picked him up, and you were so relieved the call was about something stupid that all you could do was stammer incoherently into the phone in a sloppy mix of gratitude and joy and love. That was grace pouring out, pouring out from the universe, drenching you and spilling out of you, bringing ease into the darkness: grace coloring everything the sapphire blue of a midsummer night pierced with stars.

Life, like religion, is a cascade of mysteries. Grace, to me, is the deepest of these. The concept of it has roots in the secular, religious, and spiritual realms, and it travels easily between and among them. Just look at the scattered bumblebee flight of John Newton's hymn through the ages, and how grace has figured in faith traditions around the world. That is what is truly amazing about grace: its infinite distribution.

The uplifting effects of grace. Margot Fonteyn charms retired admiral Thor Hanson.

CHAPTER 16

LEAP INTO GRACE:

TECHNIQUES FOR GRACEFUL LIVING

Alack, when once our grace we have forgot,
Nothing goes right.

—William Shakespeare, *Measure for Measure*

Grace is the purest of style. There is really nothing complicated about it.

If we make ourselves aware of other people and consider their feelings, as our mothers told us to do; if we make an effort to be absorbed by their stories, their needs, and not only our own—the door to gracefulness opens wide. We will stand, beautifully, on the threshold.

So far so good. Then what?

Well, let's check our stance. In essence, your posture is your point of view. How you stand reflects your attitude to life. How you feel affects how you move.

"With a back we can discover a temperament, an age, a social position," wrote art critic Edmond Duranty.[1] His good friend Edgar

Degas was fascinated with backs, Mary Cassatt's in particular. Degas made two paintings and a dozen works on paper of his artist colleague gazing at paintings in the Louvre. They constitute one of his most intense examinations of a single motif.

He was clearly intrigued by Cassatt's posture, for she stands in the same position in every work. Most of the works depict her from behind, where the full length of her spine is in view. The sinuous curve of her back; the way her shoulders are thrown back yet relaxed, with one arm loose, the other casually braced on an umbrella; the thoughtful inclination of her head; the graceful harmony of all her parts: these elements all make plain her confidence, her independence, and her at-home-ness in rooms full of gilt-framed paintings, an environment that some might find overwhelming or intimidating.

Posture is the foundation of moving gracefully. "I like to work on movement," the famed dance teacher Maggie Black used to say, "but I can't work on movement until we are standing up correctly."[2] Dancers from all the major New York companies filled her classes from the 1960s through the 1990s because she taught from an anatomical approach, emphasizing simple, natural movement. This is where you should begin.

Poor posture gives in to gravity. Of course, gravity is here to stay. It will get us all in the end. But graceful posture appears to defy gravity. With it, you may even seem to float. At the very least you will skim, instead of sag.

I'm a big believer in the transformative effects of posture. For childhood scoliosis, my doctor warned that I might eventually need a back brace. Well, I never did, and for this I credit ballet lessons. I started ballet when I was eight and dove into the art form intensively when I was twelve. In high school, I saw my ballet teacher more than my parents; I was taking class six days a week, two hours a day. No doctor ever mentioned scoliosis to me again. Is this proof that ballet cured it? No. But that it aligns the spine is unquestionable. Ballet is based on vertical alignment. You can tell a dancer from a block away, and the reason is posture; it is the first thing dancers work on in class, every class, no matter their age or level of experience. In classical ballet, every position of the feet, legs, and arms begins on an inhalation that lifts the spine, waist, and upper body out of the pelvis. Freedom of movement spreads outward from this elongated and airy bearing.

I stopped taking ballet in graduate school. Guess what? My back got lazy and started twinging if I walked too much. Then I had three children, and by the third one I was having a vaudeville-clown pregnancy, hand on my back, waddling and griping. Thank goodness for Velcro belly slings—yep, that's a thing. A godsend.

In the ensuing years, swimming helped strengthen my back, but what fully banished discomfort and stiffness was yoga, which, like dance, works a lot on posture. I heartily recommend it. What I like about yoga is that it also addresses the inner state of being, with attention to deep breathing and to calming the mind, both of which are essential to grace and poise. The poses are meant to open up different angles of the body to loosen tightness but also to build awareness of how the body works, and how its workings affect your mood and outlook. The breathing exercises expand your inner tissues and organs, which can be both relaxing and energizing. Breathing right, to lift your chest and inflate your belly, also elongates the spine. If you concentrate on your breathing for a few moments, really feeling your breath wash through you in slow waves, you can see how important those elastic, filling and emptying sensations are to the buoyancy and calm of graceful bearing.

I also like a book called *The New Rules of Posture: How to Sit, Stand, and Move in the Modern World* by Mary Bond, a former dancer and certified Rolfer on the faculty of the Rolf Institute of Structural Integration.[3] She describes principles of awareness, stability, and healthy motion in clear and understandable ways, with an emphasis on lightness and ease.

There are many activities that will lend you grace and improve the way you move, if you take their techniques into your daily life. It's important to find something you want to do. Swimming is the only sport I love; it just feels so crazy good to move through cool water, weightless and fully stretched. Tai chi, which focuses on slow, serene, connected motion, unbroken flow, and standing meditation, is undoubtedly the most graceful exercise. It is known to reduce stress and anxiety and increase flexibility and balance, important components of grace. I have a soft spot for it because my brother is a longtime student, teacher, and tournament champion. He has a poised, unflappable, Cary Grant kind of presence and beautiful posture. In fact, he's a very graceful guy.

The slow, deliberate warm-ups in a dance class, tai chi, or even in choral singing promote breathing together. To get the rhythm right, it helps if everyone is inhaling and exhaling at the same time. Steady breathing reduces effort and brings about a feeling of ease. A recent, albeit small, study in Sweden showed that the slower-than-normal synchronized breathing of choir members brought their heartbeats into synch too.[4] This coupling of heart rate to breathing is called respiratory sinus arrhythmia (RSA). RSA has biological soothing effects and also has benefits for cardiovascular function. By demonstrating that as soon as the singing began the hearts started following one another, the Swedish neuroscientists discovered what anyone who has ever joined a chorus knows: singing with others feels good.

Yoga classes make this point overtly. They start with guided synchronized breathing and the chanting of *om*. You don't have to buy into the many spiritual meanings of the mantra to access its basic physical function: chanting it produces a group exhalation. This can be lovely to hear, and to feel.

I have a colleague who has pain in his ankles and is convinced that you can't change the way you walk. That is absolutely untrue. You can improve your stance and your gait at any age and find a supple, graceful posture that sails you through life. This is not difficult. It is not building the pyramids or restoring the economy. Barring a condition that requires expert attention, most of us simply need correct awareness and practice. Good posture has a ripple effect: if you have young children, your posture work will help them, too. Children imitate all kinds of body language. Just as they adopt their parents' facial expressions, gestures, and loose or tense movement styles, children also copy postural habits.[5]

Posture is a constant process. It is dynamic, not fixed. Work on it, and you can improve it. But toss out any notions of ramrod rigidity. Good posture is comfortable, balanced, and fluid. You want to feel elegant and light. Here is a brief tutorial. Stand with your back against a wall. Your head, shoulder blades, and rear end should be touching the wall. Now step away and try to retain that position. Take a deep breath and feel your upper body rise up along your spine. Imagine a thread lifting you up from the top of your head. The muscles behind your neck soften. Your shoulders relax, widen outward, and float down a bit. This is a gentle, subtle action. Forcing the shoulders back and down soldier-style strains your neck and makes your head jut forward. Think of the shoulder blades gliding into place while you breathe deeply and inflate your chest a little.

Now think of your midsection and imagine a snug, shaping support around it. I once heard an actress from the *Downton Abbey* television series talk about the corsets they wear and how those period undergarments force them to stand taller and more upright. That's the image you want. No Madonna-style bondage cage. More like Spanx. We're not after rigidity; remember, the goal is movement. You just want a gentle, elastic hug around the center, as you draw your navel toward your spine.

There's been a lot of focus lately on core strength, and I won't gainsay the benefits. But six-pack abs have nothing to do with graceful movement. You do need some abdominal support to keep your upper body lifted and weightless. When you draw in those muscles, also think of lifting in the legs: imagine rising up out of the hipbones (this is subtle; no pelvis tucking allowed), perking up your quadriceps, and lifting the knees and ankles, so they don't roll in or out. Center your weight right over your feet. We tend to settle back in our heels, so you will probably need to adjust your weight forward a bit.

Roll your attention back up the body, checking in with all your parts, so they feel buoyed up on little cushions of air. You stand suspended on that air, effortlessly aligned, right up through the top of your head.

A few years ago, I had the sweet pleasure of interviewing Gillian Lynne, the choreographer of *Cats* and *The Phantom of the Opera*, two of the longest-running musicals in Broadway history. Before that, she had been a ballerina with the Sadler's Wells Ballet. Her dedication to movement wasn't over, even at eighty-two, her age when I met her for coffee.[6] She was slim, leggy, vibrant—a Roman candle of a woman. She left me with two great postural images. One is where to locate the liftedness: she stood and clasped her hands between her legs, using them as a harness around her crotch, and shouted, "Pull up! Pull up! I am not tired!"

And: think, "Nipples firing!"

"Because that's what I always yell at my actors," Lynne told me. "The first thing that enters space is this"—she inflated her chest—"and they have to be firing with energy, have to be something that lifts the audience up."

Good posture will make you look taller, slimmer, more confident and elegant. But the benefits don't stop there. Proper posture improves your health. It increases blood flow, facilitates breathing, and reduces stress on back muscles, ligaments, and discs.[7] Poor posture doesn't just look sloppy, it is bad for you. Negative health effects include neck pain and decreased range of motion, lung capacity, and circulation.[8] A study published in the August 2007 issue of the *Journal of Neuroscience* suggests that strained neck muscles, which can occur with misaligned posture or slumping at a desk, may contribute to higher blood pressure.[9] Similarly, sitting too much leads to more than ungraceful hunching and slumping, which affect your posture. Sitting has been shown to be dangerous for your health, too. In a 2012 study published in the *American Journal of Clinical Nutrition*, researchers found that the participants with the most sedentary behaviors were at greater risk of death from cardiovascular causes and cancer.[10]

So fire those nipples and sally forth with grace. It's good for you.

"Walking," wrote Hippocrates, "is man's best medicine."

Good posture is an uplifting feeling. A good walk is next. But if you watch people walk, most of us sink into our hips. To counterbalance a sagging core, our shoulders, neck, and head jut forward. This is not graceful. If you are pulled down, sinking into your hips, you cannot also be pulled up.

Your midsection is your source of propulsion, and if you collapse there, you're crushing all your power. There should be a comfortable tension in the torso: it lifts the abdomen and hips against gravity, while it also helps relax and ease the shoulders down slightly, so you don't look like you've got a coat hanger stuffed under your skin. Think of the front and back planes of the body as sandwiching your middle, with that satiny little corset hug.

Walking ought to be a pleasure. It is perhaps the most primal and profound expression of grace that we have. Walking carries us through life; it carries us into the world, sending our bodies out to explore and contemplate and interact with other people and feed our nervous systems and our souls. Ease in doing it radiates throughout your whole body and your spirit. This is your grace, the buoyancy to which you are entitled. Walk as much as you can.

A good walk is also energizing to watch.

If it is not your habit, begin gently. I am a daily swimmer and consider myself to be pretty fit, yet when I decided to take up serious walking several months ago—marching along sidewalks a couple of miles a day, in a pair of sneakers that had been sitting in a closet for half a dozen years—I quickly acquired a case of achilles tendonitis. I was reminded of what I love about the water: no pain. Proper shoes make all the difference in walking.

For long fitness-type strolls, get professionally fitted into a good pair of running shoes. They are all neon nowadays. Even my shoe guy, a college-age cross-country runner, despaired of the color choices. But I've grown to love my new lime-green-and-road-crew-orange kicks.

No matter the occasion, if you want to be graceful you must wear shoes in which you can walk. Otherwise, abandon the idea that grace will be yours. Jeanne Moreau makes this clear in *Elevator to the Gallows* (*L'ascenseur pour l'echafaud*), the 1958 Louis Malle film in which the melancholy beauty minces tightly through the streets of Paris all night long in pointy-toed high heels. We are meant to believe her despondency is because she is searching for her lover in vain, but her mood is surely souring because of those teensy little torture chambers. The effect is dramatic, which must have been Malle's intent; I cannot watch Moreau's constrained stride without wincing.

I see many Moreaus every day on the streets of Washington: women walking stiffly, awkwardly, their posture bent at ungainly angles. One winter's day I spied a young woman who belonged in a comic strip; she had a clunky, crouching, bent-kneed gait because she was crossing a busy street in the snow in four-inch-high peep-toe pumps while staring down at the phone she held with one hand, and dragging her kid along behind her with the other. It was a perfect storm of postural catastrophes. It hurt to watch her. Every step was an effort because she was trying to position the movable architecture of her body on a severely tapered and unsteady base. It cannot be done, my friends, unless you are Beyoncé or a drag queen. You need uncommon strength, height, and length of foot to manage the angle of sky-high heels. Four-inch heels feel less extreme when the steepness is spread over a size eleven shoe. Even then, your feet will be killing you.

Grace will not happen if you are tottering about on stilettos. Instead, you will experience a big night of backache, and everyone watching you will feel uncomfortable, too. Confidence and ease, ladies: find the heel height that allows this and doesn't wreck your body alignment. Shelve the rest.

You do not need to wreck your feet, knees, and natural grace in order to appear sexy, youthful, and elegant. Top fashion designers are wise to the appeal of graceful movement, and some have recently turned to the comfortable footwear that allows it. In their 2014 fashion shows in Paris, Chanel and Dior both sent couture-clad models down the runway wearing cute, upscale sneakers. In a gorgeous fall print ad, barelegged models in colorful Chanel skirt suits sprint across the page wearing coordinated running shoes, with the broad, open shoulders and nipped-in waists of the runners memorialized on ancient Greek amphorae.

The Greeks knew how to emphasize the beauty and grace of the body; it's clear in the amphorae with which they paid tribute to their naked, godlike athletes, and it's also clear in their sculpture, as we saw with Praxiteles's nudes. They used drapery to bring graceful movement into stone, emphasizing and concealing, enhancing curves and flowing lines, covering awkward transitions. You can achieve this with clothing, if you bypass skinny jeans and bandage dresses and instead choose clothes that move.

Wrote the painter and decorative artist Maria Oakey Dewing in her book *Beauty in Dress*: "Let every woman remember that it is harmony of color and grace of cut that makes a dress beautiful, and its fitness to the style and needs of the wearer, not richness of material or costliness of ornament." Her words, from 1881, apply today.

Clothes that move well liberate the body and attract the eye. They can also carry a sense of drama. In A-line skirts, fluid trousers, and shirtdresses, a skillful mix of air and fabric can create rhythmic play with every step.

I once spoke with designer Carolina Herrera about clothes that move after a show inspired by the bold energy, simplicity, and modernity in Bauhaus art of the 1930s.[11] Of all the designers who show during Fashion Week in New York, her designs appeal to me the most. You will never find the avant-garde at a Carolina Herrera show. But you will find timeless style, clean elegance without overembellishment, and a soft-edged grace that doesn't push itself at you. Designing clothes that move well stems from her view of femininity, Herrera said.

"A woman likes to feel like we're not a structure," Herrera said, describing a box in the air with her hands. "Not a blazer, very square." Besides, she added, "you move better when you're wearing something that moves well. That's what I was thinking when I made the Renee dress"—the backless gown of flowing gold lace that actress Renee Zellweger wore to stunning effect at a Metropolitan Museum of Art Costume Institute gala.

The graceful ease of clothes that move can help telegraph to the world that you are at home in it and with yourself, even if that isn't yet entirely true. In the early 1900s, French designer Paul

Poiret was the original bra burner—before there were bras. His fashions—T-shaped gowns, Greco-Roman and kimono-inspired dresses—celebrated the uncorseted woman in her natural grace. Decades later, Halston picked up on Poiret's loose simplicity. To enhance your grace, toss aside those body-hugging knits and tight pants for chemises and skirts with a little swing.

"Life has become so casual," designer Mark Badgley told me at a showing of a Badgley Mischka spring collection that featured more curves than a water slide and just as much fluidity. Tulle tops floated over chiffon pants; long, lean gowns cut on the bias featured sumptuous folds. When a woman puts one on, Badgley said, "she is inspired to carry herself differently than when running around in jeans and a T-shirt." And a gentle hip sway is the only accessory she'll need.

Men, too, benefit from a more graceful, movement-friendly cut. But in menswear, what impedes grace is an overabundance of fabric that leads to bagginess. I spoke with top-tier designer Michael Bastian about the fabric, cut, and motion of a suit, and how it should feel when a man puts it on.

"American men have been, in the past twenty years, wearing clothes that were too big for them," Bastian told me. "There was too much movement of the wrong kind." A higher armhole in a jacket can be more comfortable, reducing bagginess so "every time you move around you're not dragging the whole thing with you. . . . You just need a centimeter or two between the jacket and the body, so that what you see is what's inside; it's not a lot of fabric."

Cary Grant was famously picky about every detail of his suits and shirts, from fabric to buttons to the spread of the collar. The

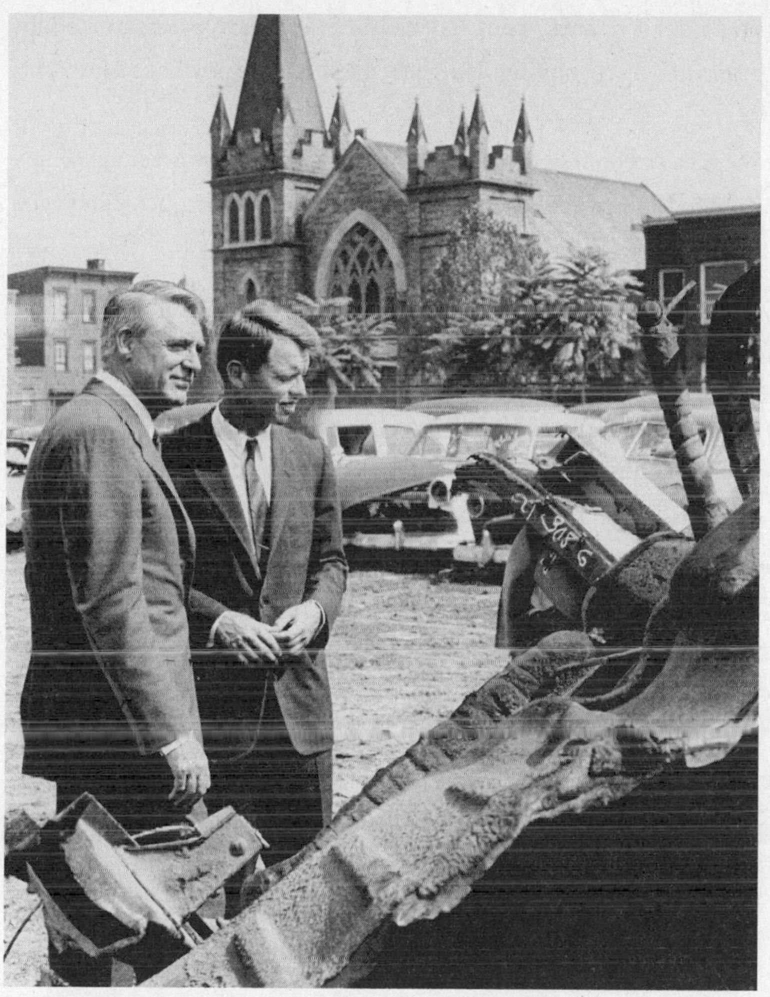

Two gentlemen of the junkyard. Cary Grant and Attorney General Robert F. Kennedy survey an impound lot being considered as a playground to help curb juvenile delinquency in Washington, DC. Smartly dressed, with an air of approachable ease, they make looking great anywhere seem like a cinch.

drape of his clothes—not too snug, never floppy—accentuated his graceful way of moving. He knew all about the power of a good fit.

We take freedom of movement for granted, but it is precious. Enjoy it. Stand tall, walk comfortably; let your natural grace carry you forth without obscuring it.

Americans have made a cult of casualness, but that can spill over into a tacky appearance, slouchy bearing, coarse manners. By contrast, if you've taken care to present yourself well, you will naturally be inclined to keep up that image in every aspect, from how you move to how you behave. Europeans place a great deal more emphasis on making the best of themselves before venturing out among others. They have more of a sense of occasion. I saw this very clearly on October 3, 1990, the day that the border separating East and West Germany officially dissolved. John and I were living in Germany at the time; he had a fellowship, and I was freelancing. At midnight the night before, we had joined the young Berliners who celebrated reunification by shoving themselves through the Brandenburg Gate, a symbol of the political divide ever since it had been closed off by the Berlin Wall. It was more than a little scary to be part of that stampeding crowd, marking passage to a new era in an especially physical way. But the next day, everything changed.

We returned to the Brandenburg Gate in the morning to witness a very different celebration: euphoria had been replaced with contentment. Germans of all ages were simply enjoying a pleasant stroll along the broad, tree-lined avenue called Unter den Linden, which stretched from the triumphal arch into what used to be East Berlin. How wonderful to explore the open space with a good, long walk! This freedom of movement was a historic act, an expression of national pride, and pure pleasure. Most of the passersby were dressed up, as if they were on their way to church or to brunch, in good coats and hats and lovely scarves. They ushered in a new era with grace.

The leisurely stroll has been all but lost as a pastime. In my travels I have joined audience members in Germany, France, and Russia in ritualized promenades around the spacious lobbies and halls of theaters at intermission. They stretch their legs and put themselves on display in their evening finery, they discuss the performance and encounter friends—all while moving in a slow, harmonious mosey that gently sweeps everyone together and adds to the elegance and grace of the occasion. Walks in the hills, walks along the coastline—these were part of the year I spent studying abroad, and none of my French friends or members of the family I was living with would be caught dead ambling among the olive trees in bulky sweatpants.

But the point is this: step into the stream of life, be carried away, and enjoy it. In a recent conversation about grace, the celebrated Italian ballerina Alessandra Ferri let me in on what she considers the secret to her country's reputation for relaxed, sunny ease: "There is less fear about enjoying and taking risks, and that's a freedom."

She's right. And that freedom comes by choice. You achieve grace, inner grace and outer grace, because you want to. It is all in your grasp. Some measure of ease in your body, elegance in your appearance, and ease and enjoyment among others can be cultivated with a little desire. It starts with observation, by being in the midst. Notice and be aware of the grace around you, in your neighborhood, in the park, in what you see on social occasions, in works of art, or in your travels.

"Let the great book of the world be your serious study; read it over and over, get it by heart, adopt its style, and make it your own,"[12] wrote the Earl of Chesterfield in *Letters to His Son*. The rewards of this study are rich. Grace allows us to walk lightly and easily, to treat others sweetly and gently, to receive and savor the gentleness of others. Grace in all its dimensions exists so that we can move well through life.

CONCLUSION

"This evening I have learned, my dear, that in this beautiful world of ours, all things are possible."

GENERAL LORENS LÖWENHIELM, IN *Babette's Feast*

GRACE SWOOPS IN where you least expect it, where highs and lows collide. One day, perhaps some breakthrough string theory of the heart will explain why awkwardness and elegance can be perceived at the same moment, why gloom and enchantment can hit you at once.

But until then, let's just call it grace.

AS MUCH AS GRACE is about inner strength—Cary Grant possessing the generosity and character to rescue a young friend from awkwardness, or Margot Fonteyn having the will to nurse her husband despite his infidelities—it is also about frailty. It is about exposing our flawed, fragile humanity to others just as flawed and fragile. It is about baring ourselves, in some small way, and making a connection with body and spirit.

That's the origin of the word *revelation*—to lay bare. Perhaps

At the juncture of ease and vulnerability, a moment of revelation: the great ballerina Diana Adams, in "Pillar of Fire" by British choreographer Antony Tudor.

that's why Ekaterina's naked grace was so illuminating. (That, and the sequins.)

Grace—whether we behold it in someone giving us a happy greeting as she walks up the street, or we feel it in the relief that washes over us when someone we've kept waiting forgives us with a smile, or we detect it inside, like a shift in the atmosphere—grace is a moment of revelation. Reality does a striptease for you. No, not a tease, but the full monty. A person or an event is laid bare, scrubbed of the gunk that typically clogs our perceptions.

Some people have an unusually attuned emotional radar. Like cats. I have a runty, skittish little calico one—a true 'fraidy cat, who jumps when the floor creaks—and she's not inclined to cuddle. But if I'm sick or low or sleepless at night, she appears matter-of-factly beside me, purring a salute as if she's reporting for duty, dispatched by the Marine commander of the force. The human equivalent is the wise maternity nurse who sits at your bedside while you're nearing your second day of labor, still trying to muscle your way through the Marin County natural childbirth fantasy of your dreams. The nurse sits with you and rubs your back and, without making you feel like an idiot, reasons you into taking the drugs, because the pain isn't accomplishing anything.

Michael Jackson was a troubled man, but he was often so graceful as a performer it was as if he had entered a quieter, more peaceful, more perfect world onstage. Jackson and his moonwalk will be forever linked, the man inseparable from his slipperiest and subtlest move. What more perfect expression could there be of this most elusive celebrity, of the mystery that always surrounded him? In the thundering melee of a live concert, amid a singularly strange life, Jackson would underscore his cool remove with a shift into reverse, coasting backward across the stage, step by gliding step, as if on a cushion of air. With his signature walk, Jackson left behind everything mundane, messy, and predictable. Inscrutable, silent, he always escaped us, as surely as the moonwalk pulled him away.

But there was connection even in that escape, in the way that grace can crash two feelings together at once. That gliding signature move forged a visceral connection with the public, filling in part of the picture that Jackson's music didn't fully capture.

Grace is a way of connecting with one another as we spin forward in this world that is indifferent and so often cruel. We are all in this dance together. As I think back on Jennifer Lawrence's fall and splendid recovery, on the rumpled Buddha singing out his request that we make room for him in the crosswalk, I realize there are thousands of acts of grace floating secretly—and not so secretly—around us.

But I keep coming back to Cary Grant, making people feel larger rather than diminished, taking care of those in his midst.

And suddenly, I'm aware that I have known him, have met his graceful doppelgangers all throughout my life. One instance looms in my memory, a time when a bright, piercing newness came into the everyday. Or rather, into a night, a dreary, sloppy night when it seemed humanity had turned its back.

It was several years ago, when John and I were living overseas. Among our adventures was a six-week trek through the south of France on crappy bikes we'd bought from the German equivalent of Kmart. We traveled the ancient Roman roads, lived on wine, chocolate, and lots of espresso, and camped out under the stars. Except when it rained.

One wet evening, we arrived in a town in the southeastern mountains and, as usual in bad weather, started looking around for a cheap hotel. There was only one, and it was closed.

By the time we discovered that, it was pouring and pitch dark; we could barely see the road in front of us. A hilly, ancient village up ahead called Bargemon was the last bit of civilization before a great climb up the Col du Bel Homme, which stood in the way of the next closest town. Our screaming legs informed us we'd never make it in the rain. Bargemon, in other words, was our last hope.

But all the inns there were either closed or full. At the only restaurant we could find, the bartender suggested we try the nursing home or the church. The nursing home turned us away. Wet, pathetic-looking, and a teensy bit anxious, I was about to knock on the church door when an eager young man ran up to us and, in halting English, offered us a bed in his house.

Call it coincidence, magic, or a message from God; we simply called him Charly, which was how he introduced himself. He'd heard about us at the bar.

Wiry and compact, our savior for the evening could have been a subject for Caravaggio. I caught sight of his hands, which were meaty, with stubby fingers. His face was chiseled and scruffy.

I felt two things at once: fear and relief, the latter of which was stronger. Something about Charly—the sincerity in his eyes, his open manner—made us trust him. Here was our Cary Grant, offering us rescue. We had been seeking him all along. And he had sought us.

And so we found ourselves drying off in front of Charly's fireplace after a hot shower, drinking his wine, and staying up until the wee hours listening to tales from his job repairing the local roads and riding in the Paris–Dakar race every year. He told us about the wife in Sainte-Maxime who had left him, taking his kids with her.

Did Charly need us as much as we needed him? No doubt, we were an attentive audience and had our own tales to share. He was delighted to have the company, and maybe it felt good to unburden himself a bit to strangers. But I think there was an imbalance in our favor. We slept on a featherbed in a spare room, tucked into linen sheets as fine as old handkerchiefs.

In the morning Charly was gone. He'd made coffee for us and set out a basket of fresh rolls. In a note under the jam jar, he asked us to leave the key with the bartender.

Our state of astonishment at our host's freely given grace only deepened. What had we done to deserve this? Not one thing. We bought him the biggest bottle of Johnny Walker we could find and left it on his kitchen table along with our address in the States and our hopes that we'd see him again someday.

That was many years ago, but Charly's act of grace stays with me. He was the companion we sought without knowing he existed, one who understood our plight, took us under his wing and into a perfect world.

That morning after we met him, as we stepped outside Charly's narrow rowhouse and into the sun, the village that had felt like a thousand closed doors the night before seemed to sing out its welcome. The sky was a brilliant, cloudless blue as we set off on our bikes, and we were surprised at how easily we managed the climb up the mountain.

TIPS FOR MOVING WELL THROUGH LIFE

SOMETHING ABOUT THE NATURE OF GRACE seems to elude fixed meaning. It encompasses so much and can seem so difficult to attain. It is visible and intangible; it is rooted in movement, but it can exist without movement, in stillness and silence and nonjudgmental acceptance. Distilling it further, at the heart of grace is ease. Defying gravity, smoothing your actions, reducing friction. Releasing your gifts to the world. Lightening the burdens of others.

Ease, however, is not always easy to master. It is a dynamic practice. With that in mind, consider these points:

1. Slow down and plan. There's no way to be graceful when you're rushing around haphazardly.
2. Practice tolerance and compassion. This goes along with slowing down. Take time to listen and understand.
3. Make room for others—on the sidewalk, at the bus stop, in a coffee shop, during a business meeting, and in your life.

4. Strive to make things easy for people, even in small ways.
5. Make things easy for yourself. Be easily pleased. Accept compliments, take a seat on the bus if someone offers it to you, embrace any kindness that comes your way. This is graciousness, and it is a gift for someone else. You are giving another person the gift of being graceful.
6. Lighten your load. Shed painful shoes, disencumber yourself of heavy purses, backpacks, and briefcases. Let the bad stuff go, physically and emotionally.
7. Take care of your body. The more you move, the better you'll move. And the better you'll feel.
8. Practice extreme noticing. Look for grace where you least expect it.
9. Be generous. It's a lovely thing to anticipate and fulfill someone's hopes.
10. *Enjoy.* Raise a glass, as Lionel Barrymore did in the movie *Grand Hotel,* "to our magnificent, brief, dangerous life—and the courage to live it!"

Margot Fonteyn, at ease in the world.

ACKNOWLEDGMENTS

As I REFLECT on the years-long process of writing this book, I keep thinking of George Santayana's observation that the family is one of nature's masterpieces. Mine is adaptable, irrepressible, and wonderfully tolerant, and to this clan I owe my deepest gratitude. Special thanks to my lionhearted and stunningly kind husband, John, who spoils me with outpourings of coffee, wine, and love, and to the enchanting, profoundly decent people we have the honor of calling our children: Zeke, Asa, and Annabel.

For her tenacious and cheerful help in hunting down photographs, my sincere thanks to Eddy Palanzo, the *Washington Post*'s prized photo librarian and researcher. I am also deeply grateful to the *Post*'s Richard Aldacushion for his generosity in granting permission to use the photos, and to the gifted photographers whose work I am thrilled to include here. For additional assistance, I gratefully bow to Matthew C. Hanson of the Franklin D. Roosevelt Presidential Library, to Donna Urschel of the Library of Congress, and to Richard Valente.

So many of my current and former *Post* colleagues have inspired and assisted me, especially my editor, Christine Ledbetter, a class act and one of the most graceful people I know; also the great Henry

Allen, friend and guiding spirit, and Michelle Boorstein, Marcus Brauchli, Michael Cavna, John Deiner, Robin Givhan, Peter Kaufman, Ned Martel, Kevin Merida, Chris Richards, and Neely Tucker.

I'm grateful to all those I interviewed and mentioned in these pages for their patient answers to endless questions, and to so many others whose insights informed my thinking, including University of Maryland English professor and historian Jane L. Donawerth, sociologists Priscilla Parkhurst Ferguson of Columbia University and Cary Gabriel Costello of the University of Wisconsin-Milwaukee, yoga teachers Maria Hamburger and Barbara Benagh, and baroque dance specialist Catherine Turocy, who generously shared her knowledge of European court traditions and body language and what we can learn from them today. For their insights on grace and other wonders, my thanks to Dana Tai Soon Burgess, Alessandra Ferri, Judy Hansen, Tony Powell, Amy Purdy, Xiomara Reyes, and Rebecca Ritzel.

Effusive thanks to my agent, Barney Karpfinger, who believed in this book steadfastly, cheered me on like crazy, and freely bestowed valuable ideas while setting his own example of kindness and grace. I am enormously indebted to the outstanding publishing team at W. W. Norton & Company, and particularly to the exquisitely sensitive editing of Alane Salierno Mason, the gold standard. I could not have dreamed of a more artful, perceptive, or dedicated collaborator. I'm grateful also to the amazing designers, and to Remy Cawley, Alice Rha, Jessica R. Friedman for her legal expertise, and Camille Smith and Stephanie Hiebert for their sharp eyes and incisive suggestions in copyediting the manuscript.

Loving thanks beyond words to my parents and heroes, Richard and Catharine, to dearest Dilys, to my brilliant brother David, and to Harvey, a font of calm. Thanks also to Larry, Patricia, Ellen, and to my sister-in-law Sabine, who, at her wedding lo these many years ago, kindly entrusted me (a somewhat shy not-yet-member of her family) with her bouquet as we exited her dressing room, high on M&Ms and hairspray. Her simple gesture of inclusiveness filled me with the flush of gratitude that this book is all about.

NOTES

INTRODUCTION: THE BODY ELECTRIC

1. Warren G. Harris, *Audrey Hepburn: A Biography* (New York: Simon & Schuster, 1994).
2. Nancy Nelson, *Evenings with Cary Grant: Recollections in His Own Words and by Those Who Knew Him Best* (New York: HarperCollins, 1991).
3. Ibid., 117.
4. Marc Eliot, *Cary Grant: A Biography* (New York: Harmony Books, 2004), 305.
5. Ibid., 284–85.
6. Ibid., 210.
7. For the various lines I have quoted, I have chosen the most beautiful language from these two translations: Miriam Lichtheim, *Ancient Egyptian Literature: A Book of Readings*, vol. 1 (Berkeley: University of California Press, 1973); and Battiscombe G. Gunn, *The Instruction of Ptah-hotep and the Instruction of Ke'Gemni: The Oldest Books in the World* (London: John Murray, 1906).
8. Keith O'Brien, "The Empathy Deficit," *Boston Globe*, October 17, 2010, http://www.boston.com/bostonglobe/ideas/articles/2010/10/17/the_empathy_deficit.
9. Pamela Paul, "As for Empathy, the Haves Have Not," *New York Times*, December 30, 2010, http://www.nytimes.com/2011/01/02/fashion/02studied.html.

CHAPTER 1: FLAIR TO REMEMBER

1. Sarah Kaufman, "One-Man Movement," *Washington Post*, January 11, 2009, http://www.washingtonpost.com/wp-dyn/content/article/2009/01/09/AR2009010901212.html.

2. Eric Pace, "Cary Grant, Movies' Epitome of Elegance, Dies of a Stroke," *New York Times*, December 1, 1986, http://www.nytimes.com/1986/12/01/obituaries/cary-grant-movies-epitome-of-elegance-dies-of-a-stroke.html.
3. Frederic La Delle, *How to Enter Vaudeville: A Complete Illustrated Course of Instruction* (Jackson, MI: Excelsior, 1913).
4. Cary Grant, "Archie Leach," *Ladies' Home Journal*, January/February 1963 (part 1), March 1963 (part 2), and April 1963 (part 3).
5. Ralph Waldo Emerson, *The Conduct of Life* (Boston: Ticknor & Fields, 1860).
6. William Hazlitt, *The Collected Works of William Hazlitt: The Round Table* (London: J. M. Dent, 1902). 45.
7. Sarah Kaufman, "Rita Moreno on Strength, Stamina and the Power of a Killer Body," *Washington Post*, July 10, 2014, http://www.washingtonpost.com/entertainment/theater_dance/rita-moreno-on-strength-stamina-and-the-power-of-a-killer-body/2014/07/10/5882a6a6-0858-11e4-8a6a-19355c7e870a_story.html.
8. Peter Bogdanovich, *Who the Devil Made It: Conversations with Legendary Film Directors* (New York: Alfred A. Knopf, 1987).
9. David Thomson, *The New Biographical Dictionary of Film* (New York: Alfred A. Knopf, 2004), 361.
10. Sarah Kaufman, "The Man Leaves His Audience Breathless; Jean-Paul Belmondo's Physicality Defines Landmark Film," *Washington Post*, July 9, 2010.
11. Garth Franklin, "Interview: Cate Blanchett for *Notes on a Scandal*," Dark Horizons, December 31, 2006, http://www.darkhorizons.com/features/183/cate-blanchett-for-notes-on-a-scandal.

CHAPTER 2: GRACE AMONG OTHERS

1. Nancy Nelson, *Evenings with Cary Grant: Recollections in His Own Words and by Those Who Knew Him Best* (New York: HarperCollins, 1991).
2. F. Scott Fitzgerald, *The Great Gatsby* (New York: Scribner, 2003), 52–53.
3. Sylvia Plath, *The Bell Jar* (New York: Bantam Books, 1981), 33.
4. "Kyle Sandilands Was Devastated after Being Snubbed by Prince William and Kate," News.com.au, April 22, 2014, http://www.news.com.au/entertainment/celebrity-life/kyle-sandilands-was-devastated

-after-being-snubbed-by-prince-william-and-kate/story-fnisprwn-1226892041914.

5. Not his real name.

CHAPTER 3: GRACE AND HUMOR

1. Sarah Kaufman, "Michelle Obama's 'Mom Dancing' Genius," *Washington Post*, February 24, 2013.
2. Ian McEwan, "Margaret Thatcher: We Disliked Her and We Loved It," *Guardian* (London), April 9, 2013, http://www.theguardian.com/politics/2013/apr/09/margaret-thatcher-ian-mcewan.
3. Patrick Sawer, "How Maggie Thatcher Was Remade," *Telegraph* (London), January 8, 2012, http://www.telegraph.co.uk/news/politics/margaret-thatcher/8999746/How-Maggie-Thatcher-was-remade.html.
4. Margaret Thatcher, interview with the *Daily Graphic*, October 8, 1951, Margaret Thatcher Foundation, http://www.margaretthatcher.org/document/100910.
5. Margaret Thatcher, House of Commons speech: "Confidence in Her Majesty's Government," November 22, 1990, http://www.margaretthatcher.org/document/108256.
6. Margaret Thatcher, Conservative Election Rally, Plymouth, speech: "The Mummy Returns," May 22, 2001, http://www.margaretthatcher.org/document/108389.
7. Sarah Kaufman, "In Mildred Holt, 105, Johnny Carson Met His Match," *Washington Post Style Blog*, May 16, 2012, http://www.washingtonpost.com/blogs/style-blog/post/in-mildred-holt-105-johnny-carson-met-his-match/2012/05/15/gIQAsaW7RU_blog.html.

CHAPTER 4: GRACE AND THE ART OF GETTING ALONG

1. *Diary of John Adams*, vol. 1, the Adams Papers (Boston: Massachusetts Historical Society), http://www.masshist.org/publications/apde2/view?mode=p&id=DJA01p10.
2. Benjamin Spock and Robert Needlman, *Dr. Spock's Baby and Child Care*, 8th ed. (New York: Pocket Books, 2004), 439–40.
3. William Kremer, "Does Confidence Really Breed Success?" *BBC News Magazine*, January 3, 2013, http://www.bbc.com/news/magazine-20756247. See also Jean M. Twenge and W. Keith Campbell, *The Narcissism Epidemic: Living in the Age of Entitlement* (New York: Atria Books, 2010).

4. Jena McGregor, "The Oddest, Worst and Most Memorable CEO Apologies of the Year," *Washington Post*, December 23, 2014, http://www.washingtonpost.com/blogs/on-leadership/wp/2014/12/23/the-oddest-worst-and-most-memorable-ceo-apologies-of-the-year; and Sam Biddle, "F*** Bitches Get Leid: The Sleazy Frat Emails of Snapchat's CEO," *Valleywag*, May 28, 2014, http://valleywag.gawker.com/fuck-bitches-get-leid-the-sleazy-frat-emails-of-snap-1582604137?ncid=tweetlnkushpmg00000067.
5. Julie Johnsson, "Boeing Profit Rises, but Tanker Program Worries Analysts," *Seattle Times*, July 23, 2014, http://seattletimes.com/html/businesstechnology/2024139521_boeingearningsxml.html.
6. Elizabeth Woodward, *Personality Preferred! How to Grow Up Gracefully* (New York: Harper & Brothers, 1935).
7. Hortense Inman, *Charm* (New York: Home Institute Inc., 1938).
8. Emily Post, *Etiquette in Society, in Business, in Politics and at Home* (New York: Funk & Wagnalls, 1922).
9. Battiscombe G. Gunn, *The Instruction of Ptah-Hotep and the Instruction of Ke'Gemni: The Oldest Books in the World* (London: John Murray, 1906).
10. See Miriam Lichtheim, *Ancient Egyptian Literature: A Book of Readings*, vol. 1 (Berkeley: University of California Press, 1973), 78, n. 29.
11. For a good discussion of this, see the introduction to Giovanni Della Casa, *Galateo, or the Rules of Polite Behavior*, ed. and trans. M. F. Rusnak (Chicago: University of Chicago Press, 2013).
12. I have taken my quotations from the Da Capo Press, New York, & Theatrum Orbis Terrarum Ltd., Amsterdam, 1969, facsimile of the version published in England in 1576, titled *Galateo of Master John Della Casa, or rather, A treatise of the manners and behaviours, it behoveth a man to use and eschewe, in his familiar conversation. A worke very necessary and profitable for all Gentlemen, or other.*
13. Baldesar Castiglione, *The Book of the Courtier*, ed. Daniel Javitch, trans. Charles S. Singleton (New York: W. W. Norton, 2002).
14. She used this term in her terrific, piercing 1939 short novel *Old Mortality*, collected in Katherine Anne Porter, *Pale Horse, Pale Rider: Three Short Novels* (New York: Modern Library, 1998).
15. See the 1901 version of the original, *Letters to His Son on the Fine Art of Becoming a Man of the World and a Gentleman*, 2 vols., the Earl of

Chesterfield, with an introduction by Oliver H. Leigh (Washington, DC: M. Walter Dunne).

16. For a thorough discussion of this, see C. Dallett Hemphill, *Bowing to Necessities: A History of Manners in America, 1620–1860* (New York: Oxford University Press, 1999), 70ff.
17. Arthur M. Schlesinger, *Learning How to Behave: A Historical Study of American Etiquette Books* (New York: Macmillan, 1947), 12.

CHAPTER 5: SUPERSTAR GRACE

1. Joseph Joubert, *Pensées of Joubert*, trans. Henry Atwell (London: George Allen, 1896).
2. Lynn Normont, "The Untold Story of How Tina and Mathew Knowles Created the Destiny's Child Gold Mine," *Ebony* 56, no. 11 (September 2001).
3. Maxine Powell, "Rock 'n' Role Model," *People* 26, no. 15 (October 31, 1986).
4. John Cohassey, "Powell, Maxine 1924–," *Contemporary Black Biography, 1995*, Encyclopedia.com, March 5, 2015, http://www.encyclopedia.com/doc/1G2-2871000059.html.
5. Paula Tutman, "Motown Reacts to Miley Cyrus Performance Last Night," WDIV Click on Detroit, August 26, 2013, http://www.clickondetroit.com/news/motown-reacts-to-miley-cyrus-performance-last-night/21657208.
6. Mike Householder, "Maxine Powell, Motown Records' Chief of Charm, Dies at 98," Associated Press, October 14, 2013.
7. Interview with Jane L. Donawerth, English professor and historian, University of Maryland, December 3, 2013.
8. Anna Morgan, "The Art of Elocution," in *The Congress of Women: Held in the Woman's Building, World's Columbian Exposition, Chicago, U.S.A., 1893*, ed. Mary Kavanaugh Oldham Eagle (Chicago: Monarch Book Company, 1894), 597.
9. Martha Reeves, "Maxine Powell Remembered by Martha Reeves," *Observer* (London), December 14, 2013.

CHAPTER 6: EVERYDAY GRACE

1. Natalie Angier, "Flamingos, Up Close and Personal," *New York Times*, August 22, 2011.

2. William H. McNeill, *Keeping Together in Time: Dance and Drill in Human History* (Cambridge, MA: Harvard University Press, 1995).
3. Sarah Kaufman, "At CityZen, Chefs Cook Up Sweet Moves," *Washington Post*, May 9, 2012. Eric Ziebold closed CityZen in December 2014 and in 2015 opened two new restaurants in the Mount Vernon Square neighborhood of Washington, DC.
4. Sarah Kaufman, "Behind the Scenes at Verizon Center: Building the Set for J-Lo and Iglesias," *Washington Post*, August 1, 2012, http://www.washingtonpost.com/lifestyle/style/behind-the-scenes-at-verizon-center-building-a-set-with-136000-pounds-of-equipment/2012/08/01/gJQAYkAtPX_story.html.

CHAPTER 7: GRACE IN ART

1. See the master on this subject: Kenneth Clark, *The Nude: A Study in Ideal Form* (Princeton, NJ: Princeton University Press, 1972).

CHAPTER 8: ATHLETES

1. See, for instance: Christopher Clarey, "Federer Beats Murray, and Britain, for Seventh Wimbledon Title," *New York Times*, July 8, 2012; Barney Ronay, "Andy Murray Gets Closer to the Affections of the Wimbledon Crowd," *Guardian Sportblog*, July 8, 2012, http://www.theguardian.com/sport/blog/2012/jul/08/andy-murray-wimbledon-crowd-2012; Bruce Jenkins, "Federer Wins 7th Wimbledon, but Murray's Progress No Small Feat," *Sports Illustrated*, July 8, 2012; Liz Clarke, "Roger Federer Beats Andy Murray to Win Seventh Wimbledon Title," *Washington Post*, July 8, 2012; and Martin Samuel, "Murray Lost to a Master of the Universe, the Tennis Equivalent of a Pele or Ali," *Daily Mail* (London), July 8, 2012, http://www.dailymail.co.uk/sport/tennis/article-2170656/Wimbledon-2012-Martin-Samuel--Andy-Murray-lost-master-universe.html.
2. Sarah Kaufman, "Beauty and the Bicycle: The Art of Going the Distance," *Washington Post*, July 24, 2004, http://www.washingtonpost.com/wp-dyn/articles/A10570-2004Jul23.html.
3. Quoted in the documentary "Joe DiMaggio: The Hero's Life," written by Richard Ben Cramer and Mark Zwonitzer, directed by Mark Zwonitzer (PBS, *American Experience* series, 2000).
4. From the program "Stories of the Olympic Games: Gymnastics," directed by Alastair Laurence (BBC Two, *Faster, Higher, Stronger* series, 2012).

5. Sarah Kaufman, "Ripped from the Plié Book: Football and Dance Have Much in Common," *Washington Post*, September 20, 2009, http://www.washingtonpost.com/wp-dyn/content/article/2009/09/18/AR2009091802513.html.
6. From the program "Vision and Movement," written, directed, and produced by John Heminway (WNET/New York, *The Brain* series, 1984).

CHAPTER 9: DANCERS

1. Frequently quoted. In *Edgar Degas Sculpture*, produced by the National Gallery of Art (Princeton, NJ: Princeton University Press, 2010), authors Suzanne Glover Lindsay, Daphne S. Barbour, and Shelley G. Sturman write that it was benefactor Louisine Havemeyer who remembered Degas making the statement as an explanation for why he painted dancers, as recounted in her *Sixteen to Sixty: Memoirs of a Collector* (New York: Ursus Press, 1993).
2. Quoted in the documentary *Margot*, directed and edited by Tony Palmer (Isolde Films, 2005).
3. Richard Buckle, *In the Wake of Diaghilev* (Holt, Rinehart & Winston, 1982), 276.
4. Meredith Daneman, *Margot Fonteyn: A Life* (New York: Penguin Books, 2004).
5. Sarah Kaufman, "Ballerina Natalia Makarova: 'Being Spontaneous, It's What Saved Me,'" *Washington Post*, November 30, 2012, http://www.washingtonpost.com/entertainment/theater_dance/ballerina-natalia-makarova-being-spontaneous-its-what-saved-me/2012/11/29/68f72692-32da-11e2-9cfa-e41bac906cc9_story.html.

CHAPTER 10: WALKING WITH GRACE

1. Sarah Kaufman, "At 18, Model Karlie Kloss Conquers the Runways at New York's Fashion Week," *Washington Post*, February 15, 2011, http://www.washingtonpost.com/wp-dyn/content/article/2011/02/15/AR2011021503549.html.
2. Virgil, *The Aeneid*, Book I, trans. John Dryden, 1697, http://oll.libertyfund.org/titles/1175.
3. Ethan Mordden, *Ziegfeld: The Man Who Invented Show Business* (New York: St. Martin's Press, 2008), 143.

4. Sarah Kaufman, "A Singular Vision: Nearing 80, Paul Taylor Is as Moving a Dance Figure as Ever," *Washington Post,* July 18, 2010, http://www.washingtonpost.com/gog/performing-arts/paul-taylor-dance-company,1034041.html.
5. Michael Munn, *John Wayne: The Man behind the Myth* (New York: New American Library, 2005), 166.
6. James Thomas Flexner, *Washington: The Indispensable Man* (Boston: Little, Brown, 1974), 41.
7. Doris Kearns Goodwin, *Team of Rivals: The Political Genius of Abraham Lincoln* (New York: Simon & Schuster, 2006), 6.
8. Thomas Jefferson to Dr. Walter Jones, 2 January 1814, quoted in William Alfred Bryan, *George Washington in American Literature, 1775–1865* (New York: Columbia University Press, 1952), 49.
9. John Adams to Benjamin Rush, 11 November 1807, available on the Gilder Lehrman Institute of American History website, https://www.gilderlehrman.org/collections/c937ec94-4d4b-4b48-a275-240372288363?back=/mweb/search%3Fneedle%3DGLC00424.
10. Benjamin Rush to Thomas Rushton, 29 October 1775, in *Letters of Benjamin Rush,* vol. 1, ed. L. H. Butterfield (Princeton, NJ: Princeton University Press, 1951), 92. For more on Washington's formative years, see also the engaging biography by Willard Sterne Randall, *George Washington: A Life* (New York: Henry Holt, 1997).

CHAPTER 11: THE PRATFALL EFFECT

1. Steven Berglas, "The Entrepreneurial Ego: Pratfalls," *Inc.,* September 1, 1996.

CHAPTER 12: WORKING AT GRACE

1. Frederic La Delle, *How to Enter Vaudeville: A Complete Illustrated Course of Instruction in Vaudeville Stage Work for Amateurs and Beginners* (Jackson, MI: Excelsior, 1913).

CHAPTER 13: "TO BECOME UNSTUCK"

1. See the Dance for PD website for more information and to find a class: http://danceforparkinsons.org.
2. Sarah Kaufman, "Amy Purdy's Bionic Grace on 'Dancing with the Stars,'" *Washington Post,* April 12, 2014, http://www.washingtonpost.com/entertainment/theater_dance/amy-purdys-bionic-grace-on

-dancing-with-the-stars/2014/04/10/e4575b48-bdd7-11e3-bcec-b71ee10e9bc3_story.html.

CHAPTER 14: THE SCIENCE OF GRACE

1. See, for example, Heidi Godman, "Regular Exercise Changes the Brain to Improve Memory, Thinking Skills," *Harvard Health Letter,* April 9, 2014, http://www.health.harvard.edu/blog/regular-exercise-changes-brain-improve-memory-thinking-skills-201404097110. Godman reports on a study conducted at the University of British Columbia, which showed that regular aerobic exercise appears to boost the size of the hippocampus, the brain area involved in verbal memory and learning.
2. Christy Matta, "Can Exercise Make You Smarter?" PsychCentral, http://psychcentral.com/blog/archives/2012/11/09/can-exercise-make-you-smarter.
3. Carl Ernst et al., "Antidepressant Effects of Exercise: Evidence for an Adult-Neurogenesis Hypothesis?" *Journal of Psychiatry & Neuroscience* 31, no. 2 (2006): 84–92.
4. Deborah Kotz and Angela Haupt, "7 Mind-Blowing Benefits of Exercise," *U.S. News and World Report Health,* March 7, 2012, http://health.usnews.com/health-news/diet-fitness/slideshows/7-mind-blowing-benefits-of-exercise/3.
5. IOS Press, "Tai Chi Increases Brain Size, Benefits Cognition in Randomized Controlled Trial of Chinese Elderly," *ScienceDaily,* June 19 2012, www.sciencedaily.com/releases/2012/06/120619123803.htm. See also Gao-Xia Wei et al., "Can Taichi Reshape the Brain? A Brain Morphometry Study," *PLOS ONE* 8, no. 4 (2013), e61038, doi: 10.1371/journal.pone.0061038.
6. "Stay Physically Active," Alzheimer's Association, http://www.alz.org/we_can_help_stay_physically_active.asp. Accessed February 6, 2015.
7. Albert Einstein to his son Eduard 5 February 1930, quoted in Walter Isaacson, *Einstein: His Life and Universe* (New York: Simon & Schuster, 2007), 367.
8. See neuroscientist Daniel Wolpert's entertaining and informative TED Talk, "The Real Reason for Brains," July 2011, http://www.ted.com/talks/daniel_wolpert_the_real_reason_for_brains?language=en.
9. Yuri Kageyama, "Woman or Machine? New Robots Look Creepily Human," Associated Press, June 24, 2014, http://bigstory.ap.org/

article/new-tokyo-museum-robot-guides-look-sound-human; and Will Ripley, "Domo Arigato, Mr. Roboto: Japan's Robot Revolution," CNN, July 15, 2014, http://www.cnn.com/2014/07/15/world/asia/japans-robot-revolution.

10. Daniel L. Gebo, "Primate Locomotion," *Nature Education Knowledge* 4, no. 8 (2013): 1.
11. Emma E. T. Pennock, "From Gibbons to Gymnasts: A Look at the Biomechanics and Neurophysiology of Brachiation in Gibbons and Its Human Rediscovery," *Student Works*, Paper 2, May 3, 2013, http://commons.clarku.edu/studentworks/2.
12. Adam Smith, *The Theory of Moral Sentiments*, 3rd ed. (London: G. Bell & Sons, 1767), http://books.google.com.
13. Herbert Spencer, "Gracefulness," *Leader* magazine, December 25, 1852; reprinted in *Essays: Moral, Political and Aesthetic* (New York: D. Appleton, 1871).
14. Ibid.
15. NPR staff, "Cate Blanchett Finds Humor in the Painfully Absurd," January 10, 2014, http://www.npr.org/2014/01/10/261398089/cate-blanchett-finds-humor-in-the-painfully-absurd.
16. Riitta Hari and Miiamaaria V. Kujala, "Brain Basis of Human Social Interaction: From Concepts to Brain Imaging," *Physiological Reviews* 89, no. 2 (April 2009): 453–79, doi: 10.1152/physrev.00041.2007, http://www.ncbi.nlm.nih.gov/pubmed/19342612.

CHAPTER 15: AMAZING GRACE

1. For a comprehensive account of the history and spread of the song, see Steve Turner's very interesting *Amazing Grace: The Story of America's Most Beloved Song* (New York: Ecco, 2002), 147ff.
2. Bhagavad Gita, trans. Swami Paramananda, chapter 18, verses 58–62 (Boston: Vedanta Centre, Plimpton Press, 1913), https://archive.org/stream/srimadbhagavadgooswamgoog/srimadbhagavadgooswamgoog_djvu.txt.
3. Ibid., chapter 9, verse 28.

CHAPTER 16: LEAP INTO GRACE

1. Edmond Duranty, *La nouvelle peinture* ("The New Painting"; Paris: E. Dentu, 1876).
2. Rachel Straus, "Black Magic: Maggie Black's Transformative Approach

to Ballet Training," *DanceTeacher* magazine, April 1, 2012, http://www.dance-teacher.com/2012/04/black-magic.

3. Mary Bond, *The New Rules of Posture: How to Sit, Stand, and Move in the Modern World* (Rochester, VT: Healing Arts Press, 2007).
4. Björn Vickhoff et al., "Music Structure Determines Heart Rate Variability of Singers," *Frontiers in Psychology* 4 (2013): 334, doi: 10.3389/fpsyg.2013.00334.
5. Riane Eisler, *The Power of Partnership: Seven Relationships That Will Change Your Life* (Novato, CA: New World Library, 2002).
6. Sarah Kaufman, "A Mover and Shaker, Still in Motion," *Washington Post*, July 6, 2008, http://www.washingtonpost.com/wp-dyn/content/article/2008/07/03/AR2008070301510.html.
7. "Tips to Maintain Good Posture," American Chiropractic Association, http://www.acatoday.org/content_css.cfm?CID=3124. Accessed April 10, 2015.
8. "How Poor Posture Causes Neck Pain," Spine-health, http://www.spine-health.com/conditions/neck-pain/how-poor-posture-causes-neck-pain. Accessed April 10, 2015.
9. Ian J. Edwards, Mark L. Dallas, and Sarah L. Poole, "The Neurochemically Diverse Intermedius Nucleus of the Medulla as a Source of Excitatory and Inhibitory Synaptic Input to the Nucleus Tractus Solitarii," *Journal of Neuroscience*, August 1, 2007, http://www.jneurosci.org/content/27/31/8324.full.
10. Charles E. Matthews, et al., "Amount of Time Spent in Sedentary Behaviors and Cause-Specific Mortality in US Adults," *American Journal of Clinical Nutrition* 95.2 (2012): 437–45.
11. Sarah Kaufman, "At Fashion Week, Spring 2012 Collections Showcase Movement," *Washington Post*, September 13, 2011, http://www.washingtonpost.com/lifestyle/style/at-fashion-week-spring-2012-collections-showcase-movement/2011/09/13/gIQAkzrfQK_story.html.
12. See the 1901 version of the original, *Letters to His Son on the Fine Art of Becoming a Man of the World and a Gentleman*, 2 vols., the Earl of Chesterfield, with an introduction by Oliver H. Leigh (Washington, DC: M. Walter Dunne).

ILLUSTRATION CREDITS

PAGE 2
Cary Grant and Katharine Hepburn in *The Philadelphia Story*. Photograph courtesy of the Everett Collection.

PAGE 23
Cary Grant with Attorney General William French Smith and his wife. ©1982, Harry Naltchayan/The Washington Post.

PAGE 29
Eleanor Roosevelt welcomes UNESCO representatives to her home. Photograph courtesy of the Franklin D. Roosevelt Presidential Library, Hyde Park, NY.

PAGE 35
Cary Grant and Rosalind Russell in *His Girl Friday*. Photograph by Mary Evans/COLUMBIA PICTURES/Ronald Grant/Everett Collection.

PAGE 37
Jackie Gleason was a beautiful mover. Photograph courtesy of the Everett Collection.

PAGE 88
Smokey Robinson gracefully smoothed over racial tensions at a 1963 concert in Alabama. ©1988, Craig Herndon/The Washington Post.

PAGE 106
A Roman copy of Praxiteles's Satyr Pouring Wine. Photograph courtesy of the Walters Art Museum, Baltimore.

PAGE 109
A Roman copy of Praxiteles's Aphrodite of Knidos. Photograph courtesy of the Walters Art Museum, Baltimore.

PAGE 111
The Three Graces of Botticelli's *Primavera*. ©BeBa/Iberfoto/Everett Collection.

PAGE 112
Raphael places his sisterly trio in a barren field. ©BeBa/Iberfoto/Everett Collection.

PAGE 116
Roger Federer, a prince among tennis players. Photograph by Robin Parker Fotosports International Photoshot/Everett Collection.

PAGE 128
Julius Erving—"Dr. J"—offered an antidote for life's encumbrances. ©1973, Frank Johnston/The Washington Post.

PAGE 133
Olga Korbut, in command of herself and the forces of gravity. ©1973, Larry Morris/The Washington Post.

PAGE 137
The peerless English ice dancers Jayne Torvill and Christopher Dean. ©1984, Joel Richardson/The Washington Post.

PAGE 149
Serene self-possession was Margot Fonteyn's gift. Baron/Hulton Archive/Getty Images.

PAGE 158
Natalia Makarova and Mikhail Baryshnikov. ©PBS/Courtesy of the Everett Collection.

PAGE 172
South African President Nelson Mandela. Mirrorpix/Courtesy of the Everett Collection.

PAGE 173
Canny politician Margaret Thatcher. ©1985, Dayna Smith/The Washington Post.

PAGE 203
Amy Purdy lost her legs to meningitis. Photograph by Dave Kotinsky/Getty Images.

PAGE 220
A Borneo orangutan and her baby. ©Thomas Marent/ardea/Everett Collection.

PAGE 243
The Madonna, by Martin Schongauer, c. 1490–91. Courtesy of the National Gallery of Art, Washington, DC.

PAGE 245
Noah Leading the Animals into the Ark, by Francois-Andre Vincent after Giovanni Benedetto Castiglione, 1774. Courtesy of the National Gallery of Art, Washington, DC.

PAGE 254
Margot Fonteyn charms retired admiral Thor Hanson. ©1983, Harry Naltchayan/The Washington Post.

PAGE 267
Cary Grant and Attorney General Robert F. Kennedy. ©1963, Bob Burchette/The Washington Post.

PAGE 272
Diana Adams in "Pillar of Fire." Photograph by Alfredo Valente.

PAGE 279
Margot Fonteyn, at ease in the world. ©1965, Vic Casamento/The Washington Post.

INDEX

Page numbers in *italics* refer to illustrations.